The sociology and politics
of development

International Library of Sociology

Founded by Karl Mannheim

Editor: John Rex, University of Aston in Birmingham

Arbor Scientiae
Arbor Vitae

A catalogue of the books available in the **International Library of Sociology** and other series of Social Science books published by Routledge & Kegan Paul will be found at the end of this volume

such change. However, I must confess that my theoretical inclina-
tion is not that of a 'positivist' or, for that matter, even of a 'system
theorist.' During the days of my graduate work in sociology at
Columbia University, I picked up a copy of *Value in Social Theory*,
by Gunnar Myrdal (edited by Paul Streeten), and this has
sustained my original faith in system-changing rather than system-
equilibrating kinds of analyses.

Let me return to the story of this book. In the 1950s, the debate
on modernization hinged around Malthus and Marx. Theorists in
the West thought that capitalism could provide the basis for solving
the various problems of the developing countries including the
Malthusian problem of population explosion. Theorists in the
Soviet countries and some in the West claimed that Marxism alone
could solve these problems, and the countries in the Soviet orbit
were offered as examples of success in such endeavors. The Soviet
model of development took individual forms in Russia, China,
Yugoslavia, and Cuba. A variant of the capitalist model called
mixed economy took divergent directions in countries like India,
Indonesia, Egypt, and Ghana. The Latin American countries,
whose independence (and modernization) began over a century
ago, also showed a mix of capitalism and state enterprise in the
economic field. Military dictatorship was an added feature in this
case. The disappointment of some Marxists, as for instance of
Milovan Djilas in Yugoslavia, and the unworkability of the early
romantic capitalist view (of, say, the techno-determinists) have
provided the background in terms of which my own ideas have
been spelled out in this book.

It helps to look at the problems of the developing countries from
the perspective of the planners also. In the 1950s, the mood of the
planners was euphoric. With some aid from the United States (as
well as from the erstwhile imperial countries from which they gained
independence) and technological help from the United Nations
through its specialized agencies, the bureaucrats, technocrats, and
politicians of the developing countries felt sanguine about turning
the corner in their march to progress. However, this 'decade of
rising expectations,' as it was called, was created more by and for
the older as well as the newer elites than for the masses. Social
scientists were generally responsible for this unrealistic optimism
by manufacturing instant theories of national development.

The decade of the 1960s was somewhat sobering as thousands of
developers gathered in meetings such as those of the Society for
International Development to tell the stories of their successes and
failures. The *International Development Review*, of which I was for
some time a consulting editor, remained technological in its
approach, whereas *Economic Development and Cultural Change*

Preface

This book has been in preparation for years. I should therefore indicate what has gone into the making of this succinct volume. First, of course, is my professional interest in modernization theory going back over a decade. Second, and no less important, is my concern about the ongoing attack on social science theories alleging that they are not of much use in guiding policy decisions.

The students who read books on modernization theory are in a quandary. They need to review the thinking of social science on problems of modernization which outflank disciplines. Sociology, economics, political science, psychology, anthropology, history as well as other humanistic disciplines have engaged in much discussion of these problems. It is difficult for a student of a single discipline to ferret out ideas which are seminal. Therefore, I had to expand the scope of this volume to provide some guidance on the literature existing in these fields. It is a comprehensive text in the sense that it gives a summary of the existing literature.

As a theorist, it has long been my practice to discard interdisciplinary boundaries and to go to any source which may have something important to say about the topic I am investigating. However, this can be done only if one has a point of view and a certain focus of one's own. I look at the problems of social change in general and modernization in particular from a committed point of view. I have taken pains to spell out the grounds of my theorizing and commitment so that I may not be accused of any hidden biases.

It is to Robert K. Merton that I owe my gratitude for having turned me from a believing activist to a practising theorist. It is important for a theorist to think systematically and to articulate the problematics of a field. This is often a different kind of enterprise than to believe in social change and to formulate plans for guiding

Contents

It is mainly through theorists that the maxims regulating the policy of advanced countries become known to the less advanced countries. In the advanced countries, practice inspires theory; in the others, theory inspires practice.

Bertrand Russell, *A History of Western Philosophy*, 1945

The country that is more developed industrially only shows to the less developed, the image of its own future.

Karl Marx, *Das Kapital*

If real modernity of outlook were to be expressed in this most modern of modern civilizations, *how* should it be expressed? Should it be expressed in the racism of the White people or the counter-racism of the Black people? If this country were really modern would there be this problem before you, discrimination between man and man?

Jayaprakash Narayan, Address to the Conference on *The United States in a Revolutionary World*, Princeton University, 1968

For
Ravi and Sarita
who will be the beneficiaries of modernization
visualized here

First published in 1980
by Routledge & Kegan Paul Ltd
39 Store Street, London WC1E 7DD,
Broadway House, Newtown Road,
Henley-on-Thames, Oxon RG9 1EN and
9 Park Street, Boston, Mass. 02108, USA
Set in phototronic Times 10 on 11pt
and printed in Great Britain by
Unwin Bros Ltd

British Library Cataloguing in Publication Data

Varma, Baidya Nath

The sociology and politics of development.
– (International library of sociology).
1.   Underdeveloped areas – Economic conditions
I.   Title   II.   Series
330.9'172'4'   HC59.7   79-41254

ISBN 0 7100 0428 1

The sociology and politics of development:
A theoretical study

Baidya Nath Varma
Graduate Center and the City College
of The City University of New York

Routledge & Kegan Paul
London, Boston and Henley

took a more scholarly and somewhat detached attitude toward practical problems of modernization. What is important to note here is that the scholars and the technical experts of the West working in the Third World could not match with their theory and deeds the accomplishments of Russia (especially when its liberalization policies took effect after Stalin's death), or China (despite its earlier closed-door policies), and later on Cuba in the Western hemisphere.

The decade of the 1970s has brought to the fore some harsh facts. The capitalist countries of the West are not interested in the global solution of problems of economic development, environmental pollution, or population pressure, if these entail a risk to their own economic or military viability. The Soviet countries can provide the key to success only by dislodging the existing leadership of non-socialist countries. The theorists of the West counsel for change through entrepreneurship and mass education (admittedly a slow process), but the theorists of the Soviet world exhort us in the name of Marx and Lenin to create revolution first and then to rebuild society through non-market mechanisms of production, collectivization of socio-economic life, and mass indoctrination.

As a theorist, I have felt it my duty not only to criticize existing theories but also to advance a theoretical model for modernization, which may guide the destinies of nations in the last quarter of the twentieth century. I have a commitment to democracy and a commitment to equalitarianism. I believe that a democratic constitution is not enough; and that individual autonomy and freedoms as well as community growth and prosperity for all sectors of population are essential ingredients of modernization. I feel that a theoretical approach incorporating these objectives can provide guidance for policy decisions in the coming years.

A word needs to be said about the organization of the chapters of this book. First, I pose the problem of the scope of modernization and examine the general criteria used for evaluating the modernization process. Next I provide the general paradigm of modernization and my own model for it. I show how problem-finding is often a function of the value stance or the open or tacit ideology, which any researcher or theorist adopts. I indicate how some theorists adopt models which openly propound ideological theories, which encompass either the revolutionary model or the evolutionary model. In the following chapters, I examine in detail the problematics arising in each one of the models used by theorists for articulating modernization. These models encompass ideological theories, social scientific theories, and activistic theories. In discussing the ideological models, I provide a brief examination of the actual responses of the developing countries to such models. Next, I consider it necessary to examine the problems of the theoretical and methodological sophistication expected from any social scientist who builds models for modernization.

In later chapters, I give extensive summaries of the views on modernization of theorists in various social science disciplines. I discuss the nature of the variables used by the theorists as well as the interconnections of these variables; I also examine critically representative models of each discipline. However, the problems I select to highlight are not discrete but have a direct bearing on my own model of modernization. In a separate chapter, I spell out the ingredients of the activistic theories of modernization, which is the focus of this book. As will be evident, the emphasis in this particular chapter is on theoretical problems of planning and national reconstruction. Finally, I summarize the main features of modernization theories in terms of the guidance they provide for policy decisions affecting the economy, the polity, the educational system, and the bureaucracy in a developing country. My own views on how the modernization process can be expedited globally are outlined in the chapter entitled, 'Modernization for what?' I hope the reader who examines this chapter reaches the same general conclusions as I do.

In reviewing the works of the 'greats' in this book, I have often been very critical. This was necessary because the 'reigning views' in the field have been dictated by such authors. I have earlier pointed out how modernization theories and the specialists who practice them have got into a morass. To rescue theory from aimless wandering and to convince the sceptics of the viability of social theory are additional reasons for undertaking this study. In the end, I have called my own contribution a humanistic manifesto for modernization because I think that humanism is the praxis of the modern world. I also believe that theory and praxis are inevitably intertwined. So any practical guidance must flow from the marriage of theory to praxis.

The present study will whet the appetite of many groups, which are actively involved in bringing about social change. Politicians and social workers will find the ideas presented here as challenging as advanced students and researchers in academia. The environmentalists, the counter-culture people, the New Left, and student activists will also find something useful here as will the town planner, the architect, and the generalist. However, the true value of this book will be appreciated by those who are encouraged by it to plunge into the vast literature on modernization, of which very select items appear at the end of this volume.

I should like to acknowledge my debt to several scholars who read parts of this book. Frank Bonilla and Y. Damle read the whole manuscript and gave valuable suggestions. Dennis Dalton read the section on political science theories, Conrad M. Arensberg reviewed the chapter on anthropological theories, Ranbir Varma guided me through economic theories and J.B.P. Sinha read the section on psychological theories. The ideas incorporated in the book were also discussed with scholars at the Indian Institute of Advanced Study, Simla, and at Jawaharlal Nehru University, Delhi University, and the A.N. Sinha Institute of Social Studies, Bihar. The comments and criticisms arising from these discussions have been duly incorporated in the book. I am sorry that it is not possible to mention the names of all scholars who contributed in this way. However, I would like to express my gratitude to Professor S. C. Dube, then the Director of the Indian Institute of Advanced Study and to Professor Sachchidananda, Director, A.N. Sinha Institute of Social Studies, for providing me with the facilities of their respective institutes, in the revision of this manuscript.

I had the privilege of lecturing at the First Summer Institute on Modernization and Social Change in Asia for college and university professors sponsored by the American Association of State Colleges and Universities and funded by the National Endowment for the Humanities. It was held at the University of Texas at Dallas in summer, 1978. The thrust of the argument of this book was presented at the Institute and critically reviewed by my other colleagues, who were specialists on China, India, and Japan. Their comments and criticisms goaded me on to write the Epilogue which is the final chapter of this book.

I would be remiss if I did not record my appreciation for Ashoka Varma, my son, who looked at the style of presentation of material through his Oxonian eyes and to Rani Varma, my daughter, who did some of the typing for this book. My wife, Savitri Devi Varma, was a helpful companion throughout the hectic period when I was sifting the grain from the chaff.

Baidya Nath Varma

'Mithila'
Yonkers, New York

1 General perspective

A common question being asked today is 'Modernization for what?' In the industrial countries, the question reflects extreme disparities in income, the disenchantment of youth with the material pursuits of their elders and the despair of the conservationists at the destruction of nature. In the non-industrial world, the question also arises. There, the older generation, not being able to cope with rapid change, asks if modernization means the destruction of all of its cherished values and traditions. The younger generation, on the other hand, sees in modernization a stranglehold of the new elite (the first beneficiaries of industrialization) on the masses and asks, would industrialization lead to more of the same? And, both in the industrial and the non-industrial world, what the question really implies is: can modernization create wealth in such a way that it will eradicate poverty and still maintain individual autonomy and community strengths? These are big questions whose answers cannot be provided without studying the sociology and politics of development.

No definitive answers can be given until more data are available and many more countries have arrived at the so-called 'modern stage,' more than the present count of roughly three dozen out of the nearly 200 countries of the world. However, we cannot wait because time is of critical importance in providing some guidance in these matters to both the modern and the modernizing countries, now. It is with that end in view that we have undertaken a comprehensive analysis of the present situation.

Dimensions of modernization

Political and economic

There are two crucial dimensions of modernization, one political,

1

the other economic. The political dimension involves the setting up of a nation-state, inculcating loyalty among its citizens, and creating national institutions of politics, law, education, and voluntary associations, which should penetrate into regions and localities. In this context, the literature on modernization deals with the questions of tribal, ethnic, caste and kinship particularisms, which stand in the way of nation-building. At the start of political modernization regional, linguistic, and other rivalries which may divide a country horizontally come to the fore quickly, and the strategy adopted in regard to satisfying the mounting pressures from these groups determines whether the nation will remain stable or not. Every nation on the road to modernization has also a rural–urban difference in its population and a rigid class structure, which starts tumbling down because of the impact of modernizing forces. Universal adult suffrage creates an altogether new dimension in the distribution of power and privilege.

The economic dimension of modernization refers to industrialization, specifically to questions of capital formation and its investment; to the availability and use of other resources of land, labor, management, and entrepreneurship; to the emerging problems of urbanization, such as employment, health, housing, transportation, and education; and to the magnitude and direction of industrialization. The availability of commercial, banking, and marketing facilities plays a key role in economic development. International assistance and trade are other important considerations to be taken into account.

Planning

A question often raised in this context is 'Is planning necessary for development?' The answer would be an irrevocable yes, if by planning one meant the coordinated enterprise which is necessary for the private or public sector to arrive at its stipulated goals. However, planning usually means the setting up of national plans, in which outlays are carefully worked out by the national government for more than a year, such as in the five-year or seven-year plans which are ubiquitous today. It involves governmental allocations of resources for private as well as public enterprises. In this sense of the term, some people question the value of planning. These sceptics believe that the shorter route to modernization is through private enterprise in a *laissez-faire* economy, where individual entrepreneurs will have the incentive to take bold steps which will bring the country sooner to the 'take off' stage of development. If, in following this path, political or labor unrest develops, a recourse to authoritarian leadership is not considered harmful. In such countries, change in the class structure will be slow and gradual, although, after 'take off,' there would begin an expansion of the urban middle class and a shift of the surplus labor from the farms to the urban and industrial enterprises.

On the other hand, those who believe in national planning emphasize some kind of state control even over private enterprise, for instance, through licensing and restrictions on exports and imports. They also stipulate at least partial allocation of entrepreneurial roles to the managers and bureaucrats of the state administration. Such an economy is either mixed or socialistic in character and may prosper or lag behind depending on the leadership of the political elite, the initiative of the bureaucrats, and the discipline of the workers as well as the sacrifices of the consumers. Planning could be highly authoritarian as in the Soviet countries or some others ruled by dictatorial regimes, civil or military. Planning could also follow the democratic path through mixed or socialistic enterprise, where the need for the cooptation of the tribal, ethnic, caste, agricultural, business and other well-established groupings will be great. Often consumerism, production of luxury goods for the elite and the middle class, as well as irrational investments in non-growth-related enterprises, present key problems in national planning in such countries.

The economic and political modernization of a country depends a great deal on the availability of scientific and technical education, a trained bureaucracy and a skilled labor force. The determination of priorities and the manner of allocation of national resources among these sectors have to be clearly thought out and carefully designed. However, much would depend on political gamesmanship. For instance, Japan, despite its fast industrial growth restricts college education in a way which India, in spite of its somewhat lagging economy, is not able to do, thus creating mounting problems for the educated unemployed in India. However, most modernizing nations face a shortage of trained managerial and technical personnel as well as important deficiencies in the skills of the labor force. Another set of problems these nations face is connected with the growth of labor unions. As unionism gains ground, the union leaders may escalate demands in such a way that it may be beyond the capacity of the industries, private or public, to meet such demands.

Barriers

The barriers to modernization are many. Some of these stem from traditional folkways and mores, such as familism or casteism, or

3

attitudes such as fatalism or otherworldliness. These traits develop over centuries and the socialization of the young takes place in terms of these values. However, today a new breeze is blowing over the continents, what with advances in mass media and international exchange of ideas and people. Every year, more and more tourists from industrial countries descend on the far corners of the earth. People in the modernizing nations experience this and other changes in their environment. Consequently, everywhere they are seen raising their level of aspiration both for themselves and for their children. The success of modernization depends very much on how a high level of aspiration among the population is transformed into a new kind of motivation. This motivation must be channeled in the direction of developing technical skills, self-discipline in the labor force,. an entrepreneurial group, a well-trained bureaucracy, and an enlightened leadership. The issues of barriers and motivation have been extensively discussed in the literature as we will show later.

We have highlighted above some of the key issues raised in the context of modernization. The issues are many, the resolutions are few. However, this will not prevent us from taking a bold and committed attitude toward modernization. In order to do this, we will formulate our own model for the general paradigm[1] of modernization and seek to discover its consonance with various other models presented in the social science literature. It is important to scrutinize these other models in a systematic way, in order to provide some solutions, however tentative, to the issues raised above. Hopefully, this will also help us answer the question, 'Modernization for what?'

The literature on modernization is enormous and it is not our intent in this book to review it all. Instead, the strategy adopted here is to be interdisciplinary in approach and to include as many viewpoints in our framework as will sustain its strength and expose its weaknesses (if any). We do not intend to present an integration of modernization theories, because such an effort, laudable as it may be on its own account, does not provide enough scope for delineating the problems and problematics in the field. Our approach is critical in the sense that we will examine the potentials and the shortcomings of the various theories; it is also imbued with a sense of value because we believe that the phenomenon under investigation – to wit, modernization – is too important and urgent to be left at the mercy of some objectivity-seeking scientists or sceptical philosophers.

Focus

Modernization implies a special kind of social change. This change

4

first permeated the values, attitudes, beliefs and actions of Western man and transformed the institutions and goals of Western societies. The institutions and goals of the West, which carry the banner of modernization, are articulated as follows: individualization; urbanization; mass education; representative government as well as expanding GNP; increasing employment; growing income for all classes; and provisions of welfare for the disabled and the needy.

After the Second World War, a large number of colonies acquired independence and they, too, became imbued with the spirit of modernization. The above-mentioned institutions and goals were quickly introduced into the vocabulary of the elite of these new nations in what William McCord aptly describes as their 'springtime of freedom.'[2] Other independent non-Western countries had already joined the ranks of modernizing nations. However, in three decades the ideology of modernization has now reached and is standing against the Himalayan wall of the 'national interest' of big powers and currently the mood is sobering and the euphoria of freedom is disappearing.[3] It is against this background that the present analysis of the problems and prospects of modernization is presented and the guidelines for a new direction are provided.

In reviewing the literature in the field, our effort will be to scan the entire spectrum of intellectual thought on modernization. However, we have to exclude two areas from detailed investigation because they fall outside our present purview of theoretical analysis. One is the general area of applied research, whether it is agricultural, industrial, technological, or administrative. The other area is the arena of the humanist, the philosopher, the artist, and the architect. We will, however, incorporate some of their thinking in our perspective as an additional input; but detailed accounts and evaluations of these fields cannot be undertaken here.

We will focus our attention mainly in the field of the social sciences, especially in the disciplines of sociology, economics, political science, anthropology, and psychology. The viewpoints of the behavioral scientists in these disciplines[4] will be examined carefully, because they are the ones who have contributed most to an understanding of the processes of development and change.

We believe that modernization is both an ideology as well as a structure of social relations, which is constantly being articulated, refined, and advanced by the change agents. Modernization is impelled by the necessity of directional change. At its worst, it implies change for its own sake. At its best, it is a process of value-directed change, which never ends.

Before we go on to the more substantive areas of modernization

5

theories, we want to delineate the canvass of modernization in terms of its scope and criteria.

Scope

Modernization can be viewed so broadly as to include all major social changes in history. In such a view, the early Greek states were also modern, and so were the centralized bureaucratic empires of Rome, China, and India. In its narrow sense, modernization starts with the Renaissance and Reformation movements in Western Europe, and gains momentum with the industrialization of England in the second half of the eighteenth century and its spread to Western Europe and North America in the nineteenth century. It is this narrow range of the spectrum that we will be mostly concerned with, because in it are encapsulated the values and the goals as well as the organizational and the scientific 'know how' of the process of modernization, which has overtaken the world in the twentieth century. It should be noted here that this process has accelerated immensely since the Second World War.

The beginnings of modernization in the West were in the fields of the fine arts and architecture as well as in religion, business, government and administration. Literature and culture (especially acquiring freedom and novelty as self-conscious cultural values) were affected later. The developments in science were both a cause and a consequence of the spirit of modernity[5] which had pervaded the West since the beginning of the sixteenth century.

In some fields, the modern trend was clear from the start. For instance, modern architecture began in the nineteenth century. Buildings designed after 1800 reflected the acquisition of technical control over nature and they culminated in the 'cacophonies of architectural styles' of the twentieth-century cities. In painting, however, the new trend arose later, i.e. at the end of the nineteenth century. It was one of unfettered individualism. No doubt, theorizing about color vision by physicists like Helmholtz and Young influenced the gush of the first new art form, viz. impressionism. And as Horace M. Kallen points out: 'This art reconciles science and machinery with painting, using the one to develop the other.'[6] However, it should be noted that post-impressionism is not reconciliation with science but secession from it, for in it the artist completely rejects painting life-like appearances, which can be achieved better through the science of photography. Instead, he pours out his emotions into the picture. Thus, the modernist in painting goes on either 'to seek or to repel reconciliation with science.'[7] The rebellion against technology is often observed with modernity in the West.

The above brief excursion into the realms of architectural and artistic trends is meant to highlight two main criteria of modernization: the application of science to all human endeavors and the principle of individualism. It is also helpful in alerting us to a special issue in the problematics of modernization, viz. the fusion of tradition (especially its feelings and emotions) and modernity (when its impetus derives from rationality and developments in science and technology).

We will now spell out the general criteria for modernity. The special criteria in terms of institutional development will be discussed later in the context of interdisciplinary theories.

General criteria

An inspection of the literature on modernization suggests the following general criteria in terms of which the state as well as the stage of modernity is judged: (a) rationality, (b) individualism, (c) secularism, (d) the application of scientific principles for advancing technology as well as personal goals, and (e) equality. We will elucidate each one of these criteria briefly.

(a) *Rationality* In its dictionary sense, rationality is the possession of reason. However, reason can be fathomed in many different ways. Socrates used cross-examination to arrive at the truth, Plato postulated absolutes, and Aristotle used syllogistic reasoning for the same purpose. Hegel indulged in dialectic for the articulation of the Concept, which, according to him, was *'self knowledge,'* which 'unites essence in *truth.'* Machiavelli gave reason the garb of cunning and Freud demonstrated how *rationalization* (i.e. concocted plausible reason or socially acceptable reason) could be used to protect one's belief or practice, when it is under attack. However, sociologists and political scientists also use the concept of *rationalization* in another sense, viz. the development of standardization, consistency, and coordination in organizational structures.

The concept of rationality as an attribute of modernity gains special momentum at the hands of Max Weber, who has been credited with the seminal investigation of many institutions of *gesellschaft* society, which today is synonymous with modern society. We made a content analysis of some of the major works of Max Weber and discovered that he denotes the phenomenon of rationality in human behavior and social affairs by at least a couple of dozen indicators. These range from seeking order in general to increasing theoretic mastery of reality by precise concepts to methodical attainment of practical ends.[8] There is a mixture of the

Aristotelian and the Machiavellian views of rationality in the Weberian formulation.

For our purposes, rationality may be said to occur in goal-directed actions if suitable means are used to arrive at practical ends. Practical ends, if they are empirical, can be achieved through tangible means. However, many practical ends are in the realm of values, whose achievement is mediated by ritualistic behavior.[9] The articulation of such behavior will involve the notions of operational indicators of values (both instrumental and moral), which are used as variables, the connections among these variables established in a logically consistent way, and the coherence of the system which is delineated by the variables under consideration.[10] To know that every action has consequences and that individual actions are embedded in a system of actions is a necessary attribute of the modern attitude.

In modernization literature, rationality is often also used in the sense of seeking private ends, which includes self-interest, the profit motive, success as the overarching goal, and even self-aggrandizement. But these concepts are directly linked with individualism, which we will discuss next.

(b) *Individualism*   In its generic form, individualism refers to the *laissez-faire* doctrine in industrialism and market economy, and the free enterprise of individuals and firms in capitalist states; it includes the creative and the radical activities of scientists, artists, entrepreneurs, and innovators; it incorporates the freedoms espoused by the liberals of the nineteenth century; and it also upholds the golden rule of self-help and self-control by which conservatives abide at all times.

However, the individualism we refer to is the set of doctrines which advocates the liberties and rights of the individual as against the demands of the collectivities to which he primordially belongs. This principle also bestows dignity on the individual and demands respect for his self. It helps to mobilize him for pursuits whose beneficiary will be the individual himself, irrespective of who else benefits from such efforts.

The individualism most emphasized in the context of modernization is the conglomeration of factors considered necessary for progress by the international staff of developers and planners, who came into being in the second half of the twentieth century. These factors include: individual orientation and initiative, self mastery, ability to act alone, continuous striving for targets set voluntarily by one's self, and faith in the efficiency of self-directed action. It is important to note that these ingredients of individualism, joined effectively with some of those discussed earlier under rationality, have produced most of the modern institutions of the Western society.

The growth of individualism in the West led to the break-up of a person's ties with many groups, like his extended kin and the tribe, which acted as his primary groups when he needed security; but, more important, it also influenced his future goals and actions. This process of emancipation from sacred ties has been referred to as 'individuation' by sociologists. Individuation opened the way for new loyalties, which created 'organic solidarity' (a term coined by Emile Durkheim) for the changing society. However, individuation often created 'anomie' or normlessness in society.[11] The pathological aspects of individuation have become quite pronounced in 'mass society' (which is a variant of modern society), as we will show later on. The process of individuation is closely linked with secularism, which will be discussed next.

(c) *Secularism* Secularism, in its doctrinaire form, rejects all faith in religion and in the worship of the supernatural. However, for our purpose, it refers to the continual separation of worldly matters from the domain of religion (or the 'sacred'), as knowledge is acquired about the empirical bases, causes, and functioning of much of human affairs, which previously were accounted for in religious terms. The secular trend in social and political affairs started when scientific and intellectual developments created the Age of Reason (seventeenth century), the Age of Enlightenment (eighteenth century), and the Age of Progress (nineteenth century), and especially when empirical knowledge of worldly events and phenomena gained ascendancy over traditional and religious explanations.

It was Durkheim who made the important contribution of drawing the line between 'the sacred' and 'the profane' in explaining the functions of religion in all societies.[12] Later, Howard Becker built the typology of sacred-secular society by stipulating that in the secular society the primary values are utilitarian and rational, which promote innovation and change. Becker distinguished between two types of secular societies, one which brings about change according to some secular (modernizing) principles and the other which advances change for its own sake. He claimed that in the secular society, religious tenets have no more efficacy than any other institutional values.[13] We have identified elsewhere a third category of secular society, where religion no doubt becomes coequal with other institutions of the society, but where the whole society is also imbued with some ultimate values, which derive primacy from the tenets of the religion practiced by the dominant group of the society.[14]

9

Secularization can be said to occur in society when the cluster of roles a person occupies at the same time (Robert K. Merton calls such multiple roles a 'status set,' which is incorporated in his provocative 'theory of role-set'[15]) belongs to multiple organizations, whose goals are incongruous, if not contradictory. Roles in a secular society are differentiated in terms of the organizational goals; their rational integration occurs only in the framework of institutional demands and needs. The individual often may find himself in the precarious situation of occupying positions in various institutional set-ups, which may put contradictory demands on him. The first thing he learns is to rescue his secular roles from the demands of his sacred obligations. Even then there may be many contradictions in the role-demands made on him. In such situations, he does not necessarily become neurotic as Karen Horney claimed,[16] but can keep on functioning in an integrated way through the mechanism of compartmentalization, as Leon Festinger has shown in his 'theory of cognitive dissonance.'[17]

Secularism, when joined by individualism and rationality, moves the individual in the direction of modernity. However, in order to be truly modern, he must learn to apply scientific principles to obtain his own private ends. The same applies to groups and societies, if these move in the direction of modernization.

(d) *The application of scientific principles for advancing technology as well as personal goals* Science, in explaining the cosmos, provides rational ethic, individual self reliance, freedom from religious dogmas, and perhaps a faith in the perfectability of human nature and society. Technology has been an important impetus in moving mankind toward a destiny which science promises is possible. One variant of that destiny is portrayed by the term 'modern'. However, science has also brought with it some gloom, with an atomic holocaust always looming on the horizon, and the continuing pollution of the environment, which may make human life impossible on this globe. We cannot recount here the possible dangers of science and technology in today's world. Our aim is to select and give attention to that facet of science and technology which can help man to accommodate himself to nature, and which can also guide him in establishing better relationships between man and man, It is with regard to the latter endeavor that the principle of equality is judged to be an important criterion of modernization.

(e) *Equality* In a sense, the tenet of the equality of all men is ingrained in all the major world religions. The equal status of 'believers' is also affirmed by all major religions, including

Hinduism (for example, in the concept of *tattwamasi* or Thou art He, as we have demonstrated elsewhere[18]). However, when one moves from a consideration of the individual's religious status to his social status, one sees many gradations and hierarchies in societies. It is here that the concept of equality takes on a special meaning for modernization.

The slogan, *liberté, égalité, fraternité*, which was raised during the French Revolution in 1789, brought into focus a new concept of 'equality', which ever since has been constantly expounded and expanded in the context of world revolutionary change. In France, it was the Third Estate (the bourgeoisie) not the Fourth (the masses), which under the slogan gained equality with the nobility and the clergy. Similarly, in England, it was the bourgeoisie which sought equality with the aristocracy and the squirearchy during the Industrial Revolution. These upheavals led to equal access to power by organized groups. But they did not create equality of status between all men of whatever vocation or profession.

The equality that has often been propounded as a gift of modernization by the West means the equality of persons before the law. It also refers to the gradual concession to the masses by the rulers of certain basic freedoms, like the freedom of speech, and certain fundamental rights, such as that of universal adult suffrage. The story of the extension of other human rights has a long past but a short history; this is not the place to recount the struggles that went into this achievement. What we wish to emphasize here is that the struggle for equality has not yet ended. In fact, it has a long way to go, even in the United States, as is clearly evident from the third quotation placed at the masthead of this book.

A modern society, as we will show later, needs a more radical conception of equality than the ones that presently obtain in the West. Equality in the eyes of the law or in the exercise of civil rights is not enough. Equality means freedom from prejudice and discrimination; it means the end of the exploitation of one's fellow men; and it is a vital part of the dignity of the individual, which is associated with the feeling and confidence of being equal. Often it can come only with equality of wealth. The basis of such equality may emerge if, for instance, society considers all producers as being equal and remunerates them accordingly. Whatever else equality may mean, it must be translated into *fraternité* or brotherhood. We will show the importance of this point when we discuss ethnic renaissance in a later section. We merely want to note here that equality takes on special meaning because every nation today is more or less polycentric,[19] generally hoping to be polyarchical,[20] and definitely multiethnic.[21] Thus the role of brotherhood conceived

11

on the principle of equality becomes crucial in organizing social relations in the present world.

Equality has been given a still different meaning by Karl Marx. The proletarization of the world which he visualized creates equal status for all men. Sociologically, this status cannot be wished into existence; it has to be claimed and actively worked out, as Marx clearly pointed out himself. Short of revolution, which Marx preferred, the only way of working out any program for such equality is through national planning. Some nations believe that providing equality of opportunity will do; for others, nothing short of equality of consumption for all citizens will be acceptable. These policies become ideological matters as will be shown when we discuss various theories of the reconstruction of society.

We have discussed above the various dimensions of modernization so that the theoretical paradigm may be sketched out in the next chapter.

2 The paradigm and the problematics of modernization

The paradigm

Definitions

In order to develop the general paradigm, it is necessary to consider some definitions of modernization. The term 'modernization' has been defined so many times and in so many ways that it is analogous to the situation in anthropology, where it seems that almost every theorist feels compelled to define the term 'culture' (the stock-in-trade of the anthropologist) in his own way.[1] Instead of examining the definitions of modernization from the unitary perspective of an economist, a political scientist, or a sociologist, we will select three definitions which have been provided by scholars who have an orientation to more than one discipline. Modernization is a multidisciplinary subject and so this strategy may be helpful in examining the scope and interconnections of its problems.

The economic philosopher Robert L. Heilbroner reviews the terms of the challenge he calls The Great Ascent, and believes that for economic development to take place there must be political and social changes; that such changes will not lead to social contentment; and that, in fact, the obstacles are so great that there is no assurance of success. He comes out with the conclusion that 'the price of development is apt to be political and economic authoritarianism.'[2]

It is clear that Heilbroner is not merely talking about *economic* development, which he defines as 'the deepening flow of incomes and the widening flow of production,'[3] but also about the modernization of a tradition-bound society. He goes into details about the shackles of backwardness, but his emphasis in this whole process is on the economy. We feel that putting incomes for all ahead of production for profit is a step in the right direction, although he has no firm views on the equality of income, a problem discussed by us earlier.

We will now turn to Daniel Lerner, the sociologist-cum-communications expert, who was entrusted with writing the article on modernization for the *International Encyclopedia of the Social Sciences*.[4] Lerner says: 'Modernization is the current term for an old process – the process of social change whereby less developed societies acquire characteristics common to more developed societies ... The process is activated by international, or intersocietal, communication.'[5] The criteria, which he discusses in this and his earlier study,[6] are increasing urbanization, rising literacy, increasing media exposure, wider economic participation (per capita income) and political participation (voting).[7] He goes on to say that this 'model evolved in the West is an historical fact ... the same basic model reappears in virtually all modernizing societies on all continents of the world, regardless of variations in race, color, creed ....'[8]

The ardor and the faith with which Lerner presents his model is part of the 'rational and positivistic spirit,'[9] which, he points out, is necessary for modernization. However, to close the parameters of modernization with four key variables, urbanization, literacy, media exposure, and 'empathy' – the last one of which he discusses at great length in his book and also brings up as 'self-things seeking' and 'self-other seeking' in the *Encyclopedia* article – seems premature, especially because the last three variables follow one from the other. In addition, economic growth is considered to be a prerequisite for political development by Lerner. One important question that has been raised about his presentation is, how ethnocentric and temperocentric is his model?

Manning Nash, an anthropologist who has perspectives of folk, peasant, pre-industrial as well as industrial societies, presents the definitions in the following way:

> Modernity is the social, psychological framework which facilitates the application of science to the process of production. And modernization is the process of making societies, cultures, and individuals receptive to growth of tested knowledge and its employment in the ordinary business of daily living.[10]

The emphasis on productivity and the instrumental use of scientific knowledge would perhaps put Nash in the category of a cultural monist, who sees the direction for the future in the cultural history of the West, more than in the category of a cultural relativist, who projects other values as well for modernizing societies.[11]

Whatever their terms of reference for articulating the modernization process, it is clear that all the three scholars put the primary emphasis on production (rather than on its equitable distribution), which they feel is related to political stability (which enmeshes more and more people in political participation), and which is directly related to scientific knowledge (its growth and dissemination) and to the improvement of one's economic and social status.

The five general criteria of modernization, which we discussed in the last section, are openly or implicitly acknowledged by these writers. However, they do not focus their attention on humanitarian problems of a global nature which is our added interest. In their praise for modernization, they take their cue from the West and completely ignore what the Western model has done to the human habitat by ruthlessly replacing the village community with the city, and the urban human community with the statistical areas of industrial planners.[12] It is in order to improve the existing Western models and to remedy some of their shortcomings noted above that the following model for the general paradigm of modernization is proposed.

The Model

Modernization refers to the process of directed change through which a nation achieves economic growth, political development and autonomy, and social reconstruction based on the principles of equality, fraternity, enhancement of freedoms, and satisfaction of basic needs. The principles of social reconstruction are articulated by individuals and cumulated by groups working often in the short-run through revolutionary methods but in the long-run through consensus and democratic consent. The model stresses individual autonomy and community growth.

As we proceed in this essay, the implications of our model will become clear. At this point, we will merely comment on a few aspects of it. We believe that modernization is a continuing process and has not stopped for the West. It is true that the maxims of modernization emanate from many practices of the advanced countries; it is also true that these maxims guide the behavior of all modernizing nations. As Bertrand Russell reminds us in relation to philosophical ideas in the epigram quoted at the beginning of this book: 'In the advanced countries, practice inspires theory; in the others, theory inspires practice.' However, the new theory of modernization dictates new practices even for the advanced countries if they wish to avoid man-made natural and social catastrophes, which are becoming increasingly common today.

In terms of our model, one finds that true fraternity and effective

15

satisfaction of basic needs for all are still lacking in the most modern of modern nations. Part of the reason may be the lags in culture or defects in the mechanisms that are created to take care of such needs. It is also possible that, short of changing the structure of the society, such goals of modernization cannot be realized. In this connection, I am tempted to put before the reader a question which was thrown at me in many different contexts and on many different occasions in my recent trips to India, 'Why should health, food, education, and work be made commodities to be bought and sold and not to be the birthright of every person?' Capitalism would be hard put to answer this question to the satisfaction of someone who is sick without medicine, hungry, illiterate, and out of a job. There are other issues connected with freedom and equality which need to be solved by the so-called modern nations, as I will show later on.

The problematics of modernization

I propose to discuss some of the problematics of modernization as they are related to the ideological, the social-scientific, and the activistic analyses of this phenomenon. Since these questions or problematics arise constantly in the process of modernization of a nation, we have to pay attention to them despite the fact that there are few agreed solutions.

It should be noted here that I classify all writings about modernization in three categories. One category is called 'ideological,' where the author consciously or subconsciously propounds a framework of inquiry which articulates some program of change. The other category is called 'social-scientific' because social scientists use varied schema in terms of their disciplinary interests and often claim objectivity for them. The last category is called 'activistic' because it is the change agents who recommend this framework. In some parlance, the second category is called pure theory and the third is considered to be the application of pure theory. However, we wish to stress that we do not believe that any social analysis can be completely value-free; whether there is a heavy input of ideology in a schema is another matter which has also to be examined.

Problematics in ideological theories

In ideological theories, we include both the Soviet and the Western industrial capitalistic versions of modernization. The modernization of the West took place under conditions of imperialism, when the imperial countries were able to use for their own benefit the raw

materials and resources of the colonies. One of the crucial questions posed today is how the ex-colonies can overcome the economic,
educational, and cultural deprivations created by colonial rule.
There are two answers: one is revolution, the other evolution.

The argument for revolution to remedy these ills is clinched by
pointing to such existing factors in the modernizing nations as: the
exploitative grip of many of the old imperial nations on the present
economy of the ex-colonies; the Western-educated elite, who wish
to continue their prerogatives and power; the system of values
fostered by the elite which emphasizes private property and due
compensation if deprived of it by the government; a legal system,
which is too engrossed in formalism and is little interested in
justice; and finally the emphasis on the military and the police for
maintaining law and order for the benefit and the advancement of
the status of the 'haves' in society.

On the other hand, the arguments for evolution point to these
crucial factors: revolution is destructive; even after revolution, a
nation needs reconstruction; reconstruction is possible through
planning and crash programs; there will always be elites in society,
the question is one of social mobility and the circulation of the
elite; there are many nations competing to provide international
help and assistance for all; one can pick and choose between donor
nations without upsetting the stability of the political system;
nationalization and socialistic redistribution are means which are
considered quite legitimate today; and finally, law will always be
needed for order as well as justice, and in the present set-up of
nations, the military cannot be abolished.

If one looks at the arguments, pro and con, for evolution or
revolution, or for choosing between the Western model of modernization based on evolution and the Soviet model based on
revolution, there hardly seems adequate rational ground on which
to choose. Perhaps each nation will go its own way, partly groping,
partly impelled by forces at home, and partly dictated by the
constraints of the international situation. Whether modernization for
these nations will be successful in the long run, no one can say, but we
believe that the process can be autonomous, and consequently at least
satisfying to the nations concerned, if our model is followed.

Problematics in social scientific theories

Social scientific theories refer to the various taxonomies of
modernization developed in the social science disciplines. There are
two kinds of problematics we wish to discuss in the context of these
disciplines. One refers to the question of values and the other to
that of means. In the value field, the issue appears in the form of

elitism versus democracy.[13] A modern society is geared to democracy with its freedoms, opportunities, and satisfaction of minimum needs for all individuals. Elites come in the way of democracy if they perpetuate their prerogatives; often they are a hindrance to the realization of basic equalities.

However, some of the benefits of democracy are inevitably linked to the expansion of consumer goods and services, which come about only in a self-sustaining economy, in whose development the elites have a major role to play. The elites are thus a means to modernization. In the past they (the industrial or the ideological elite) have been a crucial element in the growth of all nations, capitalist or Soviet ('the new Soviet elite'), and it seems that it may be difficult to abolish the elites from a society where production and consumption go beyond the subsistence stage. Therefore, the pivotal question is how to make elites socially conscious and individually accountable for whatever societal tasks they perform, and for whatever benefits accrue to them because of this.

Problematics in activistic theories

The activistic theories refer to directed change in institutions as well as to a positive policy toward change agents. Institutional change is brought about by large-scale planning and it is necessary that nations make decisions on two crucial issues. One concerns the question of tradition versus modernity, and the other, the issue of community autonomy versus bureaucracy. The older literature on modernization condemned all traits bearing the imprint of tradition;[14] the newer literature tries to assess if and how a traditional trait is a barrier to modernization, at which stage of the developmental process is its weight most felt, and how a traditional trait can be harnessed in the service of modernization.[15]

The issue of community autonomy versus bureaucracy translates itself into problems of decentralization versus centralization. Following Max Weber, one is aware of the important role of bureaucracy in organizing the affairs of a large, complex, urban, or urban-industrial society. However, one notices that everywhere bureaucratization leads to: centralization; routinization of charismatic leadership as well as movements; an emphasis on due process and rules and regulations; and mechanisms of rigid control even in political, as distinguished from administrative, matters.[16] Such trends in society may help economic growth or political stability but they may also crush individual autonomy and development of the community; they may ultimately affect the vital freedoms of a modern society.

On the other hand, the change agents of modernization, whether they are scientists, innovators, entrepreneurs, or 'marginal men'[17] often need protection and perhaps some extra consideration because of their crucial role as a catalytic factor in modernization. This may raise problems of favoritism, elitism, and even authoritarianism, which need to be resolved in all modernizing societies.

Further thoughts on problematics

It may seem that some of the problematics we have delineated may be insurmountable barriers toward the modernization of new nations. However, we do not believe this to be the case. A 'positivist' may claim that stagnation, elitism (in the sense of creating an insurmountable barrier between the elite and the masses), tradition, and community autonomy – the four variables discussed in the last two sections of the problematics – form a syndrome which goes against the grain of modernization. By this argument economic growth, democracy (in the sense of non-existence of elites, admittedly a difficult case to find), modernity (the cluster of traits on the opposite spectrum of tradition), and bureaucracy form another syndrome which truly advances modernization. Although the interrelations of the variables within the syndrome are intelligible and the latter syndrome appears to be highly recommended by modernization theorists, we believe that modernization is a dialectical process and emerges from the interplay of so-called opposed syndromes. Moreover, some of the factors which may be considered antithetical to modernization may turn out to be desirable, to which individuals, groups, and societies may wish to return after they have had a taste of modernization.[18]

The problems and the problematics of modernization are many and the guidelines for resolving them are few. But this is no reason for despair; instead what one needs is more energetic and value-committed action on the part of intellectuals, developers, and all others who are interested in this Modern Ascent.

We now turn our attention to the substantive theories of modernization. In discussing the theories, we shall try to ascertain how they relate to issues of ideology, the structural framework of modernization, and the treatment of the agents of modernization. We first review the master models of the ideology of modernization and some of the responses to such models. After that, in the following chapter, we briefly examine some issues connected with theory and methodology in modernization studies. Then, in later chapters, we discuss the social science models of the structure of modernization and their related systemic needs. Finally, we will go on to the agents of modernization, without whom the latecomers in the field may have to remain continually handicapped.

19

3 The ideological theories of modernization

Modernization theories carry a pervasive ideology, whose roots lie in the history of the West. We cannot understand the zeal of Western writers unless we comprehend the moral and intellectual roots of their being. Judeo-Christian values form the basis of their morality and the Marxian principle of revolution often suffuses them with intellectual and revolutionary fervor. It is said, perhaps without exaggeration, that Jesus Christ and Karl Marx are the two persons about whom as much has been written as about any other persons in history. It is possible that Jesus's crucifixion for his faith and Marx's propagation of world revolution in the *Communist Manifesto* (1848) may have been responsible for their fame and popularity. However, what we wish to emphasize here is not their charismatic personalities, but their ideological beliefs and dogmas, which shaped the destiny of modernization in history. The Protestant Ethic and the *Communist Manifesto* are the twin precursors of modernization. Let us elaborate on this point briefly.

First, the Protestant Ethic. Following Max Weber, there is a widespread belief in intellectual circles that capitalism developed as a consequence of the beliefs and practices flowing from the Protestant Ethic.[1] That the capitalist nation of England was the first to industrialize in history and that most processes of modernization started there is not in doubt. The story of the economic growth of England, Western Europe, the United States, and other nations of the West has been well-documented by economic historians. Our purpose is not to highlight the economic facts but to point out that political development in the West followed as a consequence of economic development and, as such, the emergence of capitalism was an important landmark in the history of the world.

Reinhard Bendix, among others, carefully reviews the transformation of 'the estate societies of the Middle Ages to the absolutist regimes of the eighteenth century and thence to the class societies of plebiscitarian democracy in the nation-states of the twentieth century.'[2] He shows how individualistic authority relationships replaced the traditional relations between masters and servants and how a nationwide system of public authority emerged in which governments went through a process of bureaucratization and adapted to conflicting group pressures in Western democracies.[3]

Modern society was born under the impetus of the beliefs of a particular Christian sect – the Puritans; their ideas were carried forward in the efforts of the 'inner-directed man,' as David Riesman calls him.[4] Some have questioned whether 'the inner-directed' man or 'the other-directed man,' another term in Riesman's typology, is the type needed for economic growth and modernization.[5] The issue is not pivotal here because one may consider both types as instrumental in bringing about modern society, perhaps one following the other. It is 'the tradition-directed man' who is the prototype of traditional society.

There is another variant of modern society of which Karl Marx is the godfather rather than Jesus Christ. This society flourishes in the Soviet World, which provides a competing model for the modernizing nations. It seems to us that the key to Marx's revolutionary ideas are in the *Communist Manifesto*, and that his earlier writings were a preparation for it and his later writings a justification for the revolutionary program announced therein.[6] The theme of revolution was further elucidated by Lenin[7] and others and it has no doubt gripped the minds of the young in all succeeding generations. We shall therefore dwell on it briefly.

In so far as social change is dependent on revolution, we believe that history will definitely remember five major revolutions. These are the American Revolution (1776 and the adjoining years), the French Revolution (1789 and the adjoining years), the Russian Revolution (1917), the Chinese Revolution (1949), and the Cuban Revolution (1959). The American Revolution was anti-colonial and its ideas have worked continuously for two centuries to establish the freedoms needed for a self-governing country.[8] The French Revolution was anti-aristocracy and helped to instill the fundamental concept of equality in the minds of men everywhere. The Russian Revolution was anti-state and created the proletarization of society. It also propagated the idea of a unified destiny for mankind. The Chinese Revolution was anti-elite, and works for constant reshuffling of the prerogatives of the elite so as to equalize them with the masses. It is also the first experiment in history for a dual-centred economy in which the rural and the urban regions will have equal opportunities for growth and fulfillment. The Cuban Revolution was anti-capitalist and is working feverishly for the

21

emancipation of the poor and the building-up of communities.[9] The impact of these revolutions is bound to guide the choices of all modernizing nations.

So far we have observed that a modern nation is born either through evolution, e.g. England, or through revolution, e.g. Russia. Now we wish to focus on their ideologies, which provide the motive force as well as some of the guidelines for directed change in the new nations. We will begin with the revolutionary model first.

The revolutionary model

The revolutionary model, as we indicated earlier, takes its primary cue from Marx and Engels's *Communist Manifesto*, where the workers are exhorted to rise against the ruling class and to capture the power structure of the society. The model stipulates a post-capitalist phase of socialism,[10] which requires nationalization of all means of production and liquidation of private capital, and builds toward communism, which when fully realized will mean 'from each according to his capacity, to each according to his needs.' The abolition of class distinctions is necessary in this model, but the equalization of incomes is not, in the beginning. An elaborate series of national plans is called for, which in some cases as in Russia, builds an industrial and a city-oriented life; in others, as in China, the stress is equally on industry and agriculture, so that people's aspirations in rural areas are not necessarily city-oriented. In the case of Cuba, there is emphasis on education and agricultural production, but a de-emphasis on urbanization and consumerism.[11] Food, shelter, health, education, and recreation are provided for all without distinction of status between a producer and a consumer. This is one of the basic differences between the revolutionary model and the evolutionary one.

The evolutionary model

It is the industrial-capitalist countries of the West which hang on to the evolutionary model and hope that it will be a beacon for the Third World of Asia, Africa, and Latin America. Japan, as a latecomer, is usually offered as a test case for modernizing successfully in terms of the evolutionary model. Not only the consumption levels of the industrial-capitalist countries, but their entire social system including class structure (especially an expanding middle class) is deemed proper for emulation by the modernizing nations. The high levels of literacy, enhanced life styles, political mechanisms of democracy, labor's proficiency in skills and the professional's competence in science make the Western countries very attractive to the new nations. However, after initial experiments with the evolutionary model, there does not seem much hope that any new country will make the grade of the West. Japan is an exception and seems likely to remain an exception at least for this century, for several reasons which we do not wish to investigate here.

What have been some of the responses to the two master models of modernization? From among the many responses, we have made a representative selection of some general models, which have guided the peoples of Latin America, the Middle East, Africa, and Asia. It should be remembered that when we talk about master models and the responses to them, we think of composite constructs, which abstract from reality the main features of the case under consideration. Also responses do not mean that there were conscious efforts on the part of an individual, a nation, or a region to respond to the two master models of the West, but only that the impact of Western modernization played some determinate role in the development of the specific ideological or social movements, which we refer to as the responses.

The responses

The Catholic model

In the nineteenth century, Pope Leo XIII expressed the Catholic position with regard to the social framework of modern society. His doctrine emphasized the God-given nature of order in the universe, which science and technology also make clear. He elaborated on the role of consensus and free will. He recognized the liberties of speech and association, the freedom of movement, and the choice of the political community. He praised the role of the worker and women, and enjoined the state to undertake economic development in order to provide adequate food, housing, sanitation, and leisure for all. He proclaimed that religious life must be guaranteed and the worker paid justly for the fruits of his labor. He called for the abolition of racism and stipulated that state authority must become a moral force because it has its roots in God's authority. Finally, he decreed that laws in contradiction with the divine order lack moral force and cannot command the obedience of the people.[12]

It is clear that parts of the ideology in the Catholic response to modernization are in consonance with the goals promulgated in the American Revolution, and some are antithetical to the Russian Revolution. A large section of Latin America (predominantly Catholic) imbibed this model and emphasized the liberal ideas embedded in it, but sections of the clergy and the laity there have shown partiality to certain aspects of the Soviet model. They admire especially the latter's revolutionary approach to problems of land and labor, because they feel that the evolutionary model of the West does not seem to bring about needed changes.

The Kemalist model

Kemal Ataturk's modernization of Turkey marks an important chapter, in the history of Islamic states. The abolition of the Caliphate in 1924 and the removal of religious objections against social reforms were important aspects of Ataturk's fifteen-year rule of Turkey. He adopted the Western style of mass education, but did not tolerate opposition parties. Some of the legal and cultural reforms (the abolition of the *purdah* or the veil for women) were unsurpassed in Islamic history, except perhaps in Egypt.

Throughout the Near East, the primary loyalties up to the nineteenth century were dynastic and religious, as well as local and tribal. It should be noted that in Islam, the state existed together with or even before the church, so the monopoly of the power of the government over the people was well entrenched. Spurts in the direction of modernization were taken in several Islamic states, but Kemalism did not gain roots outside Turkey. In Turkey, the mass literacy program, the development of transportation and communications, a viable bureaucracy, and the adoption of Western dress and morals are considered the main legacy of Kemalism.

Recent developments toward Pan Arabism[13] and Muslim Brotherhood[14] have led to the translation of the Islamic faith into acts which affirm brotherhood and militate against the age-old distrust of foreign elements. They have been dubbed 'anti-modern' but they have also encouraged the founding of schools, workshops, and cooperatives.

The African socialist model

The thrust toward socialism seems to be a universal feature of the new nations, which have been born in the era of nationalism after the Second World War.[15] However, African socialism is a distinct phenomenon. There have been leaders of African states who were socialists, such as Kwame Nkrumah of Ghana, but the true example of African socialism is found in the writings of Julius Nyerere of Tanzania,[16] whose experiments draw the interest of many Africans. Nyerere sees socialism as a logical extension of tribal collectivism.[17] Nyerere emphasizes mass education, better health services, and an improved life for small farmers. In

Tanzania, key industries are state-controlled, although some private investment is permitted in governmental partnership. Cooperatives or 'Ujamaa Villages,' as they are called, have been formed in which 15 per cent of the country's population live the same kind of life as in the *kibbutzim* of Israel.[18]

It is believed by some that African socialism can skip the intermediate stages of growth and can lead a country directly from tribalism into socialism. Tom Mboya, for instance, claimed that in African tribal life there is 'the logic and the practice of equality, and the acceptance of communal ownership of the vital means of life – the land.'[19]

The Gandhian model

In India, Gandhi's philosophy of *sarvodaya* has also been called Gandhian socialism.[20] However, *sarvodaya* means 'everyone's growth.' It implies the free and full development of every individual. Gandhi was against any coercion of the individual even in the interest of the good of the majority. He wanted to build a social order based on non-violence, where the individual's rights would be properly safeguarded. He propagated individualism in the form of self-reliance and self-help.

Gandhi felt that the individual's real merit lies in what he gives beyond anything he receives. This is the ancient Indian principle of *dán* or gift. Based on this tenet, Vinoha Bhave, a holy man who calls himself one of Gandhi's disciples, introduced the movement of *bhóodán* (landgift), whereby rich land owners make a gift of a part of their land to the poor.[21] The movement of *bhóodán* led to *grámdán* (gift of whole villages), in which production and distribution in the community are managed by cooperatives. Jayaprakash Narayan, who has been the moving spirit behind this movement, reported that by 1968 50,000 villages or one-tenth of all Indian villages, were donated to the cause.[22] Gandhi felt that cooperative enterprise was an extension of individualism.

Gandhi believed in decentralization of the economy and mass education for all; the latter he called basic education, whereby a person learns arts, crafts, and worldly knowledge through doing things himself. He did not favor massive industrialization, but he had advanced the idea of intermediate technology long before the Western economists coined this term.[23] Gandhi believed in the withering away of the coercive state as Marx did. But while the Communist Party tries to impose coercive organizations on the individual, which only helps to strengthen the state, the Gandhian ideal strives to take away from the purview of the state as much of the common affairs of the people as can be conveniently managed

25

through the cooperatives. The cooperative structure, he felt, must grow up from below, and must not be imposed from above. On the basis of these principles, the followers of Gandhi, aided by the government, have started massive programs of village government, rural self-help, cottage industries, and the uplift of the poor in India. The Panchayati Raj movement, as it is called, has been exported to other countries as well.

It should be clear from the above general responses to the two master models of the West that the paths to modernization are many and that in the last three decades, experiments in the modernizing nations, except in a few cases, have neither followed strictly the Marxist line, nor the dictates of the capitalist-industrial West. If anything, the majority of nations has been eclectic in its approach. The arguments for revolution are weighty but the costs are fearsome. The persuasion for evolution is reasonable but the prospects of immediate results are poor. The hopes of working with the evolutionary model began a new kind of psychological revolution after the Second World War, which was dubbed by Eugene Staley in 1954 the 'revolution of rising expectations.' However, in less than a decade, the hopes turned into a 'revolution of rising frustrations.'

Our effort in reviewing the ideological models has been made to show that scientific theories of modernization have necessarily some roots in political ideology.[24] Marx and Engels were not afraid of proclaiming their ideology for the future of mankind as is clear from the following words: 'Let the ruling classes tremble at a communist revolution. The proletarians have nothing to lose but their chains. They have a world to win. Working men of all countries, unite!'[25] Similarly undaunted is the Western economic historian, W. W. Rostow, who made a decision as an undergraduate at Yale University in the mid-1930s to refute Marx. A quarter-century later, in 1960, he came out with his economic-cum-ideological book, *The Stages of Economic Growth*, and subtitled it *A Non-Communist Manifesto*.[26] We shall review his thesis later on when we examine economic theories; here we only want to point out that a whole group of scholars, from Max Weber to Rostow, have felt it important to attack Marx, either for his theory, or for his methodology, but always more importantly for his ideology.

The claim on the part of the social science scholars has been that their own works are scientific whereas Marx's and his followers' works have been ideological. One is constrained to point out that lately this position has become quite untenable even on the testimony of social scientists. From the Right, comes criticism from scholars that the use of the comparative method, which is the key to understanding modernization, is ethnocentric. They point out that the 'stages of economic growth' theory commits fallacies of the evolutionary school.[27] From the Left, comes the attack that modernization theorists think of the destiny of nations in terms of the capitalist image of society, in which the existence of the market system, private property, class differences, and the role of the elite for guiding the destiny of a nation are absolutely necessary.[28] These charges cannot be dismissed lightly in view of mounting evidence on this score.

We will therefore turn next to a general discussion of the theory and the methodology of the various social science disciplines which deal with modernization. We will assess their potentialities and limitations for diagnosing the modernization process.

4 On the theory and the methodology of modernization studies

On theory

Before going into the substantive theories of modernization in the fields of sociology, economics, political science, anthropology, and psychology, a few words ought to be said in a general way about theory and methodology pertaining to the modernization field. Most scholars of modernization build a model along the lines of the ideal-type construct of Max Weber[1] to articulate a modern society, a modern economy, a modern polity, a modern culture, or a modern man. This construct of 'the modern,' in whatever field it has been attempted, bears a close resemblance to the features of the Anglo-American societies (often also to the Soviet societies) and hence the charge that it is ethnocentric.[2] In view of the evolutionary history of modernization discussed earlier, this charge cannot be avoided. However, our attempt here is not to apologize for the ethnocentric bias in some of the models, but to outline broadly the ingredients and assumptions of scientific theories of modernization.

There are several strategies used by the theorists. Either they build a construct of a modern society in its ideal-type form and compare every known society to their hypothetical construct; or they articulate a set of variables, which they consider crucial for modernization and build taxonomies out of them. A master taxonomy of the latter type will lead to the ideal-type construct mentioned above. But sub-taxonomies will delineate specific structures and processes of modernization in various areas of behavior. For instance, a certain combination of variables in the pattern variable schema of Talcott Parsons[3] can be called the master model of modernization, whereas the interest aggregation and rule-making schema of Gabriel Almond[4] falls in the category of

28

sub-taxonomies. Generally, the emphases in such theorizing are on systems and on taxonomies. They help analyses of the structural-functional kind, or the cybernetic kind (as, for instance, in the input-output analysis), exemplified in the works of Gabriel Almond,[5] David Easton,[6] and Karl Deutsch,[7] among others.

Another strategy of theorizing adopted by scholars of modernization is called propositional inventories or propositional analyses.[8] There is no hard and fast difference between this and the earlier form of theorizing (often the same scholar combines both), except that taxonomies emphasize definitions and use the diagnostic method, whereas propositions emphasize the empirical relations between variables and work toward verificational studies.[9] There are also scholars who use dialectical analysis;[10] their work is generally qualitative rather than quantitative.

On methodology

As far as methodology is concerned, we wish to point out that each scholar is more or less guided by the canons of his discipline; for instance, an economist will be generally more quantitative, and a political scientist generally more qualitative in his approach. However, quantitative studies in the area of modernization show more predilection for simple correlative analysis than for other advanced techniques such as factor or path analysis.

Structural-functional framework

A few limitations of the various forms of theorizing need to be kept in mind when we examine the works of various theorists. Structural-functional analysis provides an explanation of units in terms of other units, whose significance for man and his condition cannot be truly fathomed in so far as this kind of analysis avoids historical and moral issues. It is also generally non-causal in its approach. Since most of the literature on modernization falls into this category, it would be useful to describe the nature of the relationship between the variables in this framework. Following Zetterberg, we will call it the interdependent relation, which he explicates as follows:

> Let ΔX and ΔY be small increments in variables X and Y, respectively. An interdependent relation is present when the following conditions are met:
> *If X changes from X_1 to X_2, and $X_2 = X_1 + \Delta X$, then and only then, Y changes from Y_1 to $Y_2 + \Delta Y$; further, when Y changes from Y_1 to Y_2 and $Y_2 = Y_1 + \Delta Y$, then and then only, X changes from X_2 to $X_2 + \Delta X$, etc.*[11]

The important point to note is that 'the two variables are flirting with each other,' so that only small increment and reciprocal influence will advance the system but a quick gain in one variable will not lead to the required change in the other two. Zetterberg does not specifically identify this relationship as functional (because the word functional has many meanings), but we believe that it truly describes the general assumption made in most systematic and structural-functional analyses of the problems of modernization.

Propositional framework

The propositional approach is more amenable to identifying causation and as such its further development will be helpful. What we find in social science is a plethora of definitions, and little work of a propositional kind, especially in the area of modernization theory. Kalman H. Silvert and Frank Bonilla began with some useful sets of definitions and hypotheses concerning modernization and class and national integration, which were used as guidelines for the authors of *Expectant Peoples*.[12] However, there is little evidence of true verification of the hypotheses by any author in the work. Lucien W. Pye offers a model of the 'transitional' political process in terms of nine propositions but these seem to be stated at such high levels of abstraction that their confirmation, at least as offered in the book *Politics, Personality and Nation Building: Burma's Search for Identity*[13] is problematic indeed.

We would like to make it clear that most taxonomies carry some testable propositions, but the leap from illustration to verification in these studies is seldom taken. Selective evidence is enough for illustration, whereas critical evidence is necessary for verification. Unless modernization theories move in the direction of establishing causation and undertaking more verificational studies, their scientific status will be considered in doubt by the hard-core positivists among social scientists. Finally, it should be noted that dialectical analysis, like most of structural-functional analysis, also fails to allocate causal weights to any factors except in the sense that their 'primitives' (non-questionable assumptions) may themselves bear the seeds of all causation.

Critical variables

We will now turn our attention to one additional issue which will guide our search into the literature of modernization. The first wave of modernization, i.e. the modernization process of the West, is fairly well documented. But the second wave of modernization, which started for a majority of the world's countries at the end of the Second World War, is still in progress. There have been breakdowns,[14] arrests ('prismatic arrests,'[15] as they have been called), and sometimes stupendous leaps in the modernization of the new countries. Part of the explanation is in terms of system growth, where structural-functional categories are used. The other explanation may be in terms of a critical variable, which can shift the gear completely for a nation.

We arrive inductively at the following variables which have been considered critical at one point or another for the modernization process in general or for the modernization of a nation in particular: a charismatic leader (Nkrumah or Nasser); a symbolic act (the nailing of the 95 theses on the door of the castle church at Wittenberg by Martin Luther); a symbolic event (the arrival of a trader, a missionary, or independence for a colony); a strategic principle (the organization of collectives or *kolkhozes*); extending an idea from one domain to another (the application of deductively formulated legal principles to the realm of religion as in the case of changes in the *Sharia*); a strategic variable (land-grant universities or mass education); and constant experimentation for its own sake (as in the case of the United States). No doubt there are limits to the success of each one of these critical variables, if indeed they are critical; but one interested in the modernization of the Third World would like to know if some variables are in fact more effective than others.

Further assessment

Some theories of modernization, especially of the structural-functional kind, couch their ideas in terms of prerequisites, associated variables, and chain relationships. However, the notion of a critical variable, if it exists in the field of modernization, has always fascinated the developers. In the review of the literature, we will keep an eye on this point.

We would now like to turn to various disciplines. We will first indicate the variables which are considered crucial for modernization within the specific framework of a discipline. We will then examine the chief models of each discipline. In discussing these models, the interrelations of the variables will be kept in mind. Our effort, as before, will be selective so that some of the crucial problems raised by our model of modernization are answered; also the selections should bring out the critical thinking of each discipline. The issue of barriers to modernization as well as strategies for development will be constantly emphasized. Our selection of authors and ideas is guided by these general criteria rather than by the specific criterion of sampling a full representation of modernization theorists of each discipline.

The field of modernization studies is growing enormously and at such a fast pace that it is difficult to keep track of the latest developments. Also some authors change their views in the middle of the road. So, if we delineate the field rather circumspectly, it should be understood that it is because of our interest in critical thinking rather than in summarizing the latest developments. Similarly, if we associate a view with an author who may have subsequently changed his opinion, our purpose is not to hold the author responsible for it, but to show how his specific ideas at one time were influential in the development of the field.

It should be noted that the works of some authors are discussed in the context of other disciplines than the ones they profess; this is so because it is the point which we are emphasizing that is important rather than the discipline of the author. Further, the works of Alex Inkeles and David C. McClelland, among others, are discussed in the section on activistic theories rather than social scientific theories, because their ideas are being directly applied in the field by change agents. It should also be kept in mind that activistic theories are often no less scientific than social science theories, and in the case of the last two authors mentioned, there is no difference between the two types of theories.

5 The sociological theories of modernization

Sociologists consider modernization as a special case in the larger process of social change. In the voluminous literature existing today, they have no doubt examined some of the general aspects of modernization as sketched out in our model. For instance, in the field of economic growth, they generally concern themselves with the building of the economic institution and its interrelations with other institutions. National leadership, the development of the educational system, the role of labor unions, and entrepreneurship are some of the key topics with which they are concerned. In the field of political development, they emphasize the difficult facets of nation-building, such as the development of mass media and communications, popular participation in the political process, the growth and viability of the executive, legislative, and judicial branches of the government, the extension of a national legal system, the creation of consensus for public decision making, and similar problems connected with the functioning of the national polity.

The literature on social reconstruction is also extensive. It deals with the development of bureaucracy, the viability of planning and action programs, as well as with the shift from the rural to the urban milieu of a growing number of people, and consequent changes in class structure, urban pathologies, population pressures, and so on. The demands of the populace in the modernizing nations are fed by vocal interest groups, which often compete with the interests of the elite which is entrenched in power. The issues of equality, fraternity, and the enhancement of basic freedoms and opportunities highlighted in our model are related to the rise of new ideologies and reform movements. Many theoretical as well as speculative works exist on these topics.

In this chapter we do not propose to concentrate on these general topics, because such an effort would distract us from examining the substantive works of the modernization theorists whom we have selected for review. We will instead examine the works of the theorists in terms of the issues of modernization they themselves chose to discuss. However, in delineating the strengths and weaknesses of their theories, we shall constantly probe what they have to say on the above topics. After reviewing the theories in the framework of analysis outlined later in this chapter, we will return to these topics and examine them systematically in a later chapter. There we will present an integrated view of all facets of modernization.

Social change and modernization

Sociologists have been interested in large-scale social change ever since Auguste Comte[1] formulated his conceptions of the metaphysical, theological, and scientific (positive) stages in social evolution. Similarly, Herbert Spencer[2] visualized the growth of societies from the military to the industrial type. From Ferdinand Toennies's classification of *Gemeinschaft* (community)-*Gesellschaft* (society)[3] to Henry S. Maine's (a scholar of law and jurisprudence) status-contract,[4] Howard Becker's sacred-secular,[5] and Robert Redfield's (an anthropologist specializing in folk and literate cultures) 'folk'-urban continuum,[6] the effort of scholars to articulate and even predict social change has been unusually creative. However, it is to Karl Marx's classification of primitive communist-slave-feudal-capitalist-socialist-communist societies[7] that the world pays more heed today than to the other more academic schemas. We have discussed Marx earlier, and we will return to him again. Let us consider now Max Weber's analysis of industrial capitalism, which is of great value to sociologists in articulating modernization theory.

We noted earlier that industrial capitalism is synonymous with modern society in one of the master models of modernization. Weber singles out the following factors as the constituents of the modern society: the role of science based on experimental method; developments in the fine arts during the Renaissance movement; rational systems of law and administration; the modern state; and 'rational bourgeois capitalism.'[8] However, one aspect of Weber's theory, namely, his discussion of the role of the Protestant ethic in creating modern society is increasingly being questioned by latter-day scholars.[9]

We would like to note that the main differences between Marx and Weber are two: the former emphasizes 'economic determinism' as the key factor in the evolution of all societies; the latter thinks of ideas (religious ethic) as the primary factor at least in the emergence of Western capitalism. The former believes that the force of historical evolution (working through dialectical materialism) will inexorably lead to communism; the latter concentrates on the institutions of modern ‘Western society and analyses their constituent features with great theoretical rigor.

It is important for us to discuss in detail the views of Talcott Parsons, an eminent expositor of Weber's ideas, and perhaps the person who has wielded the greatest influence within American sociology as well as outside it in articulating the systemic models and in analysing the modernization process. It would be difficult to do justice to Parsons's multi-faceted and voluminous writings on theories of society in this very brief account. However, we wish to bring out the salient features of his schemas, which bear on any aspect of modernization. In the general introduction to this section we will outline his ideas on the evolution of society. When we come to the section on models, we will describe his specific schemas, which have influenced most of the social scientists who think of modernization as an integrated system of institutions and values.

Parsons criticized and abandoned the evolutionary hypotheses in his first major work, *The Structure of Social Action* (1937),[10] but came back to accepting evolutionary and comparative perspectives on society three decades later in *Societies* (1966) and in *The System of Modern Societies* (1971). In the decades of the 1950s and the 1960s, the non-North American and the non-European nations started modernizing and the non-Marxist theorists, who helped in the enterprise, increasingly adopted various Parsonian schemas for articulating their own individual paradigms. Parsons could not ignore the march of history, or his own role in it as a theorist.

Where does Parsons himself stand now? He says that socio-cultural evolution, like organic evolution, should be analysed in terms of the variation and differentiation of societies from simple to progressively more complex forms.[11] The evolution follows the principles of differentiation, specialization, and higher-order integration. For instance, in evolving societies, work is removed from family to firm or factory, and the integration of economic roles takes place through the new integrative structures of the firm or the factory rather than through the head of the family as was the case before.

Parsons divides the evolution of societies into three stages: primitive, intermediate, and modern.[12] He also talks about archaic societies (examples: Ancient Egypt, the Mesopotamian Empires) and 'advanced' primitive types (example: the African kingdoms). The intermediate (or advanced intermediate) societies are China, India, the Islamic Empires, and Rome. The system of modern society he dates from certain seventeenth-century developments in Western Europe, especially the role of religion in society, and the eighteenth-century evolution of the West toward democracy and industrialization. He states that the process of modernization began in the West and spread elsewhere by colonization or by diffusion. He calls Ancient Israel and Ancient Greece 'seed bed' societies from which transcendentalism, universalistic rationality, and a kind of practicality grew[13] – these being the keys of the thrust toward modernization.

The variables of modernization

For contemporary modern society, Parsons puts emphasis on the following sets of variables: a market system and its 'economic complex' of contract, property, and occupations; a nation-state emancipated from religious and ethnic control and functioning as a 'political complex' of leadership, authority, and regulation; a universalistic legal system; associations and interest groups; citizenship; representative government; competent administration; and nationalism.[14] He points out that mass education is a new cultural innovation in the direction of modernity.[15] Other sociologists, including Parsons in his other writings, add the following additional characteristics: an increase in the size and the scale of society; urbanization; centralization in the sense of concentration of power in national-level agencies and national groups such as trade unions and business associations; erosion of the power of ethnic groups in national affairs; proliferation of the mass media; interest-based national elites; free intellectuals; status-stratification based on achievement; secular trends in religion and society; the nuclear family; and population control. To these variables are added the securing of fundamental rights and basic freedoms for all.

The models of modernization

The pattern variables model

The most comprehensive model of a modern society is formulated in terms of the pattern variables of value orientation articulated by Talcott Parsons as follows:[16]
   (a) Universalism versus Particularism
   (b) Specificity versus Diffuseness
   (c) Performance versus Quality
   (d) Affective Neutrality versus Affectivity
   (e) Collectivity-Orientation versus Self-Orientation
   A combination of the first of these pairs of variables defines the

relational expectations or roles of what Parsons and his followers describe as modern society. For example, the evaluation of actions in a modern society is based on the principle of universalism rather than particularism; the scope of one's sympathies are specific rather than diffuse; a person is judged by his performance rather than by qualities ascribed to him at birth; a person learns to develop an attitude of lukewarmness (affective neutrality) rather than emotional responses (affectivity) toward societal objects in general; and finally the goals of collective society take precedence over personal gratification. Parsons claims that these five dichotomous categorizations of action exhaust the possibilities of modes of orientation and that their combination in paradigmatic form will provide the analytical taxonomy for societies. It should be noted that the possibilities of empirical societies may actually be fewer than what the permutations and combinations of these pattern variables may suggest.

The sociocultural system model

A second paradigm of Parsons is related to his biological assumptions about the sociocultural system. Sociocultural systems are postulated by him to be in equilibrium, so that their functioning can be explained in terms of pattern maintenance (this refers to problems of recruitment, socialization, etc., as well as to maintenance of the institutional and cultural patterns); adaptation (to the environment in terms of allocation of resources – the economy); goal attainment (formulating objectives and the procedures of arriving at them – the polity); and finally integration (the overall coordination of the values of societal community – the social system; also its integration).[17] The processes articulated above have gone through many reformulations at Parsons's hands,[18] and the scholars who use them try to fit Parsons's general model and its varied interpretations into their own empirical pursuits.

Further, the evolution of higher levels of any particular sociocultural system, as compared to its functioning which was articulated above, is delineated by Parsons in terms of differentiation, adaptive upgrading, inclusion, and value generalization.[19] These change processes are stated at very high levels of abstraction, and usually the scholars who adopt this general schema furnish their own elucidation of it.

The exposition of the models

In the following sections, we will first present further expositions of the sociological models. We will see how the elements of the

THE SOCIOLOGICAL THEORIES OF MODERNIZATION

preceding models have been used to interpret aspects of a particular modern society, viz. the United States, which is considered to be the most mature society in terms of modernization. We will then go on to the application of the models to modernizing societies and identify some of the critical problems of such societies. These problems pertain to centralization, authoritarianism, societal guidance by experts, consensus, legitimacy of the political system, bureaucratization of the society, the role of the mass media in the modernization process, the standardization of tastes and values, the participation of the masses in the political process, and the role of the intellectuals in a modernizing society. Finally, the implications of the models for selected institutions, such as stratification and social mobility, religion, and family, will be spelled out.

General modernization theories

Most sociologists use the systemic approach to modernization, and Parsons's schemas come in very handy for purposes of such analysis. Marion J. Levy, Jr., a brilliant student of Parsons, who wrote *The Structure of Society* (1953), in which he furnished the foremost explication of the Parsonian model of what he called 'structural-functional analysis,' has also come up with a treatise entitled *Modernization and the Structure of Societies* (1966), and has again focussed on the systemic view of what he designates therein as 'relatively modernized' and 'relatively non-modernized' societies.[20] Levy, like most writers in the field of modernization theory, has used in his book a large number of definitions (perhaps this was inevitable because it was written for graduate students of public administration and international affairs), and then has gone on to provide a delineation of some of the major issues in the field. However, his hypotheses, like those of Parsons, are often at such high levels of abstraction that one is not sure of their empirical referents. Also there is no way of knowing whether the hypotheses are verified or not. For instance, at one point he states:[21]

> United States society at present is far more highly modernized than is the society of the Soviet Union. [Modernization is defined by Levy only in terms of the use of energy power and technology.] It is also considerably less authoritarian as a society ... Except for the element of governmental authority, United States society is considerably more centralized than the Soviet Union.

The only criterion for centralization indicated by him in the above context is the technology of communications. The paucity of indicators in his treatise makes any evaluation of his major statements difficult, although in the above case he was merely pointing to the independence of modernization levels from authoritarianism and the limited association of authoritarianism and centralization. We believe that centralization is a phenomenon which must be measured in terms of the political as well as technological indicators; otherwise, the statements made in the quote above become simplistic. It is open to doubt if the United States is more centralized than the Soviet Union if we take the political indicators into consideration. Levy's demonstrated knowledge of the modernization process of Japan and China cannot compensate for his generally unsupported views on the Soviet Union and other societies.

Some of Levy's statements raise strong doubts as to whether he is talking about an empirical process or providing norms for it. For instance, he states, 'the further the process of modernization goes, the greater is the degree of centralization that must be achieved if stability is to exist.'[22] First, it is not clear why stability and the advancement of modernization should be equated, especially in view of the following statement of Amitai Etzioni: 'Modernization ... seems to proceed more easily in less than fully integrated regions of a country, all other things being equal (though not in highly disintegrated regions).'[23] Levy emphasizes centralization for modernization, whereas Etzioni finds the lack of the full integration of regions (which we interpret as lack of centralization) as being proper for the modernization process. It could be argued that Etzioni is talking about a strategy, whereas Levy has in mind a goal, but we do not see why stability (which is dependent on centralization according to Levy) should be the goal. It is arguments about stability which bring the charge that sociology is for the Establishment. Our main purpose, however, in discussing this issue has been to show that community autonomy and growth, an important element of our paradigm, is negated or disvalued in prognoses for modernization such as the one Levy generally prescribes.

Amitai Etzioni's *The Active Society* is a massive effort to apply the principles of cybernetics and system analysis to societal guidance. The plethora of definitions again is confusing but Etzioni makes a conscious effort to operationalize his terms and to provide the basis of an empirical test for his hypotheses. However, his combination of functional and genetic approaches seems fraught with dangers, especially when he refers to societal consciousness as 'the generalized capacity of a societal actor to be aware and not to an individual actor's awareness of societal processes.'[24] Despite his demurral against the group mind, because of such operationalizations of his concepts, one senses either reification or technological-managerial guidance of society in his programmatics for 'active society.' In answering the question, Active – For What? he says:[25]

> that (a) to the degree that a society is able to act in unison at all, it has *some mechanisms for converting the aggregate demands of its members into collective directives* ... (b) societal values may be realized in situations in which various members have conflicting, even incompatible demands so long as the society is responsive to the needs of the membership at large and not merely to those of a minority [italics in the original].

The issues are sharply posed. However, the mechanisms of policy formation, and the way the needs of the membership at large are assessed and evaluated are important questions on which much light still needs to be shed. The political scientist David Easton, in a similar context, would depend on the authority structure, as is clear from the following passage:[26]

> When we speak of the system acting, we must be careful not to reify the system itself. We must bear in mind that all systems, to make collective action possible, have *those who usually speak in the name of or in behalf of the system.* We may designate them as the authorities [italics added].

The cybernetic guidance which both Etzioni and Easton seek has not been able to come up with solutions of problems like the challenges to established authorities and the legitimacy of a new leadership; also they do not provide the rationale for the resolution of any conflict between the national leadership and the community leadership.

Etzioni's book is basically about guiding the future of the post-modern society of the West, which according to him began in 1945.[27] However, Parsons feels that the 'culminating' phase of modern development is a good way off, possibly a century, and the talk of 'post-modern' society is premature.[28]

Mature modern society analysis

Daniel Bell complains that Etzioni does not define post-modern society, except to point out the role of technology, knowledge, and energy in it.[29] It is here that Bell's own analysis of what he calls the coming Post-Industrial Society is germane. He thinks that the most mature industrial society of today (i.e. the United States) is moving in the direction where knowledge experts will control society. There is much material in his book about the structural bases of power of the scientist and of the expert in the evolving Post-Industrial Society but his description (or forecasting, as he calls it) of the new class relationship of that future society with techno-scientists placed at the top of the hierarchy seems overdrawn. However, the book carries good material on the unfinished jobs of the modernization process, especially the strains toward equality in the modern society,[30] about which Parsons had also hinted.[31] Bell discusses carefully the two meanings of equality, viz. the equality of opportunity, and the equality of results. He sees a conflict there, which he interprets as a case against meritocracy. He says that the equality of result is a socialist ethic and, in order to succeed, it must find its way into politics through a change in political philosophy.[32] On the other hand, Herbert Gans[33] outlines carefully the functions of poverty and shows how poverty is the end result of power-seeking and political compromises. S. M. Miller[34] and others[35] carefully state programs for abolishing poverty, which may lead a mature modern society toward the equalitarian ethos.

Seymour Martin Lipset's works[36] have a pivotal value in relating problems of democracy to a modern society like the United States. He has been under attack (especially from the Left), more than any other person in the field because he has perhaps dared and attempted to bite off more than he can chew. His comparative analysis of the political behavior of societies uses voting statistics as well as secondary materials, and is couched in the functional framework. Lipset explicitly used the pattern variables in some of his analyses and also the equilibrium model, as, for instance, in *The First New Nation*.[37] It is, therefore, rather strange that Talcott Parsons should impute to him an 'undogmatic Marxian frame of reference.'[38]

Lipset sees democracy as a system in which the political elite compete for the votes of a 'mainly passive electorate.' Legitimation of the rule as well as ruling positions and 'consensus – a political system allowing the peaceful "play" of power, the adherence by the "outs" to decisions made by the "ins," and the recognition by the "ins" of the rights of the "outs"' form the backbone of democracy.[39] He believes in conflict – but only mild conflict – within democracy. He shows how these principles work out in the United States, which is *The First New Nation*. He makes constant comparisons of the United States to other Western European countries, and seems to pull together diverse opinions and 'opinions *about* opinions' (tertiary sources) to make his points. As we examine his arguments, we find a general confusion of causation, correlation, convergence, and evolution in his analyses of traits and trait-complexes of modern societies.

His basic acceptance of the Weberian thesis 'that modern democracy can occur only under capitalist industrialization'[40] may color some of his perspectives and may seem to make him look like an apologist for the capitalists. Most of his analyses of the modernization process are about Europe; he talks about the Third World only in terms of generalities. He believes that the modernizing elite and the nationalists of Latin America and Asia have a leftist ideology, usually of a Marxist variety.[41] He thinks that cultural or value conflicts (of the religious type, as in Europe) are at the root of unstable politics in these countries.[42] It seems to us that these are stereotypical perceptions rather than generalizations from empirical studies, especially in the case of countries which have had a chance to work out their post-independence problems.

Lipset constantly moves back and forth from historical (unique) to comparative (generalizing) frameworks and gives the impression that his studies are full of tested (or testable) hypotheses. Here are a couple of examples: 'In general, the more rigid the status demarcation lines in a country, the more likely the emergence of explicit class-oriented parties.'[43] And also: 'The emphasis within the society on status differentiation facilitated the emergence of class-conscious groupings.'[44] Both hypotheses are negated in the case of India, where status demarcations have been rigid.

Lipset considers the roles of bureaucracies and political parties as quite benign in the United States. However, he seems to confuse values with power structure, as in the case of his analysis of the egalitarianism of the American frontier.[45] His works need detailed methodical scrutiny (because he throws in an endless array of variables) before they can be accepted or rejected as providing useful hypotheses for the modernization process. Some of his ideas on the process of change in the developing countries are clear extrapolations from the Western experience.

Some general correctives to Lipset's views on the modernization of the United States are provided by Joseph Bensman and Arthur J. Vidich in *The New American Society*. The authors discuss the situation in the United States since the advent of the New Deal, especially under the impact of Keynesian economics. They point out how authority relations are masked by democratic euphemisms and how bureaucratic authoritarianism is using the rhetoric of democracy.[46] They indicate that the major political parties are operating without goals and purposes.[47] The relationship of social structure (which in Daniel Bell's terminology means economy, technology, and occupation) to political culture, which was promised by Bell but was not carried out adequately by him, has received important attention in the Bensman and Vidich analysis. They point out how the growth of economic opportunity and the appreciation of the intellectuals by the professional establishments may have eroded their autonomy.[48] They feel that the cooptation of the scientists and the intellectuals is, however, not complete; the

42

latter can still reconstitute a new culture.[49] Bensman and Vidich have firm ideas about the need for and the protection of the autonomy of the individual,[50] which is also one of our interests as stipulated in our model of modernization. The point which Bensman and Vidich make that foreign aid must be 'genuinely altruistic in order to be genuinely selfish'[51] is borne out by experts like Albert O. Hirschman.[52]

Mass culture and mass society

Bernard Rosenberg has been a consistent critic of the mass culture which has been generated by advanced industrialism in the United States. The early origins of this concept are in the philosopher José Ortega y Gasset's *The Revolt of the Masses*, where he complained of 'the accession of the masses to complete social power.'[53] Rosenberg, however, emphasizes other facets of mass society, viz. its monotony, mediocrity, and debasement of man. He says: 'As Toynbee's Great West Wind blows all over the world, which quickly gets urbanized and industrialized ... a certain sameness develops everywhere.'[54] He shows how 'post-modern man' becomes 'an interchangeable part in the whole cultural process.'[55] He points to the dehumanization of man, and his entrapment and loneliness amid plenty.[56] He believes that the mass media play a major role in all this, because 'the mixing of the sacred and the profane, the genuine and the specious, the exalted and the debased' leaves the average American completely confused.[57]

The debate on mass culture is one of the most spirited in the United States and in the same volume, *Mass Culture* (1957), edited by Rosenberg, his co-editor, David Manning White, defends the popular arts in America, as did many other authors whose selections appear there. However, what we wish to point out is that the cult of advertising in the United States reduces man to his least common denominator (and often advances pseudo-goals for society), and that by 1951, when the debate was raging, the United States was spending six and a half billion dollars on advertising, which was a billion and a half more than on education.[58] Needless to say, advertising serves its own masters, whereas education serves the masses.

There is another aspect to the debate on mass culture which is relevant for our purposes. Mass culture is a product of mass society, mass society is often guided by the mass media, and as such the role of the mass media for individual autonomy and group welfare needs to be examined. Some theorists claim that, in American society, individuals have become atoms, very much disaffiliated from each other, and they only react to the messages of the mass media.[59] Other theorists point out that the proliferation of interest groups mediates an individual's reaction (and decisions) about whatever message is being propagated by the mass media.[60] According to William Kornhauser, this permits the individual to participate politically in a meaningful way because the interest group is close enough to the state to provide access to power.[61] Thus the mass media, the necessary purveyor of mass appeals, can either serve democracy or debase it depending on the nature of their use by their managers.

Communications theory

The mass media have been examined carefully by sociologists, political scientists, and others for their role in disseminating information and values without which no program of modernization can be carried out. Many scholars joined the bandwagon of creating a communications theory, which, if developed properly, would have been a master theory for all behavioral sciences.[62] Early efforts in this direction did not prove very rewarding. However, scholars like Lucien W. Pye, Daniel Lerner, and Ithiel de Sola Pool have not given up,[63] perhaps because of their affiliations with the Massachusetts Institute of Technology, where cybernetics was developed to such soaring heights by Norbert Weiner and his associates.

We find that communications theory (pertaining to modernization issues) is based more on faith and definitions than on tested hypotheses. Lucien W. Pye starts with assumptions such as 'communications encompasses *the bulk of social behavior*' [italics added],[64] and wishes to examine 'communications as an all-pervading aspect of social life.'[65] Such efforts, without stipulating variables, are born to be fruitless. In working toward a communications theory of modernization, all that Daniel Lerner could offer is the following schema for modernizing society:[66]

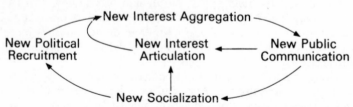

The neologism, which incorporates these terms, will be discussed in the chapter on political science; here we only wish to point out that communication in the above diagram has simply been treated as the flow of new ideas and information in the political process, and not much has been added theoretically in that endeavor.

'Cosmopolitan' and 'local'

Perhaps the most useful concepts for understanding the influencing process in modernization are the terms 'cosmopolitan' and 'local,' used by Robert K. Merton in identifying types of influential people.[67] The 'local' has influence because he understands the needs of the people around him, the 'cosmopolitan' because he knows the nature of the problem as it is related to the extra-local context and can help through his skills and expert knowledge. The 'local' is rooted in the community, the 'cosmopolitan' relates himself to the nation and the world. The linkage of these twin concepts to problems of communication, leadership, and mediation between the state and the individual (as noted earlier) are constantly being explored with quite fruitful results.[68]

Modernizing nations

We have discussed so far the problems of a modern society and the models which articulate them. We shall now turn to the application of the major sociological models to the problems of modernizing nations.

S. N. Eisenstadt's view of modernization, developed in many publications,[69] is strictly Parsonian. He recommends the leveling down of differences between the country and the city, between groups, and between regions in a modern society. He talks about eruptions, protests, and breakdowns in modernizing societies[70] and his only prescription is to remove the structural duality in these societies by absorbing the left-out groups in the consensual process.[71]

This seems to us to be either an idealistic prescription, or, actually simply to mean urbanizing these groups. Of course, the problems of over-urbanization of some developing countries are well-known and the solutions offered by some[72] are directly opposed to those of Eisenstadt.

Neil J. Smelser, a student of Parsons, and his collaborator in the book *Economy and Society* (1956), which extended the general theory of social systems to economics (the system analogy also reappears as inflation and deflation in political process), has written articulately about modernization. His first major work, *Social Change in the Industrial Revolution* (1959), was packed with definitions as are his later works, but this is nothing new for sociologists as we pointed out earlier. His analysis of the modernization process is couched in terms of the Parsonian concepts of

45

differentiation, which characterizes a social structure moving toward greater complexity; integration, which balances the divisive traits; and social disturbances, which result from the discontinuities between differentiation and integration.[73] He is candid enough to admit that his systemic analysis does not account 'for the determinants of economic development' nor can it show 'causal precedences in social change.'[74]

Some of Smelser's diagnoses seem inaccurate or commonplace, such as, 'if the educational system produces a large number of literate, skilled, but unemployable persons, this often sets up demands for economic or political adjustments.'[75] Why not revolutionary change rather than adjustment? Or apathy or fatalism, for that matter. Another diagnosis is an exemplification of the excesses of biology on sociology, as for example: 'In some cases this growth of integrative groupings in the city may be retarded because of the back-and-forth movement of migratory workers, who "come to the city for their differentiation" and "return to the village for their integration." '[76] It is not without reason that one often wonders how much of functional analysis is rhetoric and how much is plain commonsense.

The intellectuals

Edward Shils has articulated the role of the intellectual in the modern and modernizing societies.[77] He says that the modern intellectual class:[78]

> is the product of a modern society, latterly of an industrial
> society, characterized by rational, bureaucratic administration in
> the state and in economic life, widespread literacy and a high
> standard of living, an extensive educational system with wide-
> spread participation and at its peak a university system devoted
> to the cultivation of truth in science and scholarship as well as to
> the transmission of the cultural heritage.

He identifies the intellectuals as the independent man of letters; the scientist, pure and applied; the scholar; the university professor; the journalist; the highly educated administrator; the judge; and the parliamentarian.[79] Shils's intellectuals include the knowledge experts of Bell and are as well the middle classes in all modernizing societies.

There are few problems of the growth of the intellectuals discussed in his studies. His delineation of the role of the intellectual is more normative than scientific; he also ignores the important contributions of other intellectuals (who converse and work in native languages and who do not know any Western language) in the modernizing countries. Shils has been an associate of Parsons in some of the latter's theoretical works but he refrains from using the Parsonian schemas in his own writings.

Stratification

Seymour Martin Lipset and Reinhard Bendix,[80] among others, have examined the stratification system of modern as well as modernizing nations, and have unearthed some interesting findings. For instance, they point out that the rate of social mobility, i.e. the movement of children from the working class and the lower-class occupations of their parents to 'white collar' or higher status jobs is about the same (30 per cent) in the United States, Britain, Germany, Sweden, France, and Japan – all industrial nations.[81] They found that in the United States one-third (33 per cent) of the sons of professionals and associated categories of people on the same level are in manual employment.[82] The circulation of the elite and both vertical as well as horizontal mobility are considered to be key features of a modern society.

One of the chief difficulties in their framework of analysis is that it is urban-centric. The differences in the rural area are ignored or glossed over by them and it is the urban model which is applied to the entire country irrespective of its 'goodness of fit' to the norms and values of rural society.[83]

Religion

Robert Bellah has done scrutinizing work on religion in modern and modernizing nations and has shown that the Parsons-derived logical categories of differentiation and integration can be usefully applied to the sphere of developments in world religions. He sees an evolutionary process in religion, whereby the symbol systems move from a 'compact' to a 'differentiated' stage. Similarly, as religious collectivities become more differentiated from other structures, the consciousness of a religious self as distinct from the environment and daily life is developed. He posits five stages of religious development which he calls primitive, archaic, historical, early modern, and modern. He notes that 'at each stage the freedom of personality and society has increased relative to the environing conditions,' so that in the modern stage, 'each individual must work out his own ultimate solutions.'[84] This classification of religious stages is somewhat similar to Parsons's classification of evolutionary societies.[85] His book on Tokugawa religion[86] is convincing but the general framework used by him to articulate civil religion in America seems to us and to some of his critics to miss the chief point about religion that it protects man against the fear of the unknown.[87]

Family

William J. Goode is one of the few discerning scholars who has not been completely convinced by the unitary model of the modernization process elucidated by Parsons, Levy, Eisenstadt, and Smelser, among others. In his studies of the family, he provides data which no doubt show the development of the conjugal-type family in association with industrialization (as prognosticated by Parsons and his associates), but he is very careful to point out that no 'determinate relations exist between family variables and industrialization variables.'[88] He also emphasizes the theoretical importance of values or norms as bases for predicting family change;[89] he does not think that the so-called modernization process will automatically bring about the nuclear family.[90]

Goode clearly shows the gains of the extended family for the upper class in the industrial society and the costs of the conjugal family for the middle and the lower classes in the same society.[91] He exposes 'the ideology of the conjugal family' in the modern world and asks:[92]

to investigate [further] whether the Western family system, for many centuries, has been better organized than others, to take advantage of individual opportunities; and whether shifts in family attitudes may be attributed particularly to the Puritans, whose ties with industrialization are well documented?

Population: the theory of demographic transition

We shall examine one more area, i.e. population control, before we move to another discipline. The industrial revolution of the West showed a 'demographic transition,'[93] whereby population shifts occurred from high fertility and mortality levels to moderate fertility and mortality, with a time lag in the decline of fertility. Before industrialization in the West, there was a slow but fluctuating increase of population; during early industrialization, there was a phase of fast and faster runaway increase; and in the final stage, population slowed down to a moderate increase again. It was for some time the claim of demographers that this same process would accompany industrialization in other countries. However, with massive death controls, i.e. eradication of malaria, smallpox, the plague, and other epidemics in the contemporary world, and despite some efforts at birth control through natural and artificial means, the growth of population has been phenomenal during this century.[94] The modernizing nations, except Japan and perhaps a few others, have not made much of a dent in this field.[95] Demographers like Kingsley Davis now believe that short of massive governmental population control policies, the modernizing nations have no chance of getting out of the rut of massive population growth.[96] Thus, the best-known theory of demographic science – i.e. the theory of demographic transition – seems to have fallen victim to cold facts.

Some criticisms

We have reviewed the chief models of the sociological analysis of modernization and have found that although the systemic approach helps in sorting things out and putting them together, it is no substitute for propositional investigations and causal assessments. The syndrome approach and the prerequisites which are stipulated in systemic analysis remain unverified. They have a heuristic value, but they should not dogmatically be applied to the solutions of all problems of modernization. We also noted that the Weber-directed model has many issues (e.g. decentralization and autonomy) still unsettled in the sociological literature.

There is a tendency on the part of systemic analysis theorists to divide the world into traditional, transitional (a term often used by Daniel Lerner and S. N. Eisenstadt among others), and modern societies. They associate the traditional society with everything that is backward, and call the transitional societies problem-ridden and agonized societies; and so they seek to bring them to the level of modern society, mostly through the means of massive urbanization and industrialization. The frightful costs of such a change are ignored or perhaps considered necessary; also often the urban-oriented industrializing society is projected as the utopia for all societies seeking change. This attitude may, however, be changing now, what with the waste of natural and human resources and the environmental pollution overtaking the world. We find that the problems of community autonomy amid massive urbanization, and individual autonomy amid society-wide bureaucratization, two concerns most vital in our model, are also often neglected in the theorizing about modernization.

6 The economic and political theories of modernization

In this chapter, we discuss the theories of economic and political modernization. Although we deal with the works of the economists and the political scientists separately, there is a special reason for combining them into one section. They both deal with partial sectors of the society, unlike the sociologists and the anthropologists, who are involved in articulating the interrelations of all institutions of the society. Also the work of the economist or the political scientist is more specialized, partly because of his involvement in one institution alone. It is true that the concept of modernization as used in these two disciplines has its overflow in other institutions and as such several interdisciplinary issues are also under their focus. This we will notice when we examine their works. We merely want to indicate here that our selection of theories of these disciplines is guided by the general criterion of their substantive contributions to societal growth and transformation as a whole, rather than their interest in straightening out relationships between variables which involve only microscopic issues traditionally dealt with by these disciplines, such as capital formation or the development of the party system.

Economics

The special contribution of economics to modernization theories is the concept of economic growth. Simon Kuznets, one of the fathers of the concept of GNP (Gross National Product), delineates the nature of economic growth as follows:[1]

> Economic activity is concerned with the provision of goods
> needed to satisfy human wants, individual and collective. Hence,
> economic growth of a firm, an industry, a nation, a region,

means (whatever else it may imply) a sustained increase in the output of such goods ... This definition is quite general: it covers the economic growth of Periclean Athens, Augustan Rome, medieval France, modern United States, and even India and Egypt in some centuries. Being so general it is hardly useful ...
Modern economic growth of nations has two distinctive features: in *all* cases it involves a sustained and substantial rise in product per capita, and in *almost all cases* it involves a sustained and substantial rise in population ... marked rises in product per labor unit, when population and therefore labor force are increasing, are usually possible only through major innovations, i.e., applications of new bodies of tested knowledge to the processes of economic production. Indeed, modern economic growth is, in substance, an application of the industrial system ... [italics in the original].

The question of economic growth has been elaborated further by demographers, who have shown how economic growth finally leads to the stabilization of population through 'the demographic transition.'[2] Kuznets and others have articulated the economic variables of the industrial system, which are considered necessary for 'self-sustained growth.'

The variables of economic growth

The economic growth variables are: per capita income; savings or surplus or investable capital; rate of investment; productivity in agriculture; monetized sector; availability of credit; and development of financial institutions; skills, literacy rate, and economic performance of the labor force; and constant innovation in science and technology.

The interrelation of these variables is stated in terms of models in economic theory in general; there are also specific models, which point to the barriers or to the facilitation of growth in the modernizing countries. We made a survey of some of the economic and social features of the highly developed countries and compared them to those of the modernizing countries (a basic list of these countries is provided by Paul A. Samuelson, in the ninth edition of his *Economics*[3]). We noticed the following features: the total output per person in highly developed countries is $3,510, in less developed countries it is $245; the infant mortality rate (calculated on the basis of deaths per 1,000 live births) in highly developed countries is 22; in less developed countries, it is 110; the birth rates (i.e. births per 1,000 people) in highly developed countries is 18, in less developed countries it is 40; the life expectancy (years at birth) in highly developed countries is 71, in less developed countries it is 52; and education (the proportion of people literate) in the highly developed countries is 97 per cent, in less developed countries it is 40 per cent.[4] The endemic features of underdevelopment are clear from these statistics.

The models of economic growth

Hans Singer's four models   The different models of economic and social growth have been portrayed by Hans W. Singer as follows:[5]

(a) Model I is the classical puritan model, in which consumption is reduced, the saving is invested in productive capital, which in its turn produces more productive capital and more consumption goods. This model can be likened to jam yesterday and jam the day after tomorrow, but no jam today or even tomorrow.

(b) Model II is the Keynesian model, where consumption and capital formation grow and decline together, being tied to each other by the multiplier and the accelerator. Provided there are latent or unemployed resources in the economy, this model suggests that the best way of assuring jam tomorrow is to have jam today.

(c) Model III is what Singer calls the 'human investment model.' It incorporates the capital accumulation of Model I and increased consumption of Model II. However, it treats human welfare as an inducement ('human capital' is used for economic growth), and the increase in GNP or the accumulation of physical capital is considered the final value. Singer points out that according to this model, any increase in income or capital will be called 'productive investment,' but any increase in human welfare which does not do this will be called 'consumption.' In his humanitarian feelings, and on policy grounds as well, he rejects this model for the Third World, and instead offers the following model.

(d) Model IV construes 'social development' (e.g. better health, nutrition, education, and housing) and 'economic development' (measured by indices such as increased GNP or capital accumulation) as a single entity. The model stipulates that transformation curves of expenditures must be incorporated into improved levels of living, and there must be a 'feedback process,' in which improved levels of living will lead to higher productivity and higher productivity in turn will lead to higher levels of living. Singer calls this model the 'Antonine Model,' after the Golden Age of Imperial Rome, where for the first time the welfare of all people became the primary objective of the government.

The social objective of the Antonine Model is no doubt the one which most modernizing countries desire; the question is one of strategy, of planning, and of the workability of such plans. The barriers in the path of economic growth and the strategies to overcome them are many, and it is here that we need to look at W. W. Rostow's thesis on *The Stages of Economic Growth.*[6]

Rostow's five stages   Rostow stipulates five stages of the process of economic growth.

(a) Stage One is the traditional society, where a high proportion of people are engaged in agriculture; agricultural productivity is low; there are no savings; capitalization is low; and a ceiling exists on output per head. Some manufacturing may exist at low levels of productivity. Most people are illiterate and kin-oriented.

(b) Stage Two is depicted as the preconditions for take-off. These preconditions are a belief in economic progress; private profit; general welfare; and planning a better life for one's children. A centralized government and an expansion of education as well as banks and other economic institutions are felt to be necessary. Entrepreneurs emerge to participate in business as well as political activities.

(c) Stage Three is the stage of the take-off. In this stage a sufficient accumulation of capital leads to technological developments in industry and agriculture; the latter is commercialized. Industries expand, and profits are reinvested. Whereas national pride marked stage two, the enhancement of national stature through economic progress becomes the key motivation in stage three. The investment rate doubles and rises from 5 per cent of the national income to 10 per cent or more; and manufacturing takes the lead. The take-off period occurred for Britain after 1783 and for the United States about 1840.

(d) Stage Four is the drive to maturity. In this stage there is the diffusion of modern technology over the whole range of economic activity; in particular the economy demonstrates its capacity to apply resources efficiently beyond the original industries which triggered the take-off. Investment moves on to the 10-20 per cent level (and output exceeds population growth). Improvements in technology and expansions beyond early industries create a place for the country in the international economy.

(e) Stage Five is the age of high mass consumption. This stage marks the shift of the economy to durable consumers' goods and services. The income of many people helps them buy more than necessities; it is also marked by high urbanization and a shift of jobs to factories and offices. Social security and welfare programs are undertaken by the state; and the stage is marked by high mass consumption. The United States reached this stage around 1920.

Rostow's thesis was welcomed by such protagonists of capitalism as Adolf A. Berle, Jr.,[7] but was questioned by theoreticians like Simon Kuznets.[8] Kuznets examined the Five Stages in terms of the following criteria: empirically testable characteristics; clearly formulated distinctions between each stage; the analytical relation of each stage to the preceding stage as well as to the succeeding stage. He found Rostow's model deficient on many of these counts. Kuznets says that the model does not state the universe for which the generality of common and distinctive characteristics of the stages is claimed.

Kuznets further points out that many of the attributes of the take-off stage occur in the precondition stage. The line between the take-off and the self-sustained (or drive to maturity) stages is equally blurred. Kuznets faults Rostow on other counts, such as lack of a definition for 'high,' the need for stipulating manufacturing as the leading sector in the take-off stage 'unless its contributions to the country's economic growth are substantial ... no matter how high its [manufacturing's] own rate of growth.'[9] Kuznets questions the definition of the take-off stage as a generally occurring stage of modern economic growth, on the basis of aggregative data for a number of countries.

Many countries and their planners have joined the bandwagon of the take-off stage theory and their first worry concerns its prerequisites. This does not augur well for these countries, especially in view of the lengthy and rather unresolved debate by American economists on this issue.[10] There are other and better strategies of growth as we will show below.

Strategies of economic growth

We have discussed in detail two types of models of economic growth to indicate the broad range of discussion of economic problems of new nations. We will now very briefly summarize the theories of some other authors. It would not be helpful for us to examine the Malthusian, Marxian, Keynesian, or Schumpeterian versions of development, because their ideas refer to the development (and/or decline) of capitalism as such, which is not our interest here. Instead we are interested in the economic growth of modernizing countries. The Harrod-Domar growth models, often mentioned in the literature on economic growth, concentrate on secular causes of unemployment (also a problem examined by Keynes) and inflation; in addition they examine the factors determining the optimum and actual rate of capital formation.[11] They operate on the assumptions of equilibrium theory and balanced growth.[12] Harvey Leibenstein outlines systematically the 'minimum effort' thesis in development. His growth curves can be interpreted to suggest that if an initial rate of investment is continued in *both rural and urban sectors*, it would permit a jump to levels of per capita income at which steady growth can be maintained for domestic savings and investment.[13] Ragnar Nurske suggests a balanced growth which dictates 'a frontal attack ... a wave of capital investments in a number of different industries.'[14] Hans W. Singer and Albert O. Hirschman criticize Nurske's prescription of balanced growth for less developed countries and opt for a strategy of 'judiciously unbalanced growth.'

Gunnar Myrdal shows how the expansion of trade between underdeveloped and industrial nations can result in a tendency away from equilibrium, thus producing increasing discrepancies between the productivities of the industrial and the underdeveloped nations. This happens because of 'circular causation,' such that in the underdeveloped countries 'backwash' (unfavorable) effects outweight 'spread' (stimulating) effects. He shows this first in the case of regional inequities in a single country, whereby growing communities will exert an agglomerative pull on other communities, which may become stagnant or decline, with no offsetting force arising. The expansion of trade with an advanced country aggravates the process in a similar way.[15]

We discussed Hans W. Singer's view of the economic models earlier. Here we merely wish to point out that Singer favors 'strategic' investments because of shortages of resources in the modernizing countries. He is in favor of thinking big but not in favor of acting big, especially if it means balancing investments.[16] Albert O. Hirschman partly agrees with both Nurske and Singer. He emphasizes 'complementarity' among investments, and, like Nurske, believes in the overall process of equilibrium. However, his strategy for development is to combine forward and backward linkages in a series of mutually and continually destabilizing and reinforcing equilibria. Hirschman notes that the 'ability to invest' is a serious bottleneck in the developing countries, so a strategic path must be chosen. This path may suggest that it is sometimes better to invest in aviation than in building more roads, because the former will dictate needed changes in management and needed priorities in investments leading to overall modernization, whereas in the latter case, roads can be neglected and can fall back in repairs, if the incentive system remains unchanged.

The strategies of growth are many. This is a burgeoning field in developmental economics and we have merely touched on some of the prime issues here. Our aim, as before, was to be parsimonious; therefore, we have sketched out broad outlines of the conditions of economic growth and some of the crucial problems in it.

Linkages to other disciplines

The field of modernization is such that no discipline can provide all the answers. Thus we find that every discipline has a number of scholars who link the perspectives and problems of their field to interconnected problems in other disciplines. One such economist is Bert F. Hoselitz, who straddles all social science disciplines and molds his ideas on the basis of materials collected from everywhere.[17] He is the founder and was also the editor of the leading journal *Economic Development and Cultural Change*, which has now completed over a quarter century of successful existence amid great controversies over some of the issues which need theoretical guidance. Hoselitz's own works are highly incisive critiques of existent literature. His early article entitled 'The City, the Factory, and Economic Growth'[18] draws widely on historical and cross-cultural information available on the subject. He leans more toward systemic analysis and, in this, Talcott Parsons is his guide. However, his use of the Parsonian schemas is not always quite successful (for instance, when he makes achievement, universalism, and specificity – three of the five pattern variables of Parsons – the defining attributes of modern society and tries to test all traits of modernizing societies by this yardstick).[19] As the economist Everett E. Hagen has pointed out: 'There are important elements of the qualities on both sides of each dichotomous choice in both the traditional and the modern society.'[20] This raises another issue, viz. the role of tradition in modernity, on which Hoselitz holds some firm views.

Hoselitz is an important member of a school of modernization theorists, which rejects tradition completely in order to arrive at modernity. Among others in this group is Edward Shils, who claims that 'The societies of Asia and Africa have remained traditional societies – omitting for the present industrial Japan and Soviet China, where an energetic elite seeks to extirpate religion and kinship, those two seeds of traditional society.'[21] And David E. Apter confirms that 'modernity in the West attacked religion and superstition, family and church, mercantilism and autocracy,' which presumably is the way the rest of the world should go if modernization is to succeed.[22]

The de-emphasis on all elements of tradition is evident more in the early literature of the 1950s than in the later literature of the 1960s, where doubts about the Western model of modernization (especially its identification with the American economic-cum-social system) began to be raised. (The Rostow schema is an example of the early literature.) However, Milton Singer, among others, pointed out from the beginning his reservations about the idealized construct of 'traditional society' and 'traditional values.'[23] He has shown all along the importance (or at least the lack of damning effect) of some traditional values for modernity in his various writings[24] and other scholars have followed suit.[25]

Some diagnoses

We may return now from the area of the linkage of economics to other social science disciplines to the field of economics proper. Even there it seems that the early zeal of theorists to conform to the Anglo-American model of growth willy-nilly distorted many economic facts and also created some economic myths. Dudley Seers, among others, has worked assiduously to set the picture right.[26] Paul Streeten of Oxford University points out that the coexistence of rich and poor nations alters crucially the development prospects of the poor ones today. His findings militate against the 'widespread myth that international inequality *reflects*, but does not *cause*, differences in economic prospects and performance.'[27] Keith Griffin, also of Oxford, examines the traditional economic assumption that a more equal distribution of income leads to less savings, fewer incentives, and slower growth. His conclusion is: 'There is little evidence that one can find to support this view; indeed, the opposite could be true.'[28] About the myth that development requires the transfer of agricultural surpluses from the rural sector to the urban sector, Michael Lipton of the Institute of Development Studies at the University of Sussex states: 'the notion that maximum surplus transfer helps development, growth or welfare is a self-indulgent myth of those economists who are urbanists first, analysts a poor second, and empiricists not at all.'[29]

Concluding remarks

We started in this section from the models of Hans W. Singer and ended by pointing to some myths developed in the theory of economic growth. We noted that the Western (or Anglo-American) model is an important reference point for anchoring results but not necessarily a model to be copied by the Third World. The variables of economic growth were carefully delineated, but it is with regard to the developmental relations between them and the strategies of growth themselves that important questions were raised. Some of these questions are not yet fully answered, and new issues such as equalizing incomes or greater investments in the agricultural sector or greater autonomy for communities and regions are constantly cropping up. These are crucial issues in our model of modernization and we shall keep returning to them as we examine the theories of other social science disciplines. So we turn next to the field of political science.

Political science

Introduction

The field of political science went through an epochal change in the 1950s partly through what may be called the 'behavioral' revolution in the social sciences, and partly because of the need to establish comparative politics on a new footing, in order to compare the political institutions of the modernizing countries with those of the West.[30] The role of Gabriel Almond is crucial in this transformation because he and his colleagues started a neologism, which has gained such currency that it seems as if no graduate student today would walk into an examination without knowing the new terminology. We will discuss the neologism below, when we present the models. Here we wish to point out that there were two seminal influences on Almond, one being that of the social system model promulgated by Talcott Parsons and the other being the concept of political socialization, presented in a book, not as widely read as it should be, *Political Socialization* by Herbert H. Hyman.[31] We have discussed the Parsonian models earlier, and we will delineate their specific applications in political science shortly. First, we wish to point out the importance of Hyman's approach. His book made an inventory of survey data and showed how man learns his political behavior early and persists in it. The coherence of political orientation and the development of political socialization were clearly highlighted in his short monograph.

The crucial development of the 1950s was in the articulation of the terms, 'political system' and 'political development.' The 'political system' (a new name for the 'state') is linked now in a systemic framework with other concepts, such as 'political role,' 'political culture,' 'political structure,' and 'political socialization.' The new concept of 'political development' is used in two different ways. On the one hand, it denotes the forms of development of new political systems in the modernizing nations (Edward Shils, for instance, has set up the following five categories: political democracy; tutelary democracy; modernizing oligarchy; totalitarian oligarchy; and traditional oligarchy[32]) and on the other hand, it compares these forms with the 'modern' political systems of the West, especially the polities of the Anglo-American bloc.

The Anglo-American polities

The institutional structure of the English or the American polity consists of the Parliament (or the Congress), the Monarchy (or the Presidency), the Cabinet (or the Executive), the courts, the political parties, the bureaucracy, and the interest groups. The functioning of these institutions suggests the presence of the following traits: a consensual electorate, despite cultural and class diversity; public interest-oriented political parties; a responsible and neutral bureaucracy; coalition-seeking and bargain-hunting interest groups and associational blocs; and finally, a free and aggressive press and other mass media of communications. In the judgment of most political scientists, these are the ingredients of the *modern* polity or the *developed* polity. The question that is usually asked by a political scientist is: how close are the modernizing nations to these ideal-type cases of the West?

Some typologies

It is, perhaps, necessary to enumerate the various typologies of polities, in order to answer the question posed above. Tom Bottomore, a political sociologist, furnishes the following typology: (a) primitive societies (with or without a permanent political structure); (b) city states; (c) empires based on city states; (d) Asiatic states with a centralized bureaucracy; (e) nation states (democratic or totalitarian); and (f) empires based on nation states.[33] The last is nearly obsolete today. S. N. Eisenstadt has a somewhat similar classification. In his typology, he makes a distinction between early patrimonial and conquest empires; he inserts an additional category of the feudal systems in the Middle Ages; and adds two more categories to the nation states, viz. autocratic, and under-developed.[34] Both the taxonomies are highly descriptive. Compared to them, F. X. Sutton has developed an analytical schema, in which societies are classified as 'Agraria' or 'Industria.' This distinction is based on Weberian ideas of rationality and growth and draws heavily on the Parsonian pattern variables schema.[35] Almond found Sutton's formulation quite helpful in the development of his own model.

Political development

In the context of political development, it seems that the term 'modern' has an ethnocentric content. For instance, after wrestling with many shades of the meaning of 'modern,' Joseph LaPalombara suggests that:[36]

one could certainly use the Anglo-American political systems as a working example of the kind of arrangement of *institutions and behaviors that is desired* and then proceed to raise and answer questions concerning the conditions under which political development might or might not move in the desired direction [italics added].

The quotation is normative in its prescription, and speaks for itself.

In order to delineate a more objective view for 'development,' perhaps it would help to examine the ideas of the economist Joseph Schumpeter on this point. He says: 'Development ... is a distinct phenomenon, entirely foreign to what may be observed in the circular flow or in the tendency toward equilibrium. It is spontaneous and discontinuous change in the channels of the flow ... ' He gives the famous example: 'Add successively as many mail coaches as you please. You will never get a railway thereby.'[37] It seems to us that the efforts of the political scientists should be directed toward discovering the developmental potentials of the indigenous systems rather than foisting on them approximations of the Western model.

The variables of political development

The variables of political development are: the formation of the state, and the development of the executive, legislative, and judicial branches of the government; a party system; universal adult franchise; a well-informed electorate; free and frequent elections at stipulated times; some form of local self-government; and interest groups and voluntary associations, which can protect an individual from undue pressures from the functionaries of the state as well as help him to articulate and communicate his needs to such functionaries. The interest groups are a necessary buffer between the state and the individual. Besides the safeguards in the constitution and the bill of rights, the interest groups also help to protect basic freedoms and enhance individual as well as human rights in modern nations.

The models of political development

As we stated earlier, there are two senses in which the word 'development' has been used in political science; one merely refers to the setting up of viable institutions of the state, and the other implies the mobilization of indigenous resources for the growth of the polity. The latter is the Schumpeterian meaning of the term. Scholars from Aristotle to John Stuart Mill have presented an ideal model for the state, but much controversy surrounds the notion of political development.[38] The developmental models we are going to talk about get their cues from such scholars as Lasswell, who articulated the demand process of the citizenry in terms of his now-famous phrase, "Who Gets What, When, How."[39] However, the questions raised by Lasswell were mostly answered in institutional terms until the behaviorists came on the scene.

Gabriel Almond, being dissatisfied with the institutional approach to politics, adopted the 'functional' perspective and redefined some of the conventional terms. In his lexicon interest groups become 'the structures of interest articulation;' political parties become 'the structures of aggregation;' and so on. These structures are not concrete entities but have processual referents. He created other terms, like 'political system' (for state), 'political role' (office), 'political culture' (public opinion), and 'political socialization' (citizenship training), as well as the terms 'rule-making' (legislation), 'rule application' (administration), and 'rule adjudication' (judicial proceedings). Finally, Almond articulated the role of the mass media in terms of 'political communication.'[40]

The above terminology is incorporated into a model which articulates the processes and characteristics of the structure of politics, especially in the new countries, which do not have some of the institutions of the West, such as the multi-party system. However, the structures of the modernizing countries (as described in Almond's model) may perform some of the same functions as the institutions of the West but cannot be classified with them because of their differences in content.

Related to the structures is the question of the processes. Again the earlier taxonomies were ignored by Almond and other behavioralists, not because of their worthlessness, but because they could not articulate well the political processes of a 'modern' polity; nor were they helpful in understanding the politics of modernizing countries.

Almond conceives of process in terms of input-output functions, which he classifies as follows:[41]

A. Input functions
  1 Political socialization and recruitment
  2 Interest articulation
  3 Interest aggregation
  4 Political communication
B. Output functions
  5 Rule-making
  6 Rule application
  7 Rule adjudication

The citizen's demands are fed into the 'political structure' through the input route, and his satisfactions and consequent support of the leadership and the government are combined as the output process. The schema follows the outlines of Parsons's general systems analysis, as can be gleaned from the following kinds of diagnoses:[42]

> The structure and style of interest articulation define the pattern
> of boundary maintenance between the polity and the society,
> and within the political system affect the boundaries between
> the various parts of the political system – parties, legislatures,
> bureaucracies, and courts. For example, a high incidence of
> anomic interest articulation will mean poor boundary mainten-
> ance between the society and the polity, frequent eruptions of
> unprocessed claims without controlled direction into the politi-
> cal system. It will affect boundary maintenance within the
> political system by performing aggregative rule-making, rule
> application, and rule adjudication functions outside of appro-
> priate channels and without benefit of appropriate process.

It may sound overdrawn or simplistic, but the issue of new and non-institution directed demands as articulated above constantly occurs in both the 'modern' and the modernizing polities, as was noted earlier in the section on sociology when we examined Etzioni's book, *The Active Society*.

Another model is that of Fred W. Riggs, who despite the inroads of 'behavioralism' on the discipline of political science, wants to visualize 'the Gestalt of Politics,' and who still believes in the comparison of whole political systems.[43] He points to the limited value of the Almond model, because his input-output model can apply only to organizations, not to societal processes. However, Riggs himself is not untouched by the movement to redefine terms in political science. He selects four basic concepts, viz. executives, bureacracies, legislatures, and parties, and gives them somewhat special denotations; he dubs them as four *basic* types of polity:[44]

Acephaly: without executive, bureaucracy, legislature,
   party system

Procephaly: with executive; but no bureaucracy, legislature, party system

Orthocephaly: with executive and bureaucracy; but no
   legislature, party system

Heterocephaly: with executive, bureaucracy, legislature;
   but no party system

Metacephaly: with executive, bureaucracy, legislature,
   party system

Supracephaly: 'all these and more besides?'

Riggs says that there are subtypes within each one of these major types. Working with a dialectical paradigm, he shows how his model can describe any known polity and account for the endogenous as well as exogenous transformations in them. It seems to us that his is a good accounting scheme; however, in the limited discussion of his schema provided by Riggs so far, one wonders how, and how many hypotheses will flow from it.

Holt and Turner have subjected the schemas of the new comparativists (especially Almond) to a theoretical test and found them lagging in indexing and sampling, in developing non-culture-bound categories, and in the rules of interpretation as well as the criteria for admissible explanation.[45] Holt and Richardson compare the various approaches of structural-functional analysis, systems analysis, and cybernetic as well as psychological treatments of political phenomena, and find them (especially the last one) very deficient in major ways.[46] They seem to back up the rationalist approach (at least the Simon version of it[47]), but point out that without deductive theory, political science will not gain strength. We agree but we feel that their conclusion that 'the development of theory in comparative politics may depend upon innovative work in pure mathematics'[48] is not warranted, because it makes theory a handmaiden of methodology. The quantification of political science data is far behind sociology, not to speak of psychology and economics; therefore it does not behove any methodologist to counsel the discipline to await innovations in pure mathematics. Instead, what is needed is less borrowing of schemas as well as styles of theorizing, and more innovative work. It is with this aim in view that the following remarks are presented.

Promising leads

Almond's schema no doubt sensitized the five authors of the articles on Southeast Asia, South Asia, Sub-Saharan Africa, the Near East, and Latin America in the book, edited by Almond and Coleman, *The Politics of the Developing Areas* (1960), to examine political behavior according to a uniform framework.[49] However, the analyses speak more for the ingenuities of the authors than for the articulateness of the framework. It must be admitted though, that there are some theoretical leads in the articles which could not have been possible without an articulate framework like Almond's. We should like to point out in this connection that neither the Parsonian schemas nor the Almond model have provided hypotheses which have been confirmed in any scientific sense. They are merely heuristic devices for studying social and political systems.

David Apter began with a provocative model of the 'mobilization type' and the 'reconciliation type' of polities for modernizing countries,[50] but he seems to be weighed down by system fixation now. He has come to the conclusion that 'the modernization process creates such problems of coordination and control that *democratic* political systems, in the usual sense of the term, are not very relevant' [italics in the original].[51] Either this betrays a Western-centric view of democratic political systems, or a lack of better understanding of the modernization process. His attempt to redefine 'development,' 'industrialization,' and 'modernization' – the last he defines as 'the spread and use of industrial type roles in non-industrial setting'[52] – clearly shows his vulnerability on both counts.

David Easton's system analysis of political life is theoretically very weak on system articulation,[53] but is clearly in the right direction in so far as it is meant to articulate demands (of the citizenry) and supports (to the government and the polity). These are the two important political issues before modernizing nations and what is needed is continuous examination of the problems flowing from them rather than exercises into the articulation of the model for a stable polity or into finding the model for the equilibrium process in political situations (which seem to be the major preoccupation of some of the behavioral political scientists).

Karl W. Deutsch uses great skill and sophistication in creating a cybernetic model for articulating political phenomena in quantitative terms.[54] Cybernetics is the science of communications and control; it applies to all organizations. Because governments are organizations, they are subject to communications controls. The patterned relationship between events (which is called 'information' by him) is transmitted through various 'channels' for the circular flow of governmental decisions, which contribute to governmental efficiency.[55] His views on national integration[56] are similarly well articulated; we will discuss them when we come to the concept of community autonomy in a later section. Deutsch has been called 'the Aristotelian mean between Plato and a census enumerator'[57] and not without reason, if one considers not only his sophisticated approach to systems and communications, but also his sense of values as in his discussion of the kinds of autonomy, mobilization, and integration needed in a modernizing polity.

Some pivotal issues

We could go on and talk about other models, but that would not advance the discussion. Each model, as we have seen, answers a special set of questions and satisfies only partially the theoretical and methodological rigors of a scientific paradigm (in Kuhn's sense), as we noted earlier. What we wish to do now is to select issues, which have not been dealt with earlier, and which in a special way fall in the domain of political science. One such issue is that of nationalism.

Rupert Emerson, a careful student of nationalism, says:[58]

> One of the central features of the great revolution of our times which has brought the modern world into being is that the peoples of mankind in successive stages have been swept into a vivid and sometimes all-consuming sense of their existence as nations – or at least of their desire to create nations where none existed before.

Thus the quest for nationhood becomes the ruling feature of modern times. Once nationhood is attained through revolutionary or evolutionary methods, there comes the problem of nation-building. We know from recent history that revolutionary regimes emphasize economic growth more than political participation by the people in the affairs of the state. This fact is often decried by Western political scientists, although many of them believe that political development can only follow economic growth as it did in the West.[59] It is difficult for us to accept this argument, partly because political scientists and political sociologists are no experts on economic matters, and partly because of their ethnocentric application of the Western historical development to modernizing nations of today. We shall therefore ignore the issue of economic development here and concentrate on political development only.

Political development means first setting up the administrative machinery of the state and stipulating its relationship to popular participation in decision-making as well as national policy making. In this context, the distinction drawn between political function and governmental function by Gabriel Almond[60] is of great value. The former refers to the mechanisms and processes of participation by the citizens in the affairs of the state, the latter to the efficacy and efficiency of the bureaucratic structure of the government. One can easily see that the West itself is not perfect on either count and that the Western experience is not necessarily a valid guide for ordering the affairs of modernizing nations. We are of course not referring here to the necessary conditions for the existence of any polity – e.g. the minimal administrative structure, a constitution, and a legitimation of both in the minds of the citizens – but to the sufficient conditions – e.g. political action, and the peaceful resolution of conflict within the polity. If bureaucratic action is in conflict with the mobilization of a group, which one should prevail? In the modern polity, the solution is in favor of bureaucracy; in a modernizing nation the opposite solution may be better for political development.[61]

The next set of issues relates to the problems of democracy.

Lipset[62] and others have shown that traits such as average wealth, the degree of industrialization and urbanization, and the level of education are highly correlated with democracy (the case of the Soviet countries forms an exception though, in the minds of some writers), and they would therefore recommend these traits for all modernizing countries. We noted earlier the difficulty of choosing between economic growth and political development in terms of priority for a new nation. We should like to add that rather than follow the Western syndrome, it would be better for the modernizing countries to look for the critical variables of democracy. At the least, these seem to us to be the following: civilian control of the military; local self-government with the power to tax the residents for running its affairs; a two-way communication between the leaders and the masses; and a civil service recruited on an achievement basis. The empirical question is: can these elements be united in divergent types of political regimes?

Finally, we would like to discuss the role of the interest groups. The processes of urbanization and industrialization everywhere accelerate the formation of interest groups. Growth of literacy, occupational specialization, and social mobility, all create opportunities for associational groupings. The growth of interest groups needs to be fostered irrespective of the level of urbanization and industrialization in a modernizing country. One can say that there is more political education in belonging to interest groups than in the exhortation of the political leaders or in the continual flow of information through the mass media, both considered vital for an informed citizenry. Interest groups create grounds for 'political competitiveness,' which has been considered necessary for democracy by James S. Coleman.[63]

Thus, we find that the requisites for political development are to be sought more in the ideology and the leadership of a nation than in its economic and industrial status. Political scientists would do better to explore the realms of the values and motivations of new nations and find ways of institutionalizing them in the direction of modernization, than to preach the infallibility of the institutional structures of the Western polities.[64]

7 The anthropological theories of modernization

A discussion of the anthropological viewpoint on modernization is important for the following reasons: (a) anthropologists have studied a wide array of societies from the hunting, gathering stage of social organization to the settled-agricultural, peasant, first urban, and even industrial societies of today and, as such, they have a wider perspective on some of the problems facing the modernizing nations; (b) the limitations of ethno-centrism are recognized and carefully avoided by anthropologists and so the light they throw on the comparative analysis of cultures is helpful in understanding societal problems of development; (c) anthropology is generally holistic in approach, so that the nature of integration of the whole society – a common concern of modernizing societies – is subjected to special investigation by them; and (d) the community studies approach of ethnographers brings out the range of problems facing individuals in their communities in a sharper way and with a more culturally broad-based orientation than the urban-industrial view of other social scientists examining such problems.

Our review of the anthropological literature will also include two issues which have become quite controversial in anthropology today. One is the issue of the existence or the development of the state in political anthropology; this relates to a whole spectrum of problems concerning law, authority, legitimacy, and social control in the cultural evolution of societies.[1] The other is the issue of formalism versus substantivism in economic anthropology,[2] which is related to the problems of economic growth in pre-industrial societies.

It may be noted here that we will not follow in this section the general pattern adopted in discussing other social science disciplines, i.e. that of outlining the variables, describing the important models, and then providing an exposition of these models. The reason for avoiding this earlier pattern of analysis is that anthropology does not concern itself with basically one set of variables as economics does (as in the notion of 'economic growth') or as political science does (in the concept of 'political development'). Rather, anthropology, like sociology, discussed earlier, deals with the whole array of variables which comprise culture, under which all variables of all social science disciplines are subsumed. In terms of model-building for modernization problems, most anthropologists have adopted the systemic approach;[3] some have also provided clarification of the problems raised in economics or sociology, as for instance, in the discussion of social development and economic change in two Indonesian towns by Clifford Geertz, in his book *Peddlers and Princes*.[4]

In comparing the economic modernization of two towns in Indonesia, Geertz showed the following processes at work: (a) innovative economic leadership occurred in a fairly well-defined and socially homogeneous group; (b) the innovative group had crystallized out of a larger traditional group with a history of extra-village status and interlocal orientation; (c) the larger group from which innovation came was itself experiencing radical change of status; (d) the innovative group conceived of itself as the chief vehicle of religious and moral excellence; (e) the main problems faced by the innovators were organizational rather than technical; and (f) the functions of the innovator were to adapt traditional means to novel ends.[5] This is clearly a systemic approach and ties in social and psychological problems as well, as we will show when we discuss the role of the entrepreneur in a later chapter.

Evolution and development

In a sense, most anthropological theories are either about evolution or about the development of man and culture. The evolutionists of the nineteenth century postulated a unilinear evolution of culture, which seemed to lose its strength by the end of the first quarter of the twentieth century, at which time its hold on the anthropological discipline was revived by Leslie White[6] and Julian H. Steward,[7] among others. Robert L. Carneiro, in a seminal paper, clarifies some of the tangled issues of generalization in unilinear, universal, multilinear, and differential evolution.[8] In the comparison of modernizing countries with modern ones, we are faced with differential evolution, i.e. 'the tendency of societies to evolve the various aspects of their culture – economic, social, political, legal, etc. – at various rates and to different degrees.'[9] The concept 'differential evolution' also measures another aspect of cultural development, viz. 'the difference in degree to which *entire societies* have evolved.'[10] Raoul Naroll's index of social development[11] and Robert L. Carneiro's index of cultural accumulation[12] provide quantitative perspectives on the cultural dimensions of societies at various stages of transition.

Another school of anthropology, viz. the functionalists, eschewed evolutionary hypotheses and tried to articulate the pattern of a culture in terms of its constituent parts and their functions. In such a view, development was viewed more in terms of changes occurring from within the system itself and it was endogenous in nature. The imperatives emphasized by the evolutionary school, the ecological viewpoint, and the input-output interchange between the system and its environment were generally underemphasized in the earlier stages of the functionalist theory. From Bronislaw Malinowski and A. R. Radcliffe-Browne to the present, functionalism as a theory has gone through many transformations, so that now it even incorporates systems analysis, cybernetics, game theory, and large scale quantification of anthropological data. But its explanation for change has remained non-evolutionary in perspective. We would like to add here that historicism, diffusionism, and innovation-ism – the three other important branches of anthropological theory – also pose important questions of growth and change, which will be clear as we proceed. However, the controversies between these schools are about past evolution rather than future growth.

We examine now the spectrum of societies which anthropologists have scanned and the theories about their development.

'Folk' society to urban anthropology

Robert Redfield characterized the folk society as follows: 'Such a society is small, isolated, nonliterate, and homogeneous, with a strong sense of group solidarity.'[13] These attributes of folk society are more or less accepted by most anthropologists;[14] however, when it comes to delineating the sources and nature of change within such societies, very serious controversies have arisen. Oscar Lewis restudied a village which Redfield had studied seventeen years earlier[15] and raised some general issues concerning the paradigm of folk society. Lewis questioned whether the interrela-tions of the variables in it formed a system, and pointed out that causal primacy for change in folk society could be in a single variable, rather than in a concatenation of them, as Redfield had implied. Lewis also felt that the ideal-type construct used by Redfield was too narrow in focus for delineating field research.[16] Redfield accepted some of the lighter charges of Lewis, as for instance in his glossing-over evidence of violence, cruelty, disease,

69

and suffering in the village of Tepoztlán, studied by both. However, he made it clear that each of them had approached the village from different perspectives. Said Redfield, 'The hidden question behind my book is, "What do these people enjoy?" The hidden question behind Dr. Lewis' book is, "What do these people suffer from?" '[17]

Redfield makes an important suggestion, which needs to be taken into account in evaluating anthropological data. He says that 'a means to better understanding of a little community might be found in the deliberate construction of alternate and complementary descriptions of it.'[18] We will show later that this problem of the opposing evaluations of the situation occurs when one tries to deal with the applicability of the concept of the state in tribal societies. In an earlier chapter, we have already noted the opposed views on the problematics of modernization of ex-colonial countries.

As one examines the various concepts of folk, peasant, feudal, and industrial societies, one often notices important differences of opinion in articulating the structure (especially the problems of integration) of each of these types. We will briefly discuss some of the difficulties faced in the analysis of social change through the schema of folk society. One of Oscar Lewis's criticisms of the folk-urban continuum was that it 'focuses attention primarily on the city as a source of change, to the exclusion or neglect of other factors of an internal or external nature.'[19] The folk society, when it is a part of a larger cultural whole, must incorporate variables which establish its similarities and differences with other communities, which are parts of the whole culture. At this point, it should be noted that the cultural whole itself is not a folk society but a peasant society or a feudal society.

Redfield has provided an insight into the nature of the peasant community. He says: 'The culture of a peasant community ... is not autonomous. It is an aspect or dimension of the civilization of which it is a part. As the peasant society is a half society, so the peasant culture is a half-culture.'[20] He goes on to show the difference between the peasant community and that of the 'primitive band or tribe.' The crucial difference is that society or culture of the peasant cannot be fully understood without knowing 'what goes on in the minds of remote teachers, priests, or philosophers whose thinking affects and perhaps is affected by the peasantry.'[21] Redfield and Singer have articulated the culture of such intellectual and urban centers in the concept of the 'great tradition' which they compare with the 'little tradition' of the village folk.[22] We note, thus, how *tradition* and impetus to *modernity* (at least two of its elements, viz., logic and philosophy in the 'great tradition') are inextricably tied to both the urban and the rural components of peasant society.

Eric R. Wolf delineates the shift from the 'primitive' to the peasant society in a careful way.[23] The peasant is a rural cultivator, but not yet a farmer. Unlike the farmer in an industrial society, the peasant 'runs a household, not a business concern.'[24] And the surpluses of peasants:[25]

> are transferred to a dominant group of rulers that uses the surplus both to underwrite its own standard of living and to distribute the remainder to groups in society that do not farm but must be fed for their specific goods and services in turn.

Thus the conceptions of the elite, 'domain over the land,'[26] patron-client relations, a surplus necessary for the emergence of cities, and some form of government finally leading to the emergence of the state, are hatched in the womb of the peasantry.

From the peasant society to the feudal society was the next stage of development in cultural evolution. Gideon Sjoberg, a sociologist, outlines the main ingredients of feudalism.[27] A large peasant population is the backbone of the feudal society. Towns spring up, which become political, religious, and trading centers. These towns suffer fewer social disorganizations than do modern industrial cities. Besides the ruler, the feudal elite is composed of a governmental bureaucracy, a priestly and/or scholar group. A nobility, landlord group, and militarist or warrior group are found in various combinations in feudal society. The stratification is bipolar, composed of the elites (including the ruling stratum) and the masses. An institutionalized state system is a prerequisite of the feudal society. We should like to note that the state (including the legal system) of the feudal society is traditionalistic. Authority, domination, coercion, and control, all are functions of the will or the writ of a monarch or of a theocracy; they are not highly differentiated and rationally ordered principles flowing from the constitution of a modern state.

We do not wish to discuss the development of a modern industrial society here, because we have already done so. Anthropologists generally accept the variables suggested by sociologists and others in this regard. However, urban anthropology, which developed when anthropologists started studying industrial societies, is now a burgeoning field and so a few words need to be said about it. In delineating the field of urban anthropology it helps to make a distinction between 'anthropology of the cities' and 'anthropology in the cities.'[28] The former field encompasses comprehensive study of a city[29] as well as an articulation of the principle of the development of the city, as for instance, in its *orthogenetic transformation* (the city of the moral order; for example, Peiping, Lhasa) and *heterogenetic transformation* (the city of the technical order; for example, Shanghai, Washington, D.C.), suggested by Redfield and Singer.'[30]

It is, however, mostly the 'anthropology in the cities' with which the genre of work in urban anthropology is associated. Anthropologists have studied small towns in industrial civilization with anthropological tools and techniques (for example, the Yankee City series of books of Lloyd Warner and his associates[31]); they have followed a tribe or caste from its rural to its urban milieu and examined problems of its adjustment;[32] they have also studied urban families,[33] ethnic groups,[34] neighborhoods,[35] and urban pathologies[36] in the context of either a moral or scientific concern for man and his life. The study of urban pathology has provoked a lively debate in anthropology, concerning the culture of poverty hypothesis.

The culture of poverty debate

Few terms have evoked as much controversy as the term 'culture of poverty,' coined by Oscar Lewis and appended to the title of his book, *Five Families: Mexican Case Studies in the Culture of Poverty* (1959).[37] Lewis, toward the latter part of his career, specialized in perceptive studies of life in the Mexican, Puerto Rican, and New York slums; he articulated this concept carefully in his multiple-volume publications on the slums,[38] for example, in the introduction to his book *La Vida*[39] and also in the article entitled 'The Culture of Poverty,' published in *Scientific American* (1966).[40] He incorporated in this concept a large array of traits, such as higher death rates, lower life expectancy, child labor, lower education and literacy, constant struggle for survival, pawning, cramped living, lack of privacy, alcoholism, earlier sex initiation, authoritarianism, masculinity cult, orientation to the present, mistrust of government, powerlessness, and sensitiveness about status distinctions, but no class consciousness.

Lewis maintains that 'The Culture of Poverty is not only an adaptation to a set of objective conditions of the larger society. Once it comes into existence it tends to perpetuate itself from generation to generation because of its effect on the children.'[41] He sees the culture of poverty as a reaction of the poor to 'their marginal position in a class-stratified, highly individuated, capitalistic society.'[42]

When we look at the furor the 'culture of poverty' concept has created within American anthropology, it seems to us that the fault of Lewis was not in bringing to the attention of others the list of some seventy traits (with great difficulty, Anthony Leeds says he was able to count only sixty-two[43]) of poverty, but of calling it the 'culture of poverty.' Thus, Michael Harrington, with the best of intentions of helping the poor, wrote in his book, *The Other America*: 'Poverty in the United States is a culture ... a culture that is radically different from the one that dominates the society.'[44] This book had an important influence on President John F. Kennedy and on successive regimes in initiating policies for helping the poor. However, the 'labeling' effect of the term also helped racists in the United States to project a picture of the inferiority of the entire culture of the poor peoples, especially that of the blacks and Puerto Ricans.

The life of the *favelas* in Latin America, the *bidonvilles* in North Africa, the *sarifas* in the Middle East, and the urban *bustees* and *jhuggies* in India have attracted both literary and scientific investigations. The conditions of these city slums have somewhat common and generalizable features. It is only the political implications flowing from Lewis's hypotheses that have cast doubt on the usefulness of the concept of the 'culture of poverty.' As Charles A. Valentine points out: 'The complex of conceptions, attitudes, and activities that has grown up around the "culture of poverty" has had a predominantly pernicious effect on American society.'[45]

However, one should realize that concepts are not refuted on the basis of their misutilization by some groups. The conditions of the other half ('the low, the lowliest, and the lost,' as the poet Rabindranath Tagore called them) have been portrayed by novelists like Charles Dickens,[46] by people who come out of the same depressed group, as well as by social scientists. Frank Bonilla, a political scientist and an astute observer of the scene, conducted a survey in the *favelas* of Rio de Janeiro in 1961. He reports:[47]

> Despite the conflict, frequent aggression, and insecurity of personal relationships that according to the accounts of all observers are commonplace in the *favela*, the *favelado* himself feels that he is part of a fairly cohesive, solidary group. It is vis-a-vis the world outside the *favela* that he feels bypassed, forgotten, and excluded.

It would not help to criticize Oscar Lewis for the traits, universal, economic, psychological, or other, which he identified as belonging to the 'culture of poverty'. The traits are operative to a greater or lesser degree. What is called for is an arrangement of these traits as a model, which, unfortunately, with all his technical training, Lewis was not able to provide, and neither have his detractors. So it seems to us that the verdict on the 'culture of poverty' debate is best given

73

by Eleanor Burke Leacock, who presided over one such debate. She says:[48]

> To sum up, differences between the poor and the nonpoor in our society [the United States] stem from three sources. First, there are the different traditions of people with different histories; these are often reinforced by racial or religious segregation and discrimination. Second, there are realistic attempts to deal with objective conditions that vary from one class to another ... and the third, [there are] those adaptive acts and attitudes that become institutionalized, and incorporated into internalized values and norms appropriate for living in a given position in the socio-economic system. It is, of course, the last – the subcultural variations along class lines – which comes closest to what culture-of-poverty theory is supposedly documenting.

Our discussion of the culture of poverty was meant to focus on two kinds of issues, one, theoretical, and the other, humanitarian. The theoretical issue is whether the 'culture of poverty' phenomenon is one which is isolated from the larger stream of events with which urban anthropology is concerned. This could not have been the intention of Oscar Lewis, who as we noted earlier was very sceptical of Robert Redfield's rather insulated view of folk culture. Also when the debate became acrimonious, Lewis himself pulled back a little from his earlier position. He said:[49]

> The crucial question from both the scientific and the *political point of view* is: How much weight is to be given to the internal, self-perpetuating factors in the subculture of poverty as compared to the external, societal factors? My own position is that in the long run the *self-perpetuating factors are relatively minor and unimportant* as compared to the basic structure of the larger society [italics added].

Lewis could not have been cognizant of the 'political point of view' when he formulated the hypothesis. But the 'self-perpetuating factors' of the 'culture of poverty' are related to theoretical issues of causation and explanation, and these need careful scrutiny. Whether class variables affect poverty more than ethnic or cultural (or subcultural, racial, religious, etc.) discrimination is an issue still being debated; it seems to have had no resolution so far in social science theorizing.[50]

As far as the humanitarian issue is concerned, one has to remember that, according to Lewis, the culture-of-poverty syndrome is found in the urban as well as in the rural milieu. All societies from the newly independent to the modern can fall a victim to this malaise. Socialism and communism have been offered as solutions to the problem as we noted in an earlier chapter. Whether they will be true solutions in the long run is problematic. Also, to some extent, this issue often carries over into the realm of the status of a community in modern society, which we consider next.

The community in the larger society

The articulation of the community has been an important basis of anthropological field work. Redfield suggests that 'distinctiveness, smallness, homogeneity, and all-providing self-sufficiency – define a type of human community,' which anthropologists find in folk and early peasant societies.[51] When societies change in scale, the rural village or small town moves away from these qualities, but as Redfield points out, even a village in contemporary United States or Sweden may 'notably fail to realize the four qualities, *while yet retaining them in significant degree* [italics added].'[52] Perhaps the notion of a community cannot be divorced from the intimate quality of social relationship as Tönnies pointed out long ago.[53] And as Raymond Firth asserts:[54]

> The term community emphasizes the space-time component, the aspect of living together. It involves a recognition, derived from experience and observation, that there must be minimum conditions of agreement on common aims, and inevitably, some common ways of behaving, thinking, and feeling. Society, culture, community, these involve one another.

The anthropologist as well as the sociologist has to take note of the community in the larger society.

It is to Conrad M. Arensberg that one turns for a careful analysis of the structure and functioning of communities. In a series of articles, Arensberg first explored the relationship between culture and society through the intermediary concept of community,[55] and then examined the variability in the relationships of the various types of communities to the society of which they form parts.[56] Arensberg and Solon T. Kimball have now proposed to go beyond the earlier taxonomic approach, and to incorporate systems analysis, interaction analysis, and 'event analysis' in their framework in order to articulate the process and change in the community structure.[57] This new approach, they hope, will 'allow cross-cultural comparison and the formulation of general statements about culture and society.'[58]

Arensberg constructed his first typology of the community on an inductive basis. He articulated categories which must be given attention in any community study. The categories are: space, time, family structure and socialization process, attitudinal and value (including ideological) materials, institutional and role patterns enmeshed in larger eco-social aggregates, stratification, class structure and other categoric organizations which may be larger than the community.[59] The detailed operationalization of each of these concepts provided a heuristic basis for analysing historical communities of a nation. For instance, the following community patterns were identified (and analysed) in the United States: (a) the New England Town, (b) the Southern County, and (c) Crossroads Hamlets and Main Street Towns.[60] Arensberg's classification of communities, which include cities and metropolises,[61] and the mode of their structuring provides important insights into the extant nature of communities in both the modern and the modernizing nations. The latter are on various levels of development from peasant to feudal to newly-formed nation-state systems, as we noted earlier.

Anthony Leeds[62] suggests an interesting step in the direction of understanding the changing nature of communities in modernizing nations. With the formation of the state, and especially after the independence of a country, the communities as loci of power can 'enter into various sorts of interrelations with other loci of power, characterized by different conjunctions of power sources.'[63] The interrelations of the supralocal structures of power (especially the state) with the communities (i.e. 'localities,' which term is defined as 'nodes of interaction'[64]) has been dealt with in a preliminary but forceful way by Leeds.[65] This may provide an insight into the nature and conditions of the autonomy of the community, which we designated as an important attribute of our model of modernization.

Political anthropology

The question of supralocal power has concerned anthropologists throughout their studies of those tribes and peasant communities which had their source of authority centered in an institution higher than the kinship organization. Such an authority has been variously referred to as the government or the state. Lewis Henry Morgan made the distinction between the government of savages and barbarians, which he called 'a society *(societas)*' and the government characteristic of civilization, which he termed 'a state *(civitas)*.'[66] R. M. MacIver contends that 'Tribal government differs from all other political forms in that *territorial basis is not sharply defined*. In its primary sense a tribe is a community organized on the basis of kinship.'[67] I. Schapera was one of the first anthropologists to challenge this view. On the basis of evidence

76

gathered from four different groups of peoples of South Africa, Schapera showed that it was 'incorrect to maintain that "political union" was based solely on kinship in primitive societies, and on "local contiguity" in civilized societies.'[68] He went on to add that 'Both kinship and locality serve everywhere to link people together, and the most we can claim is that in primitive societies kinship is often much more important than among ourselves in the regulation of public life.'[69]

As one examines the theoretical articulation of kinship authority, territorial power, and tribal government, and their interconnections with the concepts of law and the state, one finds a whole array of divergent, and often opposed, points of view. Some believe that all these phenomena occur in all human societies; others see the evolution of some of these phenomena as societies evolved to higher levels of culture. Sometimes the debate is focused on definitions, so that in exasperation, the behavioralists, as we noted in the section on political science, have altogether abandoned the concept of the state.[70] One political anthropologist, going along with the behavioralists, has defined the political system as an aspect of the social system without mentioning the state;[71] but such a strategy fails to incorporate many issues pivotal to the understanding of the stability of the state in the newly-independent countries.

The state

Morton H. Fried has written a provocative essay on the evolution of the state, where he points out that as societies moved from the 'egalitarian' to the 'rank' to the 'stratified' stages, they still lacked the basic ingredients of the state.[72] He argues against hypostasizing the state in terms of 'some mystical concept of "people," of mass will, or of highest good.'[73] He says that 'a state is better viewed as the complex of institutions by means of which the power of the society is organized on a basis superior to kinship.'[74] The state is an evolutionary phenomenon, and it evolved in two stages, one pristine, and the other, secondary state. He notes that the key to the state is maintaining social order in order 'to defend the central order of stratification.'[75] The basic principles of its organization are 'hierarchy, differential degrees of access to basic resources, obedience to officials, and defence of the area.'[76]

Meyer Fortes and E. E. Evans-Pritchard conceived of the state as an explicit form of government. They pointed out that studies of eight African societies showed that five have had a centralized authority, administrative machinery of some kind, judicial institutions, social divisions of wealth, power, and prestige. They called the other three societies in their survey 'stateless societies,' although even these had some form of authority, administration, and judiciary practice. Such functions in stateless societies were carried on by their kinship and community groups.[77]

We have reviewed the concept of the state (including the political system) for two reasons. One was to show that the phenomenon of the state is actually an emergent case in the evolution of human societies, so that some groups (tribal or aboriginal) in some newly-formed states may not be able to construe the full meaning and scope of this phenomenon. From this follows the other concern, viz. the need to articulate the problems of centralization and decentralization in modernizing countries in the light of the needs of the state competing against the needs of 'community autonomy' discussed earlier.

Several authors in a recent symposium on Africa conclude that political coercion by one of the corporate groups in the new nations may be the main element in holding the nation together if the nation is comprised of culturally and sructurally heterogeneous societies or cultures.[78] Thus, we find that Morton H. Fried's view about the coercive maintenance of the stratification system of a society by the state (or nation-state) is partly supported by their evidence. However, Pierre L. Van den Berghe puts 'equal stress on political coercion and economic interdependence (often of an exploitative nature) as necessary, sufficient, and *mutually* reinforcing bases of social integration in plural [modern] societies.'[79] We thus come to see the symbiotic nature of communities and groups in the formation of the nation-state of today. We examine the question of economic interdependence from the anthropological viewpoint in the next section.

Economic anthropology

Our interest in briefly reviewing here the 'on-going argument' in economic anthropology is twofold: one, theoretical, and the other, substantive. The theoretical interest is whether there are standardized concepts in social science (especially in economics) which can apply to all societies. The substantive point refers to the nature of integration (chiefly economic) of the modernizing societies.

In 1927, N. S. B. Gras, an economic historian, coined the term 'economic anthropology' in an essay on 'Anthropology and Economics,' published in a volume titled *The Social Sciences and Their Interrelations*, jointly edited by a sociologist, W. F. Ogburn, and an anthropologist, A. A. Goldenweiser.[80] Gras intended this sub-field to study 'the ways in which primitive peoples obtained a living.'[81] He asked anthropologists to provide facts to the economists 'in return *for ideas and the fundamental issues* involved in getting a living [italics added].'[82] Gras's suggestion went unnoticed until the 1940s, largely because of Malinowski's 'anti-economic' and functional sway over anthropologists.

It was left to another economic historian, Karl Polanyi, to bring the issue of the application of economic theory to non-industrial economies to the fore in his series of publications, especially *Trade and Market in the Early Empires* (1957).[83] Polanyi, Arensberg, and Pearson pointed out in this book that the 'view of the economy as the locus of units allocating, saving up, marketing surpluses, forming prices, grew out of the Western milieu of the eighteenth century,' and raised important doubts about 'the generality of the market system in the realm of empirical fact.'[84] Polanyi gave a different slant to the meanings of reciprocity, redistribution, and exchange as used by the economists,[85] and he and his followers substituted the notion of 'provisioning' for that of 'economizing' in understanding primitive and peasant economics. He argued that the 'market mentality,' the central value of supply and demand, the theories of price, income, and growth were culture-specific to the industrial system and as such they could be analysed by the medium of formal economic analysis. But other forms of economic integration than the market system were found in known empirical societies. He believed that such societies were not amenable to price-setting institutions, and as such they had to be approached through substantive economics, i.e. an analysis of the sociocultural system in which the economic activity was embedded. Thus arose the distinction between the formal school and the substantive school in economic anthropology.

The literature on the controversy between the formalist versus the substantivist is growing rapidly and takes on theoretical, methodological, epistemological as well as many meta-theoretical issues.[86] These will not be our concern here. The extreme point of the formalist can be stated in LeClair's words: 'What is required ... is a search for the general theory of economic process and structure of which contemporary economic theory is but a special case.'[87] This is reminiscent of Georg Simmel's call for formal sociology,[88] or Ludwig von Bertalanffy's emphasis on laws of open systems,[89] both laudable endeavors but without much hope of succeeding so far. As opposed to the 'need-satisfying behavior of people,' the substantivist emphasizes 'the material life-process of society.' As Marshall Sahlins puts it: 'Not ... the way means are applied to ends to achieve the greatest possible utility, but the way techniques, goods, ideas and social relations, as qualities in their own right, interact to produce the observed material result.'[90]

It seems to us that the gap between the formalist and the

substantivist can be narrowed if the insights and contributions of the substantive studies of primitive and peasant economies by, among others, Raymond Firth[91] in Asia and Sol Tax[92] and Eric R. Wolf[93] in Latin America are considered along with the theoretical formulation of George Dalton,[94] one of Karl Polanyi's followers. Dalton points out how Polanyi's work on 'modes of transaction, money, markets, external trade, and operational devices ... [have] begun important new lines of analysis, and, indeed [have] allowed us to clear up some old muddles such as "primitive money" ... and economic "surplus" '[95] Dalton sees economic anthropology as part of the comparative economy and makes the distinction between primitive economies (with or without centralized polity), peasant economies (before and after modernization), and industrial economies. There is not only the difference between the scale of these societies but also the appropriateness of applying certain categories of modern economic analysis to them. In terms of economic development, Dalton makes the important distinction between 'degenerative change' (which is severe disruption in primitive economies of traditional life over several generations accompanied by social malaise), 'growth without development' (where subsistence economies become peasant economies as cash earning and market sales of crops or wage-labor grow), and 'socio-economic development' (where the structure of economy, technology, and culture advances to the point of self-sustaining growth and the local community is progressively integrated with the nation).[96] There is room for articulation of a middle ground in the general debate on community autonomy and national development in the economic theory of culture.

The community and the nation

Too often development theorists adopt the point of view of the national elite and let the communities take the results of the national decision pell-mell and as they wish. We noted earlier the charge of forced political integration of communities and the theoretical point that the state exists for and guarantees the stratification system of the nation, and guards the prerogatives of the elite. Similarly, economic cooperation is often interpreted as receiving from the rural agricultural sector its surplus of food and taxable wealth for the benefit of the urban areas in return for protection and some auxiliary services, such as banking facilities and marketing facilities. The unity of the nation and the importance of the viability of the state become prime concerns of the power-holders and the bureaucrats. The needs and expressed desires of communities and ethnic groups receive secondary attention.

80

In the context of developing societies, Manning Nash has advanced the useful concept of 'multiple society with plural cultures.'[97] He points out that this concept is not the same as J. H. Boeke's 'dualistic' economy;[98] however, it can be compared to J. S. Furnivall's 'plural economy.'[99] Says Nash:[100]

> As a social type, the multiple society with plural cultures is marked by the presence of at least two distinct cultural traditions, each significantly different in the breadth of integration. Although the entire population of the national territory is included in a single system of political and economic bonds, only a part of the population is fully aware of the national entity, participates significantly in its culture and social life, or has control over resources and communications of nationwide scope or impact.

Nash goes on to show that the national component of such a society is itself divided into classes and has rural and urban differences. But what is important about 'the multiple society' is that the subordinate societies are also locally organized, albeit with meager economic resources and inferior political power.[101] It is in the context of this difference in organization and power that the problem of national economics as well as social integration must be viewed.

The question of national integration is a key issue in the modernization of a country. Manning Nash points to the subordinate status of some regions in the development of a 'multiple society.' The sociologist Arthur L. Stinchcombe says that agricultural enterprises, such as the manorial, the plantation, and the ranch systems need to be differentiated in terms of their characteristics and the consequences of their economic behavior for the class structure of the entire society.[102] These are useful reminders of the fact that communities and regions have an autonomy which can either help or hinder the process of economic growth and national integration.

It is true that the existence of locally organized groups and the proliferation of interest groups are the ingredients of a democratic polity. But what happens to national economic growth if these groups work with their own economic ideas and practices and demand autonomy from national control of resources as well as the distribution of goods and services? Some scholars believe that national economic growth, even forced, is a prerequisite for national political viability. Others see a positive function for small-scale strifes and struggles in the power structure of the center and the periphery.[103] The filtration of ideas of nationhood from the national elite to the regional and rural elites to the masses is not

81

hampered in their opinion by the democratic processes of competition and confrontation. Still others, and this view is more emphasized within the discipline of anthropology than in other social science disciplines, assert that the autonomous value systems and ways of life of the unintegrated groups (especially the tribals) in the national economic system need to be protected at all costs. The debate on the issue is interminable and seems unresolvable at present because the question, 'modernization for what?' has not been properly answered.

In summing up the literature, into which we cannot go further here for lack of space, we have concluded that all too few studies of a theoretical nature exist which adopt the viewpoints of localities, communities, and regions, as well as ethnic, racial, and subcultural groups for understanding the modernization process of newly-independent and other modernizing countries.

8 The activistic theories of modernization

The important premise of the activistic theories of modernization is that societies and civilizations need the active guidance of men in reaching higher levels of performance and excellence and in avoiding the catastrophes inherent in the evolutionary process. This faith in man and his wisdom has characterized all reform movements in the past. However, it is only with the growth of science and technology that the process of the modernization of a society starts, if only because men 'would not ... shatter it to bits, and then remould it nearer to our heart's desire' without the know-how needed to obtain control over nature. Thus, the spirit of modernity could not truly have been a molding influence on earlier civilizations before the advent of industrial Western civilization.

We shall discuss the activistic theories from two standpoints: one, we call 'the gradualist approach,' and the other 'the revolutionary approach.' The gradualist theorists do not wish to intervene in societal change in such a way as 'to shatter it to bits' (as the poet sang), but only insist on institution-building and the effective use of man's acquired knowledge. In the process of the application of scientific knowledge, the hope is that society will be transformed in such a way that mankind will be delivered from hunger, misery, and the other vicissitudes of nature. The revolutionary approach theorists, on the other hand, believe in forceful intervention with a consequent shattering of the old social order so as to recreate from it something totally new, and perhaps unavailable at any previous period of human history. Although both kinds of theorists believe in the revolutionary potential of increased scientific knowledge, the former wish to cushion change against arbitrary shocks; the latter purposely introduce these shocks to steer man in his new course toward his first secular redemption in history. In short, the gradualist approach works through system building, entrepreneurship, and other catalytic factors of change: the revolutionary approach starts with a violent revolution, in which, after seizing power, the leaders launch a massive transformation of social institutions. They keep the revolutionary goals constantly in mind while working out their plans and programs of reconstruction.

The gradualist approach

Edward Shils exemplifies the common point of view of the gradualist approach when he calls for an estimate of 'the approximations toward, the factors leading toward, and the obstacles in the path of *the formation of society and polity, and of a coherent cultural order*' [italics added][1] in the study of the new states. In other words, the new states must evolve into a society, a polity, and a coherent cultural order, where there was none before, or where there may have been many units existing in an inchoate state. Such a study is designated as macrosociology by Shils and he emphasizes that 'consensus is the key phenomenon of macrosociology.'[2] We will show later how this is a very different view from the one held by the theorists who propagate the revolutionary approach.

System building

One of the important attributes of the modernization process is system building, in which planning plays a crucial role. Therefore, we will examine the nature and scope of planning undertaken by the new nations. We will not go into the specifics of planning and its problems for the reasons indicated earlier. Instead, we will characterize here some of the assumptions necessary for any planning of a socio-political system. These assumptions, to be discussed below, pertain to the economic and the political fields. Other assumptions of system building have already been discussed in various contexts.

Among the economists, Gunnar Myrdal has consistently focused on the mutually reinforcing nature of developmental activities for understanding the sequence of change in any society.[3] In his massive book, *Asian Drama*, Myrdal has presented the scope of the activities and performances of eleven Asian nations, from Pakistan to the Philippines, with a special eye on the future development of their economies. His faith in activism bears ample evidence in his statement, 'history, then, is not taken to be predetermined, but within the power of man to shape;'[4] and yet, despite his ten-year study of the Indian scene, his humility (and perhaps his tacit recognition of the limits of the gradualist approach) restrained him from giving any advice to Prime Minister Nehru, even though he asked for it.

Myrdal is bold enough to acknowledge that modernization theory, like all other theories in social science,[5] carries a value premise. The tenets of the modernization premise are stated by him as follows: (a) rationality; (b) development and *planning* the development (italics added); (c) rise of productivity; (d) rise of levels of living; (e) social and economic equalization; (f) improved institutions and attitudes; (g) national consolidation; (h) national independence; (i) political democracy, in a narrow sense; (j) democracy at the grassroots; and (k) social discipline in the face of 'democratic planning.'[6] These criteria guided the direction of his survey. The author of the famous book, *An American Dilemma*,[7] could not but look at 'the poverty of the nations' in socio-political terms; what is important is to note that he moves beyond the economic and political attributes of the given system (of modernization) to the issue of 'social and economic equalization,' which was emphasized in *our* model, but which generally receives scant treatment in the gradualist approach to modernization. One important criticism which has been leveled at Myrdal is that he is 'merely the recorder of failures,' and that he came to the erroneous conclusion that 'rigid social stratification' and 'absence of rationalism, institutional and attitudinal' were the root cause of the stagnation of these countries, rather than their colonial (or feudal) exploitation.[8] Despite the criticism, Myrdal's orientation to planning is in the right direction.

National planning in the revolutionary tradition goes back to Lenin but planning for revolutionary purposes was already a tenet of socialist thinkers such as Robert Owen or William Morris. One principle common to all socialists is that they believe in equality, which needs a plan of action for implementation. However, here one has to separate national planning from planning of small communities (like the ones Owen had in mind) as well as from planning of individual sectors of the economy (which is common in all industrial countries, including the United States).

The state, as an agent of change and as a vehicle of national planning, played little part in socialist thinking, except in that of Sidney and Beatrice Webb, whose views on this matter were never wholly accepted by the Fabian socialists. However, it is important to note that Beatrice Webb was very firm on this issue. She says, 'Public administration is the alternative to private enterprise, and since private enterprise is corrupt and selfish we propose to supersede it by democratic control.'[9] The activism of Myrdal, a liberal from a socialist country, is matched by that of the Webbs, socialists from a capitalist country. We believe that W. Arthur Lewis is correct in pointing out: 'In the dispute about the powers of the state the traditions of socialism are rooted in liberalism. The bias of socialists, in recent times, has come to be in favor of using the state in place of other social institutions.'[10] The state then becomes the vehicle of system building in all modernizing countries, socialist or otherwise.

Lewis, an astute scholar of planning and an advisor to many governments of modern and modernizing nations, has laid bare both the broad and the specific principles of planning in a series of studies.[11] He believes that the indictment of *laissez-faire* against national planning is all but gone. He says, 'we are all planners now. That is not to say that we believe in all forms of planning or in complete central planning.'[12] However, he cautions against complete bureaucratic direction and its control of all activities. His mistrust of centralization – an issue we have already dealt with at length – remains strong. He says:[13]

A plan cannot be made by 'the people' or by parliament or by the cabinet; it has to be made by officials, because it consists of thousands of details fitted together. Its results are embodied in thousands of administrative orders and decisions, of which parliament and ministers can have only the briefest knowledge, and which provides innumerable opportunities for corrupting the public service. The more we control from the centre the less the control that is possible. When the goverment is doing only a few things we can keep an eye on it, but when it is doing everything it cannot keep an eye on itself.

Lewis, with a democratic bent, eschews the 'overdetailed and overcentralized'[14] model of Stalinist planning, about which we will talk later. Lewis aims to preserve free markets wherever possible in order that resources may not suffer from immobility. He shows how planning by inducement helps the state to manipulate the market in securing its objectives. He is in favor of price control and of rationing only in the interest of equity. He recommends 'planning by [state] direction [of the private sector]' only to overcome immobilities and suggests that the chief instrument of planning should be the budget, unless there is marked disequilibrium between demand and supply, when more rigorous methods may be needed.[15]

The political economy of planning is the necessary condition for modernization, but the sufficient condition is entrepreneurship, if modernization is to lead a country to self-sustaining growth. So we discuss next the problem of entrepreneurship.

Entrepreneurship

Economists at all times have appreciated the need for entrepreneurship in a market economy. However, entrepreneurship is linked to cultural and psychological factors. As Benjamin Higgins notes, '*all* economists who have specialized on [*sic*] economic development recognize the importance of the interplay of these [sociological, cultural, and psychological] factors with economic factors [italics in the original].'[16] It is to the investigation of the sociological, cultural, and psychological factors in the development of entrepreneurship that we turn now. We begin with psychological factors.

David C. McClelland, a psychologist, first outlined his ideas on community development and human motivation in a paper presented at M. I. T. in 1959, in which he described the relationship between his concept of '*n*-Achievement' and economic development.[17] He has since published a book entitled *The Achieving Society*;[18] and he and his associates have provided many empirical studies of the viability of his original hypothesis and its extension in different directions.

McClelland's central thesis revolves around the idea that the economic development of a country depends on 'vigorous activities of a number of individuals who behave in an entrepreneurial fashion.'[19] These individuals have a strong need for achievement, which he terms *n*-Achievement (or *n*-A). The people with high *n*-A show a concern to do better, and to improve performance in a moderately challenging task. Such people prefer personal responsibility, they seek and utilize feedback on performance quality, and they keep on innovating to improve their performance.[20]

In *The Achieving Society*, McClelland reported that generally businessmen scored higher on *n*-A than professionals and that this pattern extended beyond industrial capitalist society to communist countries, such as Poland. He presents his case of modernization with disarming simplicity: 'It seems reasonable to expect that if there are lots of such [achieving] men in a society, it ought to begin to develop rapidly economically.'[21] He buttresses his thesis with proof from historical studies of past societies as well as empirical studies of currently modernizing societies. From individual motivational levels, he moves on to motivational levels of nations by scoring collective fantasies as counted in folk tales and children's books. He believes that 'assessing collective motivational levels may enable an observer to predict in advance what will happen to a civilization.'[22]

McClelland makes it clear that *n*-Achievement is a cause of, not a response to, increased economic opportunity and growth. He and a number of other scholars have suggested that the critical period for acquiring achievement motivation is between the ages of four and eight. McClelland has also refined Max Weber's thesis on the

THE ACTIVISTIC THEORIES OF MODERNIZATION

Protestant Ethic and the spirit of capitalism. He says that the key element in the ethic is an 'inner worldly activism.'[23] He finds some other leads in his comparative studies of entrepreneurship. One of these is the importance of ideology. He says that because ideology is 'important in raising motivation levels, one could perhaps start up economic development in a society by directly increasing the achievement motivation of a number of its key business leaders.'[24] He started the experiment in India and noted that the men trained by this method proved to be 'considerably more active: 51% of them had definitely improved their businesses in the two-year period after the course [meant to increase n-A], contrasted with only 25% of the untrained men.'[25] However, he did not find the cities to which the trained men returned any more economically improved than the cities of the untrained men, two or three years later.[26] McClelland notes some historical evidences of the fact that 'the achievement energies that produce economic development also result in domestic disorder and one-party rule.'[27]

The economist Everett E. Hagen discusses entrepreneurship in the context of innovation. Hagen defines innovation as 'arriving at a new mental or aesthetic concept ... [which] always involves creativity.'[28] He goes on to note that 'innovation involves two steps: arriving at a new mental conception, and converting it into action or into material form.'[29] He points out that in technological innovation, this second step:[30]

> may involve only design or rearrangement of some items of physical equipment or it may involve the organization of a group of human beings into a going concern that carries out a new step. In the latter case it is entrepreneurship; the concept of entrepreneurship seems always to include the management of other human beings.

It should be noted that McClelland's entrepreneur is involved with drive for performance of moderate tasks, whereas Hagen's entrepreneur wishes to take on the ordering of social relationships as well. Hagen combines the 'entrepreneurial' function and the managerial and administrative functions into one entrepreneurial task. Strangely enough, instead of seeking the cause of economic development in economic variables, Hagen locates it in a social group. In reviewing history, he notes that a relatively elite group, when deprived of status at some time, moves into risky financial ventures, which lead on to economic growth. The deprivation may ensue from the actual reduction of the group's historical status or it may even emerge from a threat of such reduction. He marshalls the following historical evidences for his thesis:[31]

In England, the agricultural revolution which preceded the Industrial Revolution was carried out by members of the landed gentry – but they were a country group to whom the urbanite group of gentry manifested a sense of superiority. The Industrial Revolution itself was carried out by *Scots,* who had been conquered by the English, and whose religion was looked down upon by the Church-of-England gentry, and by Nonconformists in England itself. The intellectuals of Russia; the Antioquians of Colombia who have been looked down upon as 'country cousins' by the inhabitants of Bogota; and immigrants in many countries, not fully accepted by the local society, provide other examples of the vigor of such lower echelon elite in their reaction to social subordination. The example *par excellence* is provided by Japan.

Hagen generalizes his findings into 'the law of the subordinated group,' which stipulates that 'only a group driven by an urge to regain or maintain a rightful social status will carry out the revolutionary actions which complete the transition to continuing technological advance.'[32] It seems a little odd that an economist, who usually deals with variables which have predictive value, should formulate a law of economic change in such a way that it could serve little predictive function. Even if Hagen is right about his judgment of hard economic events, his law will be inoperative in the future for the simple reason that national planning in modernizing countries will not provide opportunities for 'such lower echelon elites' to regain their status through such entrepreneurship. The systemic allocation of resources and their management on the national level will preclude the role of minorities in moving to the forefront of entrepreneurship, especially when system building also involves the tenet of social equality.

Alex Inkeles, a sociologist, has explored in depth the attributes of individual modernity as compared to societal modernity. He has characterized the 'modern man' as possessing the following traits: (a) readiness for new experience and openness to innovation and change; (b) disposition to form or hold opinions over a large number of problems and issues within and beyond his immediate environment; (c) a democratic attitude in the realm of opinion so that differences of opinion are acknowledged; (d) oriented to the present and the future rather than to the past; (e) planning-oriented; (f) a faith in man's ability to control nature for his own use; (g) calculability; (h) dignity; (i) faith in science and technology; and (j) distributive justice, i.e. rewards should be according to contribution.[33]

Inkeles has devised and tested six scales for measuring overall

89

modernity (he calls it, OM scale), and feels that he has 'a theoretically broad, empirically tight, administratively simple measure of individual modernity,' which can be used by researchers and planners to judge the modernity of individuals or groups in modernizing countries.[34]

We believe that Inkeles, like McClelland, has provided an important tool in the hands of nation-builders. However, what mix of 'modern man' and traditional man as also what ratio of high n-Achievement people to low n-Achievement people will take a country beyond the threshold of stagnation is something on which much work needs to be done. Inkeles's 'modern man' should be located in all leadership roles, whereas McClelland's high n-A people would be desirable mostly in business occupations. Hagen, on the other hand, implies that it is only a closed subcultural group of lower elite status that can escalate the economic development in any country. His view, in this matter, seems to have few implications for policy.

Other catalytic factors

We have discussed the role of the entrepreneur, both economic and administrative, in the development process. In this section, we wish to examine some other catalytic factors in modernization. These refer in general to the 'modernizing elite' of the newly-independent countries. Specifically, we will consider the role of the military and the leadership of the bureaucracy in the modernization process.

It would be a truism to affirm that the elite of the newly-independent country can either help or resist the modernization process. There has been a tendency in the earlier literature to emphasize the role of 'the Western educated elite' in the development of a nation.[35] No doubt, during the colonial years, such elites imbibed the liberal philosophies of individual and national freedom, rational growth of the socio-economic system, and the guarantees of basic rights for the pursuit of life, liberty, and happiness. Some of these elites became the spearhead of the ideology of nationalism, without which the liberal values could not be realized in their estimation.

When the former colonies of Asia and Africa became independent (Latin American colonies became free about a century and a half ago), these elites and the emerging ones set to the task of nation-building, which was essential to the growth of a liberal democracy. In this process, some of these neo-colonial elites became *elitists* in orientation and conceived of all plans and reforms along the lines followed in capitalist countries like the United States. Other neo-colonial elites, especially those under the impetus of ideas emanating from the London School of Economics – founded and nurtured by the socialist leader, Harold J. Laski – wanted crash programs of a socialistic nature, including state control of key public enterprises and national resources for developing the country. These elites eschewed the elitist attitude of a faith in the free enterprise system and its consequences for individual motivation and rewards; instead they became equalizers of social status, rank, and power, and set into motion massive opportunities for social mobility through educational, technocratic, and ideological reforms and programs of action. It would take us too far out of our present discussion to spell out the differing roles of the elitist and the equalizer types of the neo-colonial elites in the modernizing nations. (Both types of elites often coexist in the non-Soviet modernizing nations today.) However, what we do wish to emphasize here is that the elitist leadership is bourgeois in orientation and seeks equilibrium and stability, whereas the leadership which believes in equalization and the leveling down of class differences is usually proletarian in its outlook and looks for constant agitational methods for eliminating the scope of capitalistic inheritance of status and its perquisites.

We will now discuss the role of two elites, the military and the bureaucracy, in the modernization process.

(a) *The military*   Lucien W. Pye, a political scientist, spells out the characteristics of the army as a modern organization. He also shows how professionalism, hierarchy, specialization, and the need for efficiency create strains toward conservatism as well as rationalism in the army.[36] He concludes that:[37]

> where traditional habits of mind are still strong one might
> expect the military to be strongly conservative. Such was largely
> the case in the West during the pre-industrial period. By
> contrast, in most of the newly emerging countries, armies have
> tended to emphasize a rational outlook and to champion
> responsible change and national development.

Pye adduces some strong evidences in favor of the army as a modernizing agent. First, it is instilled with the spirit of rapid technological development, and this leads to the adoption of the methods of industrial organizations for ordering tasks within the army. Staff functions increase compared to line functions; this leads to larger numbers of officers being assigned to staff functions. Those officers trained in specialized training schools are also well versed in personnel management and procurement. Rationality guides their actions in staff functions and consequently such officers, especially the younger ones, 'are extremely sensitive to the needs of modernization and technological advancement.'[38]

Pye, however, seems to overemphasize the modernizing role of the army for both the officers and the men in the newly-independent countries. Within the army, acculturation does take place but it does not necessarily mean that all the virtues of 'the more impersonal and universalistic relationships of an industrialized society' are learned, as he claims. The examples of the German factory utilizing non-commissioned army officers as foremen; the Corps of Engineers in the United States opening up its West; the Brazilian army building roads, promoting natural sciences and protecting the American-Indian population; as well as ex-army personnel providing trained manpower, and often leadership, in India, Malaya, and the Philippines, do not necessarily provide 'training in citizenship,' as Pye implies.[39] Awareness of the political dimensions of the society is one thing, but appreciation of political action, political bargaining, and responsible nationalism is something else again. It would do well for a political scientist to avoid global generalizations on the basis of some imagined systemic link of variables; instead he should work with empirical cases. The existence of modern attitudes which are assumed for army officers and men by Pye needs to be tested against the more comprehensive model of the 'modern man' of Inkeles, as well as the distinction between 'the cosmopolitan' and the 'local' made by Merton, and discussed earlier in this essay.

The relationship between the army and the civilian leadership has been spelled out in terms of a typology by Gino Germani and Kalman H. Silvert for Latin America.[40] It is not our intent to review the presumed types of relationships of the army to the civilian rule, of which ten types are identified by the authors. We merely wish to point out that only three such relationships are pertinent to the advancement of the modernization process. These are: (a) the military as orienter of national policy (Mexico is cited as an example); (b) the military as a pressure group with veto power (Chile, before Allende came to power, and the subsequent military rule there); and (c) the military as the political arm of the state (Cuba, Bolivia, and USSR, among others, are given as examples).[41] One should note that the 'benevolent' role of the army is more of an exception or even myth, than a rule. Under certain circumstances (as in stable democracies and wherever a preponderance of 'the equalizer' rather than 'the elitist' kind of officer in the army prevails), the army may be counted on to advance the modernization process; otherwise, its role is to create either polarization in the society with the elite dominating the masses, or to back up centralization to the point where the political regime becomes dictatorial in substance, if not in principle.

Edward Shils, in making an early survey of political development of the new states, points out that among them:[42]

> Only India and Pakistan inherited large, well-trained armies experienced in warfare and governed by an *officer class with a modern military tradition* ... The armies of the Arab states of the Middle East are more recent creations with less military experience ... The Indonesian and Burmese armies are the heirs of guerilla forces. In the independent states of Sub-Saharan Africa, the armed forces are slight. African officers are, on the whole, new to their tasks [italics added].

Shils believes that if the modern intellectual class (which, according to him, as we noted in an earlier chapter, includes the professional and the middle class) consists of people with technological education, the military may regard it as an ally. He points out that military oligarchies can be successful only if they achieve the following goals: stability and effectiveness of the elite; acceptance of opposition; authority maintained with the help of the civil service; public opinion; and civil order. In sum, he rightly concludes that 'the military oligarchy is not a complete regime ... It is ... a "caretaker regime." '[43]

Morris Janowitz, a careful student of the sociological functions of the new military, agrees that the military of the new nations base their technology and organization on the Western pattern. They are also 'centrally involved in internal order and political power.'[44] The constabulary function (maintenance of law and order) and the political function (bargaining) of the military have to be carefully examined, because as he points out, one of the goals of military assistance given by the United States is 'to mobilize the armed forces of the new nations and Latin America to assist in the modernization of their countries.'[45] However, in a review of the literature of revolutions and *coups d'état*, it has been pointed out that often the army isolates itself from the mainstream of civilian life by 'providing its own educational and indoctrination programs, establishing its own economic institutions, and in some cases its own political organization.'[46] There are strong doubts indicated in this literature about the ability of the army to set up a democratic pattern of communication, to arbitrate between the conflicts of social and political groups, to accept setbacks, and especially to solve complicated economic problems.[47] The 'Western' structure of the army, preserved by a military elite, thus becomes an obstacle in the way of winning political support through political competition.

Janowitz, in reviewing the impact of technology on the military organization of the West, has unwittingly provided a clue to the solution of the democratic problem of 'the modernizing military' (wherever it is found) in the newly-independent countries. He points out that in the West (especially in the United States), the impact of technology on military organization was 'to weaken the distinction between the soldier and the civilian during the period 1900-1945.'[48] Military preparedness meant the expansion of military influence on the production process. The civilian scientist, technologist, and engineer were integrated with the military, whether they were in uniform or not. However, since 1945, the limits of 'this process of civilianization' have been reached and the newer defense systems and defense technology are so 'specialized and differentiated' that they must be compartmentalized from the larger social environment. He does not believe that there will be a complete isolation of the military, if only because 'the fusion of the military and political goals alone makes this impossible.'[49]

In so far as the war-making needs of the new nations will be paramount in view of the traditional or newer enemies of these countries, the military will continue to dominate the civilian systems of allocation and production. However, if the war-making potential increases to the point of the production of nuclear weapons (as is possible, for instance, in Israel and India) or if it is not needed in view of the geopolitical status of a country (for example, Sri Lanka), there is the possibility of disengagement of the military from civilian rule. Whether the military will ever lose influence in any country is open to doubt (Costa Rica seems to be an exception). Whether it will serve as a vehicle of modernization depends on the many factors discussed above, but this is always governed by the overall attitude of the military to the civilian authority system of a nation.

(b) *The bureaucracy* We discuss in this section the role of the non-military bureaucrat in the modernization process. Bureaucracy is necessary for system-building, because it is the ideal type of formal organization for performing complicated tasks, as Max Weber pointed out long ago.[50] And Robert K. Merton adds, 'The chief merit of bureaucracy is its technical efficiency, with a premium placed on precision, speed, expert control, continuity, discretion, and optimal returns on input.'[51] Nothing is needed more than these virtues from the bureaucrat in a modernizing country. However, important difficulties arise from another trait of bureaucracy, that is, its impersonality, and especially its lack of affectual involvements in the values advanced by the political leaders of the modernizing nations. In this section, we are not going to review the entire characteristics of the bureaucracy of modernizing countries, but only the leadership potential of bureaucracy as a 'modernizer.'

It is well-known that Karl Marx was in favor of smashing the old bureaucracy in order to realize the new goals. As he wrote, 'I say that the next attempt of the French Revolution will be no longer, as before, to transfer the bureaucratic-military machine from one hand to another, but to smash it.'[52] J. Donald Kingsley, in his study of the bureaucracy in England, points out that emphasis on the merit system and the separation of the civil service from the patronage system served more the function of the business groups, who wanted cheap and efficient service from the state.[53] Whether the movement from a *laissez-faire* attitude to a planned society attitude in the modernizing nations demands a new role for the bureaucracy or a continuation of the system of non-political permanent officials manning the higher civil service is still a debated issue. Kingsley points out that the top-level officers of Nigeria have played a vital role in the integration of that nation.[54] Ralph Braibanti describes how Pakistan built up its civil service from the rather limited administrative talent at its disposal.[55] Subsequent history shows that its role in uniting the country has been minimal, if any.

S. C. Dube, who has examined the rural and urban bureaucracy of independent India, believes that 'bureaucracy forms an important element of the modernizing elite in many of the economically less developed countries.'[56] He points out the complicated adjustment of the old bureaucracy to the post-colonial situation, when 'the supremacy of administration was replaced by the sovereignty of politics.'[57] The change in attitude needed by the bureaucracy to realize that 'it could not maintain its image of power, nor could it continue to exist as a high-prestige class enjoying exceptional privileges' is hard to make.[58] Dube asks for its closer identification with the masses and advises it to shed the paternalistic and authoritarian tone of administration.[59] This is admittedly a difficult task. Yet the resocialization of the bureaucrats is imperative if they want to be a modernizing force and not a neo-colonial *elitist* elite.

Fred W. Riggs suggests an important limitation of bureaucracy in the modernization process, which needs to be taken into account here.[60] The development of political parties depends a great deal on their ability to use the 'spoils' system as opposed to the 'merit' system for awarding some civilian jobs. In the zeal for efficiency, this may be blocked by the civil service both at the higher and lower echelons.[61] Another drawback of the bureaucracy may be the inability to decentralize administrative decisions. In a newly-independent country, decentralized administrative machinery may encourage more local and regional initiative than a centralized administration can. Providing local watchdogs on administrative agents is also a cardinal principle of democratic polity. But this leads to the larger problem of the ideology of modernization, i.e. whether it should be gradualist or revolutionary in approach. So we turn to the revolutionary approach to societal transformation, which we discuss next.

The revolutionary approach

Any people anywhere, being inclined and having the power, have the right to rise up and shake off the existing government, and form a new one that suits them better. This is a most valuable, a most sacred right – a right which we hope and believe is to liberate the world.[62]

These are not the words of Karl Marx and Friedrich Engels, or of Lenin, the architect of the Russian Revolution, but of Abraham Lincoln, who spoke these words in the House of Representatives of the United States on January 12, 1848, a short few weeks before the *Communist Manifesto*, the working doctrine of worldwide revolution, was announced on the platform of the Communist League. We wish to emphasize that the revolutionary approach to changing society is not to be associated with communist dogma alone but with other thinkers who want to shatter human bondage, wherever and whenever it appears in the course of history. However, the communist approach to revolution is based on a different premise: it identifies exploitation with the existence of classes in a society, and claims that without the overthrow of the capitalist class and the simultaneous creation of a socialist society, no revolution will succeed. The goal is to create communism, where the authority structure of the state will vanish and man will finally be free and truly creative. As Marx and Engels put it in the *Communist Manifesto*: 'In place of the old bourgeois society, with its classes and class antagonisms, we shall have an association in which the free development of each is the condition for the free development of all.'[63]

Ideology is the creator of revolutions, and ideology, as we noted earlier, is a prime force for social change in the modernizing countries of today. We also indicated in our model of modernization that revolutionary methods are appropriate in the short run, so long as, in the long run, consensual and democratic methods of social organization of work and rewards get firmly established in society. These goals are commensurate with all revolutionary schools. In this section, we first discuss the Marxist revolutionary approach, then the non-Marxist revolutionary approaches, and finally the method of goal maintenance in the revolutionary transformation of society.

The Marxist revolution

Marx and Engels preached the overthrow of capitalist and other oppressive ruling regimes in order to advance worldwide communism. The abolition of the capitalist ownership of the means of production, the seizure of the power of the state by the proletariat, the reorganization of work and production by the leadership of the party first and later by the free individuals themselves, are important tenets of the Marxist revolution. As Engels points out, with the success of proletarian revolution, 'Man, at last the master of his own form of social organization, becomes at the same time the lord over Nature, his own master – free.'[64]

In the *Communist Manifesto,* Marx and Engels provide a reasoned critique of the failure or non-workability of 'reactionary socialism' (under which they include the *feudal* socialism of France and England, the *petit-bourgeois* socialism of Sismondi, who influenced both the French and the English writers, and the *German or 'True' Socialism* of the German philosophers), 'conservative or bourgeois socialism' (reformers of the Proudhon type), and 'critical-utopian socialism' (e.g. Saint-Simon, who was in 'search after a new social science,' as well as the Fourierists in France and the Owenites in England). The discovery of 'class antagonism' and the emphasis on the 'historical initiative' of the proletariat in capitalist society were the two hallmarks of communist interpretation of historical laws, in their judgment.

Engels believed that the fundamental tenet of the *Communist Manifesto* was 'destined to do for history what Darwin's theory has done for biology ... '[65] He states the central proposition of the *Manifesto* as follows:[66]

That in every historical epoch, the prevailing mode of economic production and exchange, and the social organization, necessarily following from it, form the basis upon which is built up, and from which alone can be explained the political and intellectual history of that epoch; that consequently the whole history of mankind (since the dissolution of primitive tribal society, holding land in common ownership) has been a history of class struggles, contests between exploiting and exploited, ruling and oppressed classes; that *the history of these class struggles forms a series of evolutions in which, nowadays, a stage has been reached where the exploited and the oppressed class – the proletariat –*

97

cannot attain its emancipation from the sway of the exploiting and ruling class – the bourgeoisie – without, at the same time, and once and for all emancipating society at large from all exploitation, oppression, class distinction and class struggles [italics added].

Two facts need to be emphasized here. One, that the Marxian revolution is sceptical of all socialist reformers and planning unless the bourgeois class is abolished, and, two, that the stage had arrived in the 'series of evolutions' to take the next step (through worldwide revolution) of 'emancipating society at large from all exploitation, oppression, class distinction and class struggles.'

Lenin, the father of the Russian Revolution, masterminded a strategy which finally led to the establishment of the 'dictatorship of the proletariat' in Russia. It is true that Marx's prognosis of the revolution first taking place in the advanced capitalist countries did not come true, but that is not of much consequence so long as the revolution did take place somewhere. The way Lenin steered the revolution and started to rebuild the first true socialist society has been recounted in many scholarly volumes.

Lenin was the first national *planner* in history. Apart from some general remarks in *The German Ideology, Capital, The Critique of the Gotha Program,* and in their correspondence, Marx and Engels did not provide substantive ideas as to how the economy should be organized or the authority structure reworked after the overthrow of capitalism, or after the revolution. Lenin reflected on some of these issues, especially on the problem of the 'withering away of the state,' in *The State and Revolution,* written during the volcanically turbulent year of 1917, and had this to say:[67]

Engels speaks ... of the *destruction* of the capitalist state by the proletarian revolution, while the words about its withering away refer to the remains of a *proletarian* State after the Socialist revolution. The capitalist State does not wither away, according to Engels, but is *destroyed* by the proletariat in the course of the revolution. Only the proletarian State or semi-State withers away after the revolution.

Lenin saved the first socialist state from destruction by its enemies, including the anarchists in his own camp. He died a premature death in 1924, but had lived long enough to steer his Bolshevik Party through the civil war phase and to promulgate the New Economic Policy (NEP) in 1921, which was a compromise with capitalism, as an expedient to rebuild the tattered economy of an impoverished Russia.

It is to Stalin that one must turn to see how the first Soviet Socialist Republic was transformed from a hungry, ravaged nation into one of the two mightiest powers in the world today. The principle of 'democratic centralism' propounded by Lenin in due course led to centralized planning, when in 1928 Stalin set up the First Five-Year Plan, which was the first comprehensive case of national planning in history. The First Five-Year Plan led to the Second, and the Third, and so on, until today this manner of planning has become the *raison d'être* of the modernization process in most newly-independent countries. The ruthlessness with which Stalin implemented the plans (especially the terror of his political purges) has been criticized by all neutral observers and yet Horowitz may be right when he claims that 'Stalinism was not a simple rule of terror. Rather, terrorism was the consequence of an approach to development in which planning, decision-making, and policy determination were all centralized and expected to be realized – whatever their human cost.'[68]

Milovan Djilas faults contemporary communism on many grounds and calls such a system 'total state capitalism.'[69] He believes that People's Republics are totalitarian states, controlled by the Party and a 'new class,' which hungers for power, ownership, and the control of ideology.[70] He is right in accusing the Communist Party of over-centralization and over-zealousness in protecting its rights and prerogatives. After all, Lenin himself had said that 'a Communist Party will be able to perform its duty only if it is organized in the most centralized manner, only if iron discipline bordering on military discipline prevails in it.'[71] But that was for the period of the 'acute civil war'. It is Stalin who transformed this doctrine applicable 'in the period of struggle preceding the achievement of the dictatorship [of the proletariat]' into a dogma, which states: 'The same, but to an even greater degree, must be said about discipline in the party after the dictatorship has been achieved.'[72]

Djilas, however, seems to have misconstrued both the meaning of capitalism in the Marxian lexicon and the relevance of class in Marxist theory, or for that matter, in sociological theory. For Marx and Engels, the key to capitalism is in property relations and the power of capital in the hands of its individual owners (or the 'social relations of production' and the 'factors of production' respectively, as they are known). The political bureaucracy of the Soviet nations does not own private property for personal aggrandizement; neither does it use capital (nor 'excess profits' of the workers in the hands of the bureaucracy) for anything more than investment into the state enterprise system.

Djilas's definition of the new class is vague, to say the least. It seems that every functionary of the state falls into his category of 'the new class.' He qualifies the concept endlessly, for instance, 'this new class, the bureaucracy, or more accurately the political bureaucracy.'[73] Again:[74]

> This is not to say that the new party and the new class are identical. The party, however, is the core of that class, and its base. *It is very difficult, perhaps impossible, to define the limits of the new class and to identify its members.* The new class may be said to be made up of those who have special privileges and economic preference because of the administrative monopoly they hold [italics added].

If Djilas cannot define the limits of the class or even identify its members, it is difficult to see what sociological function such a category serves.

Most important of all, Djilas does not appreciate the importance of the fact that inheritance of private property is the basic ingredient of the formation of the class sytem. This is minimal in the USSR and other People's Democracies. In fact, the tendency to circulate people of various statuses to various levels of jobs is a common phenomenon, as is clear in the erstwhile deputation of urban workers and professionals to manual labor jobs in rural areas in the People's Republic of China. When studies in Poland showed that more members of the professional stratum wanted payment on a piece-rate basis, this was interpreted by Gomulka as leading toward class formation, and so instead of acceding to this wish as an incentive, he promulgated the opposite policy, so that the accumulation of personal gains could not give unfair advantages to the children of professionals as compared to those of manual laborers.[75] The educational system in these countries is also designed to give better opportunities to the children of people engaged in manual labor, either on the farms or in the factories.

It may be noted that it was never the intention of Karl Marx to abolish all private property, only the private ownership of the means of production. Thus private property (consumption goods) is accumulated somewhat unevenly depending on the wage differentials in the Soviet countries. In so far as these countries are still socialist (building toward communism), the principle obtaining at present is: 'from each according to his ability, to each according to his deeds.'[76] In this process, a distinction has to be made between a manual laborer on the farm or in the factory and a professional. In the Soviet Union today, for instance, there are 30 million people who perform non-manual labor tasks. Half of them have been classified as professionals, for example, the engineers, technicians, agronomists, teachers, and physicians.[77] This is inevitable in any industrial society. What Marxist revolution, especially the Leninist interpretation of it, demands is not the abolition of stratum

differences but the consequences of class formation (with hereditary perpetuation of rights and privileges) flowing from such
differences. Class is a concept rooted in exploitation; stratum is a
concept flowing from the complex division of labor in society.

The non-Marxist revolution

Barrington Moore, Jr has written a provocative book on the
making of the modern world in terms of the working out of some
historical forces.[78] He points out that:[79]

> one may discern three main historical roots from the preindus-
> trial to the modern world. The first of these [England, France,
> and the United States] leads through ... bourgeois revolu-
> tions ... The second route has also been capitalist, but culminat-
> ed during the twentieth century in fascism [Germany and
> Japan] ... The third route is of course communism, as exem-
> plified in Russia and in China.

He believes that in India a fourth general pattern may be observed in its 'weak impulse toward modernization.' As he says,
'In that country [India] so far there has been neither a capitalist
revolution from above or below, nor a peasant one leading to
communism.'[80]

Moore states that the way the landed upper classes and the
peasants react to the challenges of commercial agriculture determines the political outcome of modernization. He believes that new
social arrangements generally grow up by violence and that both
non-democratic and even antidemocratic modernization works.
The English landlord of the eighteenth century, the Prussian
Junker in the seventeenth century, and the Russian communist in
the twentieth century used violence in transforming the peasantry
but the Japanese ruling classes found that they could get their way
without destroying the peasant society. However, both for Japan
and Germany, the price for avoiding a revolutionary entrance into
modernization has been very high, viz. fascism. Moore concludes
his complex historical study by suggesting that: 'The process of
modernization begins with peasant revolutions that fail. It culmin-
ates during the twentieth century with peasant revolutions that
succeed.'[81]

Eric R. Wolf reviews the role of the peasantry in six major
revolutions of this century: the Mexican (1910), the Russian (1905
and 1917), the Chinese (1921 onwards), the Vietnamese (post-
Second World War), the Algerian rebellion (1954), and the Cuban
Revolution (1958).[82] He believes that the peasantry cannot engage
in a sustained rebellion. However, when they rebel, it is because of

three factors: the demographic crisis, the ecological crisis, and the crisis in power and authority. Like Moore, he emphasizes the role of the market and of commercialization in deranging the numerous middle-level ties between the centre and the hinterland. This results in an ever-widening gap between the rulers and the ruled. Thus counter-elites are formed with the help of provincial elites and other intellectuals, who can then lead rebellions.

The components of the peasantry who can revolt are (a) landowning middle peasantry, and (b) a peasantry located in a peripheral area outside the domain of the landlord. The rich peasant is unlikely to rebel. Wolf does not think that the peasant rebellion can be transformed into a revolution, i.e. the overthrow of the power of the society, without outside help. This confirms the hypothesis of the Marxists on this point. The peasant rebellion, wherever it succeeded, merely changed the order of the country-side, not of the state, as the following examples show: Zapata stayed in his Morelos; the 'false migration' of Pancho Villa simply receded after the defeat at Torreon; the Ukranian rebel Nestor Makhno stopped short of the cities; and the Russian peasants of the Central Agricultural Region simply burrowed into their local communes. Wolf concludes, 'Thus a peasant rebellion which takes place in a complex society already caught up in commercialization and industrialization tends to be self-limiting, and hence anachronistic.'[83]

Goal maintenance

A revolution must have mechanisms of goal maintenance, in order to succeed. The first goal is to achieve power. Sometimes, power is limited territorially, as in the case of the peasant rebellions; sometimes, it is far-flung and comprehensive, as in the case of the military (including guerilla warfare) revolutions, peasant revolutions, and proletarian (so far only mixed cases of proletarian, bourgeois, and rural sectors) revolutions. Initial success can depend on many factors, such as charismatic leadership (examples, Lenin, Mao Tse-tung), class leadership (the landed upper class in England), and armed guerillas (Cuba). However, the second goal of revolution is the consolidation of revolutionary change. It involves comprehensive planning of the type, for instance, undertaken in the USSR, China, and Cuba.

One of the crucial issues debated in the context of revolutionary consolidation is the role of the bureaucracy in it. In the case of Russia, some of the old bureaucrats fled, while others were absorbed into the new bureaucracy that was set up by Lenin and Stalin. However, bureaucrats have a tendency toward elitism unless they are constantly checked and reshuffled. Castro has often complained since 1965 about the fear of bureaucratism. The Cultural Revolution of China is often interpreted in the West as the competition for power between rival camps in the Party. It seems to us that it may also be the mechanism for reminding the bureaucrat that he is no different from any other member of the proletariat or any worker on the farm. It was not without reason that Lenin thought it necessary to teach administration to millions and millions of workers.

Before we conclude this section, a word needs to be said about democracy in the Soviet countries, which came into existence through revolution. The British Prime Minister Attlee once said that a communist election is 'a race with one horse'. And yet Lenin wrote, 'There can be no victorious socialism that doesn't practice full democracy.'[84] We have noted earlier the difficulty of judging democracy on the basis of the two-party system, or any single major criterion used in the West. If popular participation is the criterion, then here is how a Soviet sociologist describes the situation in his country today:[85]

> Millions of people actively assist in the drafting of laws and reforms and the taking of the most important decisions. Tens of millions of people took part in the discussion of the directives of the five-year plan of the economic development of the USSR in 1966-1970. A nation-wide discussion preceded the passing of the Law on Marriage and Family, of the Land Law, of the Model Regulations of a Kolkhoz. Working people are entrusted with the control over the activities of Soviet economic and public organizations. Bodies of Public Control are staffed by nearly 7 million people.

The transformation of the backward economy of Russia into a modern state and its successful competition with the most powerful industrial nation of the world, the United States, makes it an attractive model for imitation by the modernizing countries. As the quotation from Karl Marx at the masthead of this book says, 'The country that is more developed industrially only shows to the less developed, the image of its own future.' And the realization of this image is possible only through national planning in the modernizing countries, for which Russia and China have much more to offer in terms of experience than the United States. The problem of goal maintenance of a revolutionary regime is primarily solved through comprehensive planning, and this will be carefully examined in the next chapter, where we present our own views on modernization.

9 Modernization theories: a summation

Theories of modernization, as we noted in the preceding chapters, span a wide spectrum of issues concerning all aspects of social life and covering all major disciplines of social science. In this chapter, we attempt to summarize the main issues in such a way that a viable plan for modernization can emerge. Our summary takes into account the major variables, which may be considered associated with modernization either as necessary or as sufficient conditions for it.

There are four sets of variables which may be regarded as crucial for modernization and on which we concentrate here. These variables lie in the areas of economy, polity, education, and bureaucracy. We examine the full range of modernization issues within each one of these variable-sets, and so far as is possible relate them to each other in a systematic framework. Our review here pulls together various strands of thought examined in the earlier chapters and will try to knit them together in a comprehensive whole.

The economy

The economic variables like per capita income, savings, capital, investment, credit, and finance have meaning only in so far as there is a well-developed market system and high monetization of the production and distribution of goods and services in a country. We noted the controversy in economic anthropology about the applicability of this principle to all cultures. Here, we wish to reiterate the point that we are going to discuss only those economic issues which are germane to a market economy and not necessarily to primitive barter/exchange situations.

All underdeveloped countries have a 'subsistence sector' and a 'money economy,' whose interrelations have not been systematically studied so far.[1] This phenomenon is often referred to as economic dualism, where the subsistence sector is labelled as the 'traditional' sector and the money economy as the 'modern' sector of the domestic economic framework. J. H. Boeke considers sociological rigidities as the factors causing such a situation.[2] However, dualism has another meaning in economics, whereby the 'modern' sector is defined as consisting of large-scale economic units, which employ capital-intensive methods of production, and the 'traditional' sector is defined as small-scale economic units, which use labor-intensive methods of production.[3] Thus the allocation of resources to the 'modern' and 'traditional' sectors becomes the backbone of contention in economic theory.

Some economists wish to extend and adapt the neoclassical theory of equilibrium and the static theory of the optimum allocation of scarce resources for bringing about economic growth. Others apply the Keynesian macroeconomic approach including the Harrod-Domar type of macro-models to underdeveloped countries. Still others want to introduce radically new 'dynamic' approaches to deal with the changes in the long-run supplies of factors of production, as well as changes in the techniques of production and the organizational structure of the country. The new dynamic approaches link underdevelopment to the 'vicious circle' of economic stagnation and population pressure. They often prescribe the 'take off' theory, which involves doubling the investment rate and raising the investment from 5 per cent of the national income to 10 per cent or more. And the 'big push' theory emphasizes that manufacturing should take the lead, in such a way that even 'steel mills' of the capital-intensive type of Western technology are not ruled out for adoption by the underdeveloped countries. Such theorists recommend 'crash programs,' say, in education, without necessarily analysing the demand and supply factors affecting the market for skilled labor.

If economic growth is to be self-sustaining, it is important that the material 'infrastructure' should be built as quickly as possible. However, resources are limited, so one school recommends that instead of investing them all in productive capital, there should be an investment in 'human capital,' particularly education and even social welfare. This approach neglects market forces and emphasizes governmental planning of all sectors of the economy.

There are important differences of opinion among economists as to whether and how far the neoclassical or the Keynesian approach is applicable to the *economic* problems of the underdeveloped country. It is true that shortages of capital, skilled labor, innovation, entrepreneurship, management, and political experience exist

105

in various degrees in all underdeveloped countries. But that is not prima-facie evidence that economic theory, as developed for the workings of the market economy, will not apply to them if they are functioning in terms of a market system domestically and internationally. With regard to the application of the Western-industrial model to these countries, there are no doubt important criticisms about factor disproportionality, cumulative disequalizing factors, and the weaknesses of the balanced growth theory, as we noted in an earlier chapter. However, it seems to us that the allocation of resources, no matter how they are done, i.e. either through the market system or through governmental regulation, must be finally accountable in terms of the optimum theory on a given time scale. Otherwise, there is no economic accountability; instead, economy becomes a function of political demands and bureaucratic controls.

An issue which has not been given enough attention in the development of macroeconomic approaches and macrogrowth models is that all underdeveloped countries are not alike. India with its surplus of trained manpower, well-equipped bureaucracy, and relatively stable political system is very different from most other developing countries which have important lags in one or another of these areas. In this sense, Brazil and Mexico are more like India than most of the African and Asian countries. On the other hand, India's population pressure does not exist in Latin America or Africa despite their high rates of population growth. The man/land ratio and man/resource ratio put important limits on the development of the domestic economy. India can afford to produce for its domestic market, but its balance of payments would suffer if its international trade did not expand and exports lagged behind imports. On the other hand, countries with no population pressure can afford to export primary goods in return for capital and aid in the form of technology and know-how. The opportunity for emigration, as in the case of Puerto Rico, provides a new dimension to population pressure and capital formation in a country.

A word needs to be said about international aid. As most developing countries have already adopted large-scale governmental economic planning with widespread protection of infant industries at home, import controls, and deficit financing of major enterprises, the need for external assistance is growing. Despite the efforts of the World Bank, the International Monetary Fund, the International Development Corporation (and other similar regional bodies and consortiums for helping individual countries, such as India), and UNCTAD, the developing nations face a dire shortage of capital, discrimination in trade, and barriers to their viable entry into the world market. Such imbalances cannot be corrected because of the early start of the industrial countries in monopolizing trade and commerce and the control of multinational corporations which are mostly based in industrial countries. UNCTAD's failure to induce trade rather than aid is one example of the lack of bargaining power of the developing nations.

The underdeveloped countries, even though working in a democratic framework, will not succeed in attracting either governmental or private foreign capital unless they work at the same time to overcome imbalances in their own national economic systems. Most of the gross national product of these countries is in the 'traditional' sector, yet agriculture and cottage industries are usually discriminated against in terms of credit, financing, and investment compared to the modern sector of heavy industries and commerce. This leads either to the lack of motivation on the part of rural producers and/or to militant trade unionism in urban industries, where artificial barriers are created for unemployed manpower to enter the labor market. At some point, the planners must face up to the duality in the economic system, which may not only stagnate the national economy but create grounds for ethnic, regional, class, and communal discontents leading to production breakdowns and revolts and perhaps eventually to revolution.

The issues we have raised in this section are economic issues of barriers to capital formation, development of a nationally unified economy under the market system, entrepreneurship and planning, as well as the availability and use of international resources and facilities. We noted that there are no clear-cut answers, but at the same time we emphasized that economic cost-accounting must take place, in terms of optimum resource allocation in some time-bound framework. Without it, growth will be haphazard and vulnerable to political decisions all the time. In this process, we believe that a developing country does not have to adopt the orthodox economic policies of *laissez-faire*, free trade and conservative fiscal and monetary policies in order to utilize some proven concepts of neoclassical economics, such as the optimum theory. The policy of development may be pragmatic but the theory of development must be rational and subject to confirmation in the developing body of principles in economics.

The polity

The political variables include the organs of the state (e.g. the executive, legislative, and judicial branches of the government and the army), the political groupings (e.g. parties, interest groups, and quasi-governmental bodies like the *panchayat*, i.e. village assembly,

107

system of India) on national and local levels, the forms in which the citizens exercise their political rights (e.g. election, referendum, recall), and the degree of popular participation in national, regional as well as local political affairs (e.g. universal adult suffrage, limited franchise as in the case of property or residential qualifications for voting, and various combinations of direct and indirect elections, including nomination and quota reservations for ethnic or minority groups).

The problems that occur in the development of the national political system have been reviewed in an earlier chapter. There we were mainly concerned with the building of the political system. In this section, we will deal with some of the issues, which constantly crop up in the early period of nation-building, as well as some of the dangers which a new country may face in consolidating itself after independence. We also briefly relate political development to economic growth.

The problem of the creation of national identity comes first. In newly-independent countries, 'the ideology of nationalism' will dictate some kind of democratic framework of governmental and political institutions and the machinery for popular participation in them. What is of concern to us here is how the initial experience of 'self-rule' will stand up when it comes to dividing the fruits of the political 'spoils.' Will the democratic methods of bargaining, compromising, coalition-forming, and working through consensus prevail, or will there be a shift in the direction of a one party system, a strong man system, or rule by the military junta? These are crucial issues to which there are no proven answers. On the basis of the literature we have examined, it seems that one can only provide a programmatic approach to facing such issues.

The civilian control of the military is essential for democratic development. By democratic development, we mean safeguarding the political rights of citizens to participate in voting as well as contesting for public offices; rule by law and constitution; and the opportunity to receive 'a piece of the pie,' without ethnic, class, or regional prejudices. A military regime or dictatorship of one man or of an oligarchy may fulfill some of these requirements, but cannot provide them all. Whether it can be done through a one party system remains a debatable issue in political theory despite the successes in this regard of some countries like India (until recently), Tanzania, and Mexico, where generally one party rule prevails. The Soviet countries are in the same class although for different reasons. Thus the aim should be to avoid military rule and dictatorship of one or the few, and to work toward a party system.

The penetration of national institutions into regions and localities is another key issue in political development. The need for extending national economic institutions, for instance, credit and marketing facilities to the rural sector was mentioned earlier. Let us now consider another national institution, the legal system. How far and how soon the national legal system should be extended to all groups and all regions is dependent on the nature of the use of these institutions by the people, as well as on the relevance of their actions for national stability. We noted earlier that the national legal system must be universalistic in a modern country. However, in India it does not help to ask villagers to bring every legal issue to court when most of them are satisfied with the *panchayat* (voluntarily assembled judges) justice.[4] The criminal code obviously has to be universalistic because it pertains to the maintenance of civil order. In terms of a civil code it was easy for India to codify the rules of the Hindu laws of marriage, inheritance, and succession and to enact a universalistic system for them. The same has not yet been done for Muslim law. The conflict between the *shariat* and the deductive system of law was noted in an earlier chapter.

Ethnic, religious, linguistic, and regional identities create problems for the development of a national identity. The nineteenth century development of the nation-state suggested that these identities could be merged into a whole, whereby the national loyalty would take precedence over sectional loyalties in political matters. It was posited that, with the growth of industrialization, there would be the development of social classes where class loyalties would cross-cut and transcend other loyalties. The latter would prevail in limited spheres of cultural and community affairs, except perhaps religious loyalty, for which reason the distinction between the state and the church was firmly drawn by all modern nations.

In this century, especially after the Second World War, ethnic loyalties came to be reasserted both in modern and modernizing nations. In the former nations, there is a kind of ethnic renaissance today, which is a combination of the drive for a share of the 'political pie,' a movement for the 'equalization of opportunity,' as well as 'equalization of results' in the educational and occupational spheres, a sense of appreciation of one's primordial values ('self-identity') by oneself as well as by one's fellow countrymen, and finally the effort to escape the racism of the larger society, wherever it exists. In this connection, the remarks of Jayaprakash Narayan at the masthead of this book are very appropriate.

In the modernizing countries, the ethnics (as well as castes and other subcultures) generally wish to join the mainstream of national life, and if they are vocal, they also want a piece of the political pie. The religious groups show political postures mostly when it comes to persecution for religious beliefs. The linguistic groups, on the other hand, are highly politicized, especially if they perceive political deprivation in jobs and power. The regional grouping is more like the linguistic one and often the two overlap.

Tribal identity is one of the most important rivals to national identity. We have to make a distinction here between tribalism in a continent or country where the percentage of the tribal population is small, like Latin America or India, and a country where the major segment of population is tribal as in most countries of Africa. In the former case, the tribals behave like ethnics, mostly interested in a larger piece of the political pie. With the growth of education, they also demand jobs and protection as the linguistic groups do. In the latter case, as in most African countries, tribalism often invokes a new definition of the polity and a new visualization of the political process, rather than the one outlined in traditional political theory. We noted earlier the views of Julius Nyerere and Tom Mboya on the transition from tribalism to socialism without going through the stages of commercialism and industrialism. We cannot here discuss further the literature on making tribes into a nation, and only wish to emphasize that the roles of the intellectuals and of the party which lead a country into independence are the same in these countries as in other newly-independent countries. The early political leadership of a nation made up largely of tribes comes from either a charismatic leader or from a single tribe and the 'detribalized' urban population of the country. Education, military support, and rural-urban differences between various tribes seem to be more important than sheer size in playing a leading role in the national polity.

Finally, we come to the important issue of rural-urban differences in the shaping of the politics of a modernizing country. The urban groups are generally more educated and better informed and so are able to participate more knowledgeably in the political process than the rural groups. The urban population is also more likely to have a greater commitment to the nation, because its survival depends on the viability of national institutions. The rural peoples, on the other hand, remain deeply engrossed in their folkways and mores until the propaganda of political parties, the publicity of governmental organizations, and the slow permeation of the mass media of communication awaken them to the new realities. When the consciousness of the nation develops among them, they also want a piece of the larger pie. Since resources are limited and demands many, they often find their efforts thwarted and frustrated, especially if they cannot organize as well as the urban population can. It is here that the development of 'local self-government' type of institutions becomes necessary. Such institutions are necessary for creating consensus, they are necessary for bringing about national loyalty, but most important of all, they are crucial for bringing the rural population into the mainstream of national life.

A final word needs to be said about the role of the rural population in the economic development of a country. We noted earlier how this population is shortchanged in planning and even economic theorizing. It is often felt that the rural peoples have nothing to offer except underdeveloped methods of production, fatalistic beliefs and attitudes toward life, and a steady growth of population, which creates further scarcity of resources. These judgments are harsh, to say the least. The liquidation of absentee ownership of land, the expropriation of the estates of big land-owners (with or without compensation, depending on the type of national government), a ceiling on landholdings, and the develop-ment of cooperative marketing and credit facilities for them will certainly create better motivation in the rural peoples to develop the rural sector. The moneylender can be turned into an entrepren-eur, the peasant can be transformed into a farmer (producing for the market as well as for personal consumption), and the young men and women of the village can be induced to stay in the village and be productive, if they are given proper direction through education. This leads us to the topic of education, which we consider next.

Education

The question of education is crucial to modernization in two senses: education makes for better citizens, and education is needed as an input in the growth of the industrial sector in the form of providing trained personnel and scientific know-how to the country. No one can deny the value of education *per se*, but one must also consider the costs of providing 'crash programs' of education.

Let us briefly examine the educational system of India for underscoring some crucial issues of education in the modernizing nations. In 1900, there were 16,000 students in institutions of higher learning in India. Today, there are three million students registered in about 100 universities or university-level institutions and 3,000 colleges located in all regions of the country. Out of these three million students, one million will drop out after three years, either with a degree or without one. They will be looking for jobs, and if unsuccessful, will join an army of 2.3 million educated people registered as unemployed by the governmental agencies in 1971. This is the situation in higher education.[5]

Under the Directive Principles of the Indian Constitution,

111

adopted in 1950, free and compulsory elementary education is to be provided for all children up to the age of 14. Forty per cent of the Indian population (approximately 635 million in 1978) is below 15 years of age. In 1975, there were 64 million pupils (constituting 77 per cent of the age group 6-11 years) in primary school, 15 million pupils (constituting 32 per cent of the age group 11-14 years) in junior high school, and 8 million pupils (constituting 19 per cent of the age group 14-17 years) in high schools. Thus approximately 87 million students were receiving education of one form or another below the college level. The literacy rate of India in 1971 was only 30 per cent (40 per cent for males and 18 per cent for females); it had changed to 35 per cent by 1975. To these statistics, we would like to add one more set of data. There are 39 national laboratories to take care of the industrial needs of the country and 200 other laboratories for other purposes (including agricultural research). The ratio of annual Research and Development *outlay* to GNP doubled in India between 1958 and 1969. In 1967, India's Research and Development *manpower* was comparable to that of the United Kingdom and West Germany; it has kept pace in this regard.

Now let us explore the implications of these statistics. We noted in an earlier chapter that when India became independent from British rule in 1947, it had a well-trained bureaucracy and a well-developed system of education. In 1951, India started its first of a series of Five-Year Plans and, therefore, was able to plan for training its academic, technical, and professional personnel fairly well. So instead of any shortage, it is now faced with a surplus of trained personnel in many fields, so that, in 1973, there were reportedly 80,000 engineers out of jobs. Many other technically-trained personnel were working in non-technical jobs, such as office clerks and high school teachers. Where did the plans go wrong?

The answer to the above question lies in the fact that exact forecasting of the need for technical skills is difficult in an expanding economy. However, what is more important to note is that in the experience of many Asian countries with a well-endowed system of education under colonial rule, the expansion in the number of university graduates soon reaches 10 per cent to 20 per cent per annum, whereas the growth rate of national income is difficult to raise beyond 5 per cent to 6 per cent per annum.[6] If expansion of university education remains uncontrolled, it becomes difficult to provide sufficient jobs for new university graduates after the initial phase of job redistribution.

We can attempt to look at the educational problem further in the context of industrial growth. One educational need is to provide technicians, managers, and professionals for the targets established for various industries and enterprises in the national plan. Except for some modernizing countries in the beginning of their independent career (as in the case of Africa, where educational institutions were relatively less advanced), this need is quickly taken care of, because it is the 'missing component' in the mind of the planners. If there are any 'bottlenecks,' they can be quickly ascertained and managed through the allocation of proper resources. However, it is in the handling of the larger educational system from the primary to the college level that the real question of priorities arises. India needed 2.5 million teachers (including half a million women) in 1975 to educate its school-going population.

The revolution of rising expectations creates a drive among the rural, but more specially among the urban, population to send their children to school. A democratic government receptive to popular feelings cannot ignore the demand for creating facilities for education. It is perhaps cheaper to educate people than to provide them with jobs. The latter needs industrial expansion with many more necessary inputs than does the educational system. As jobs become scarcer even with high school diplomas, the drive is toward college education. In this process, standards are lowered. Political discontent created by lack of jobs puts additional pressures on academia, both from the student body and the politicians.

As university education becomes more valued, technical education receives short shrift, what with low-paid jobs and traditional cultural mores which disvalue manual labor. The 'brain drain' is another problem for some modernizing nations, although in the case of India, we do not feel it to be serious. In order to correct the imbalances what is needed is not to look at education as a patchwork of political bargaining with groups, but to make it a vehicle both of entrepreneurship development and for inculcating humane and democratic values. The role of education in the socialization of the young as well as national integration must also receive full consideration.

We can now look at education not in terms of the supply of 'skill-input' for a given level of development but as a variable which raises the rate of development. This would mean that the scientist, engineer, technician, or the administrator is not merely trained on the Western pattern, but is also able to innovate, adapt, and apply his skills to local circumstances. It is fashionable to think that the land-grant colleges of the United States (no doubt important in the early economic development of the United States) should be copied by the underdeveloped countries. The American agriculturalist is a farmer, who raises commercial crops, not a peasant, whose cultivation methods are guided by traditional norms of reciprocity and exchange with neighbors. So the agronomist of the United States is able to count on the rationality and cost accounting of the farmer. On the other hand, the agronomist in underdeveloped countries must cope with the irrationalities of the rural social system. Often, agricultural graduates seem to be attracted more by prestige, pay, and power than by an interest in solving the real problems of non-commercial agriculture in developing countries.

In the professions, the case of the medical doctor may be examined briefly. The doctor faces somewhat the same problems as the agronomist in the sense that the folkways of the village people often militate against the notions of scientific hygiene or public sanitation. The villager does not understand the germ theory of disease. And yet, unlike the case of the agronomist who is hardly welcomed in the village except by wealthy landowners, the medical doctor is much sought after by the villagers. The irony is that after years of training and investment, the doctor settles down in an urban area and is very reluctant to go to the villages. He has a greater incentive to settle in the city, because unlike the engineer or the technician, he can set up a private practice. Also some doctors emigrate to the industrial West, especially the United States, where the American Medical Association has effectively controlled the expansion of medical education, thereby creating an artificial shortage of doctors in the United States.

The need for expansion of the educational system in any underdeveloped country must be guided by the twin principles of providing the 'missing component' in development targets and the innovative approach in education, which will help the country utilize its maximum potentialities. These two goals apply to the training of scientists, engineers, technicians, doctors, and all professionals. Of course, the development of personality and social commitments can never be divorced from the educational enterprise, whether it is technical or simply intellectual and academic. One should also keep in mind that innovation in education will suffer if the best brains are all requisitioned for development purposes. Higher education (especially academic teaching) must not be deprived of its right to claim some of the best minds in the country.

Finally, the expansion of educational facilities is a question which needs careful review in terms of the resources of a country. In all countries, the size of the student population tapers off as one moves in the direction of higher education. However, the goal of 100 per cent primary education may be utopian in the early phase of development. Such a demand needs impartial scrutiny in view of the fact that, according to one study, whereas the average primary schoolteacher got less than one and a half times the per capita

114

income in the United States, he or she received three times the per capita income in Jamaica, five times in Ghana and seven times in Nigeria.[7] Of course, we are not comparing absolute incomes here. The capacity of a country to pay its schoolteachers in terms of equity as well as priority of other national needs must be taken into account. A viable educational policy is as much needed by a modernizing country as a viable bureaucracy, which we discuss next.

The bureaucracy

It is well-known that Karl Marx considered bureaucracy as an instrument of oppression, whereas Max Weber conceived of it as an instrument of efficiency. Lenin, in his *State and Revolution*, emphasized that one of the first tasks of the revolution would be to expedite the struggle against bureaucracy through such means as reducing the level of the official's salary to that of the working-man's wages and the instant revocability of every civil servant. However, after the Revolution of 1917 in Russia, Lenin could not abolish bureaucracy but made it an instrument in the service of the people. This was later changed by Stalin, who abolished the distinction between Party and bureaucracy, and shifted all power from the Soviets to the Party apparatus. We noted the incisive critique of Djilas on this point in an earlier chapter. However, what we want to emphasize here is that the instrument of bureaucracy must be made efficient, whether it is in the hands of a democratic or an authoritarian regime. This is a point on which Max Weber has much to contribute.

Following Max Weber, sociologists view bureaucracy as being imbued with rational-legal authority. This obviously refers to both public and private administration, which are both governed by principles of hierarchy, responsibility, rationality and performance norms. Most modernizing countries inherit a civil service from the colonial masters, who practice these norms. The civil service may have different degrees of weaknesses in the personnel on the highest level, imbalances in recruitment from various strata of the population, and over-zealous regard for law and order; yet it invariably tries to apply universalistic standards to all decisions. This may lead to ritualistic following of rules and procedures, which may hamper entrepreneurship and thus retard development. It may also provide opportunties for widespread corruption. But one of the main functions of bureaucracy in a modernizing country is to stabilize things and thus it works as an important agent of national integration in the early period of a country's independence.

We reviewed the leadership potentiality of bureaucracy as a

115

'modernizer' in an earlier chapter. Here we want to pinpoint some additional issues. One of the questions asked in the modernizing countries is whether the old civil service trained to be a 'generalist' can perform the specialized tasks needed for economic development. Obviously it cannot, and yet almost everywhere the specialist is supervised by the generalist and the coordination of the various specialists like the engineer, the agronomist, the doctor, and the technical expert is also in the hands of the 'generalist,' as in the case of the district magistrate or the subdivisional officer in India. The 'generalist' officer is like a layman as far as these services are concerned, but he coordinates them in terms of the maintenance of peace and order within the community. Thus he may unwittingly work more in favor of the established elite than up-and-coming groups. However, it is also true that often the non-involved civil servant has more of a sense of equity than the committed partisan, who may be a specialist dispensing services to the activistic groups, which are the recipients of such services.

The civil service is also the buffer between the cabinet minister and the public. The minister has the dual role of being the executive as well as the elected representative of the people. In the latter role, he is expected to dispense special favors for his constituency; in the former role he is sworn to provide justice and equity between rival claimants. The bureaucracy as the neutral instrument of the government can shield the minister from improper attacks as well as from the illegitimate demands of his partisan supporters.

Scholars from Weber to the present have emphasized the point that bureaucracy has a tendency to appropriate power to itself and become self-perpetuating. Many newly-independent nations like India experienced in the beginning a period of friction, if not conflict, between the elected leaders and the permanent civil service in evolving policies and implementing plans and projects. However, through mutual goodwill and after some working experience, their relationship settled down to that of a policy-maker and policy-implementer, the elected official being the policy-maker and the permanent civil service being the advisor and the policy-implementer.

One question that is often raised is how the bureaucrat with his 'aloof' attitude and shielding of personal life from public view can be made to participate in crash programs of quick change. This is a question which has no adequate answer. Loyalty to the policy-maker or to the policy itself may create commitment in the civil service. However, it seems that the specialist is often more interested in social change than the 'generalist,' especially if the leadership desires the change.

A moot question in the development of the political system is whether the bureaucracy which emphasizes order and due process would welcome popular participation in decision-making because such procedures necessarily entail turmoil and controversy. It is often found that the development of 'local self-government' is hampered by bureaucratic intransigence or its noncooperation. We noted earlier, the point that decentralized decision-making and regional autonomy are handicapped by the emphasis on centralized planning and its administration through the national civil service. It seems that the strength of the bureaucracy is in centralization so that, as already noted, it can be very effective when national integration is weak. On the other hand, where the need is the development of backward regions of a country, it would be better to leave it in the hands of the entrepreneurs and lessen the impact of the bureaucrats in such regions.

Bureaucracy is a blanket term for all officeholders who work in an organization, so it is important to make a distinction between the rank and file of the bureaucracy and the managers of public and private enterprises as well as the administrators in government, to whom most of the earlier remarks apply. As far as the lower rungs of the bureaucracy are concerned, they are mostly 'conformists' or 'ritualists' in Merton's paradigm of modes of adaptation to social situation.[8] It is often noted that the payroll of the governmental white-collar workers is padded in most modernizing nations. This is done to coopt the dissident or vocal elements of the population but it is a form of 'underemployment' or 'disguised unemployment.' There seems to be little chance of avoiding this, especially if economic growth is sluggish and/or the population is being educated faster than the economy can absorb. Such a bulging of bureaucracy in the middle creates grounds for corruption, laziness, and lack of production. The only way to avoid it is to push education in the direction where high school and college graduates will be entrepreneurs rather than traditional job seekers.

The bureaucracy of a modernizing nation is supposed to be a stabilizer as well as an entrepreneur, depending on the resource level and its mobilization in a country. The British civil service has the tradition of stability, whereas the American bureaucracy has a training in entrepreneurship. A due admixture of these two traditions can solve the problems of many modernizing countries, but the nature of the mix will remain for some time a pragmatic problem.

Modernization is as much art as it is science. We have analysed the grounds for making it into a science. The artistic input must remain in the hands of the leaders and the traditions of the people whom they lead. In the end, there is no sure road to success in modernization except the will and determination of the people themselves.

117

10 Modernization for what?

We have come to the end of a long road in the quest for modernity. The preceding review of modernization theories convinces us that the answer to the quest lies in the creative reformulation of past knowledge and this is what we propose to do in this chapter.

It is important to unravel the meaning of the word modernization, before we can answer the question, 'modernization for what?' Words have a strange way of defying articulation if one wants to cover enormous ground with a single word. Such is the case with modernization. This difficulty in the articulation of a concept is not atypical in social or political analysis. Thus Lucien W. Pye, in his 'Introduction' to the symposium on *Political Culture and Political Development* expresses a realistic and an exasperating attitude, when he says in the beginning of his note that 'Politics defies classification.'[1] Similarly, after an exhaustive treatment of the origins of democracy in the modern world, Barrington Moore, Jr., confesses to another kind of scepticism:[2]

> All these familiar facts serve to press home the point that such words as democracy, fascism, and communism (and also dictatorship, totalitarianism, feudalism, bureaucracy) arose in the context of European history. Can they be applied to Asian [one can add African and Latin American] political institutions without being wrenched beyond all recognition?

As is the common practice in social science analysis, we will assume that any generalized concept must have both a referent and a connotation before it can be adopted in the analytical protocol. We will, therefore, first establish the empirical and the conceptual bases of the term, modernization, so that we can proceed to answer the question, 'modernization for what?'

The history of modernization

All modernization in history began with some kind of revolution: bourgeois, peasant, or proletarian. There is a tendency among some scholars to be allergic to the word revolution. Such an attitude cannot help in arriving at objective analysis. After all, whatever else modernization implies, it certainly refers to the phenomenon of radical transformation of societies either in the West or in the East. The causes or the conditions of such transformation may be debated among scholars but not the consequences, which exist in empirical reality and persist before our own eyes. Any historical account of the earlier eras of more modernized societies will convince an impartial observer that the change is indeed revolutionary and could not have happened if a revolutionary (including violent) event or set of events had not intervened between the traditional society and its modern form.

The ideal-type constructs of folk, feudal, and industrial societies have to be subjected to the searchlight of history to comprehend the manner and scope of their transformation. We will concentrate here on the shift from the 'feudal' society to the 'industrial' society, because this is what modernization is generally presumed to be all about. A feudal society has two dimensions in the analytical framework, one political, and the other economic. The political dimension refers to the relationship between the king or the monarch, and the aristocrats, the clergy, the people in the cities and the peasantry in the rural regions. The economic dimension articulates the relationships of production between the mercantile class of traders, financiers, money-lenders, etc., and the landowners, burghers, artisans, peasants, and serfs. Political and economic historians do not always agree on how the shift in power took place between these classes in the process of their transformation.

Barrington Moore, Jr., believes that 'revolutionary violence may contribute as much as peaceful reform to the establishment of a relatively free society.'[3] He shows how this happened in England, France, and the United States, as well as in Germany, Japan, Russia, and China. In England, early protest movements of peasants were quelled by the landed upper classes, but the commercialization of agriculture displaced the power of the rural gentry as well as the king and culminated in a Civil War and the Puritan Revolution. After the Civil War, England settled down to rule by Parliament in the eighteenth century. The gradual incorporation in the political process of first, the bourgeoisie, and then, the masses took place by the end of the nineteenth century.

In France, where agriculture was not commercialized and where the nobility was aligned with the crown (unlike England), the bourgeois class amalgamated with the nobility. It took the French Revolution to unhinge its power, but only partially. Also, parts of the bourgeoisie joined the radical urban plebs and the resurgent peasants in the Revolution. The failure of the French Revolution could be blamed on what Moore calls the 'feudalization' of a considerable section of the bourgeoisie,[4] and it was not until the twentieth century that France could usher in the era of modernity in its socio-political framework.

In the American case, Moore claims that it is the Civil War and not the American Revolution which should be characterized as a revolution. He says: 'The claim that America has had an anticolonial revolution may be good propaganda, but it is bad history and bad sociology. The distinguishing characteristic of twentieth-century anticolonial revolutions is the effort to establish *a new form of society with substantial socialist elements*' [italics added].[5] We note here again an emphasis on equality (a crucial element in our model), which is one of the 'socialist elements' Moore implies in the book. Moore gives centrality to the Civil War because it struck down slavery just as absolute monarchy was changed by the English Civil War. He concedes that the Radical offensive on the Southern United States did not 'represent a united capitalist offensive on the plantation system. It was a combination of workers, industrialists, and some railroad interests at the time of its greatest power. *Still it would not be amiss to label it entrepreneurial and even pragmatic capitalism*' [italics added].[6] And he points out, it is difficult to believe how organized labor could have forced its way into southern slavery and established legal and political rights for all workers in American society, without the abolition of slavery.

Moore shows that in the case of England, France, and the United States, the road to modernity was through the democratic route, although the initial spurt came from a violent revolution in each instance. As for Germany and Japan, their modernity, or more properly their industrialization, came through fascism. And Russia and China launched themselves into their modern eras through peasant revolutions and dictatorships in each case.

We have discussed Barrington Moore's thesis in detail because it is a profound book written about the implications of revolution for modernization. Scholars would not necessarily agree on the central role which Moore assigns to violent revolution in the modernization of a society. For instance, Robert A. Dahl rejects his analysis for England and the United States.[7] Many political scientists concentrate on the late eighteenth and the nineteenth century political process of England and thus come to the conclusion that the English transformation of society was evolutionary. S. M.

Lipset calls the United States the 'First New Nation,' because it was the first country to disengage itself from the colonial link (although the link was one with masters of the same racial, ethnic, and religious background) through violent revolution; he goes on and talks about the consensus and mild conflicts (except the Civil War) that guaranteed the development of democracy in the United States in the following centuries.[8]

Despite the disclaimers of some scholars, the role of revolutions and crises cannot be denied in the historical transformation of societies. Most political scientists would agree today that crises play an important role in political modernization. As Joseph La Palombara and Myron Weiner put it, 'the concept of crises [is] useful for understanding the circumstances under which parties [or political democracies] first emerged.'[9] And in the context of economic growth, Bert F. Hoselitz notes that *The appearance of socially deviant behavior* stimulated by the presence of ethnically or socially marginal individuals *may thus be regarded as a necessary but, in most cases, not a sufficient cause for social change*' [italics added].[10] We note thus that historical revolutions, crises, and socially deviant behavior have been considered by many writers of various persuasions as being necessary for the modern ascent.

The meaning of modernization

The historical view of modernization is associated with the successful rise of industrialism, as we noted above. By industrialism, we mean the set of factors which govern the enterprise of production in the factory, the development of trade, finance, and banking systems, and the constant application of scientific knowledge and technology in the productive and distributive processes. The factory, the firm, and the machine are the hallmarks of industrialism. No doubt the phenomenon of industrialism could not have come about without a supportive social structure and psychological types of men ('entrepreneurs' as well as 'modern men'), but the distinctive feature of industrialism is the harnessing of science for the control of machine, man, and his environment. We wish to stress the point here that 'in the military-industrial complex' of the United States and the Soviet Union, the machine is now taking precedence over man so that 'the social organization of machines' has come to dictate the social existence of man in these societies. Some machines are prerequisites to other machines, and these in turn give rise to more machines, which process at some point starts reorganizing the life of man himself. This is the concept being used here to denote 'the social organization of machines.' There is no going back in history to simpler times for the industrial nations. The success of industrialism in providing material comforts has given rise to a worldwide movement for industrialization, whereby every nation today wishes to adopt as many practices and traits of the industrial society as possible. Thus one meaning of modernization ties in with the word industrialization.

There is another meaning of modernization which is lost sight of if one concentrates only on the experience of the capitalist or the Soviet industrial countries. This meaning comes through when one examines the ideologies of national leaders and other articulate groups in the non-industrial nations. No doubt, it is difficult to compile the basic tenets of all the ideologies, put them together, and make sense out of them, if only because they are bound to suggest contradictions. However, we believe that there is a common thread in the experiences of these nations and their expectancies, which helps us to articulate the ideology of modernization in the following terms: (a) national viability; (b) intergroup harmony; (c) economic self-sufficiency; (d) abolition of hunger, poverty, and conditions of malnutrition; (e) education; and (f) cultural autonomy as well as the pursuit of artistic excellence. It is clear that the first two factors are political, the next two are economic, and the last two are social and cultural. One can argue that all of these conditions will be satisfied better in an industrial society, but we believe it is a debatable point. The resources, the challenges, and the 'felt needs' will vary from country to country, but we think that the ideology of modernization minimally covers these six points.

We have used above the concept of ideology in the sense of a body of doctrine, often associated with a political and cultural plan for its implementation. It is in this sense that the word ideology was also used by us in an earlier chapter. The ideological theories we propounded there were ideal-type theories with an empirical base. The ideology of modernization we are presenting now is our *sociological* view of how thesis and praxis can be matched in the contemporary world.

It is the character of an ideology that the specifics of its content cannot be repudiated. The six elements of the modernization ideology we have outlined above form a cumulative whole. However, their implementation may require a system of priorities. We believe that in looking at the condition of both the newly-independent and the other modernizing nations, the top priority is political, i.e. national viability and intergroup harmony. Without either, the nation may disintegrate. The economic concerns as stipulated in the ideology receive second priority. And the educational and cultural activities come next, because adjustments in these are easier to make than in the political and economic constraints stipulated in the ideology.

The ideological imperatives have to be translated into a set of goals for immediate as well as long-range implementation. The goals are the future state of affairs sought by the nation; the ideology provides the driving force. So we turn next to an examination of the range of goals available to a modernizing nation.

The goals of modernization

We will discuss the goals in the same order as they occur in the ideology paradigm presented earlier. The prime goal in the political field is the establishment of the institutions which make for a nation-state. Thus, the executive, judicial, and legislative branches of the government are essential, and so is the army to a certain extent, both for the protection of a country from outside enemies and for giving additional support to the police force in the maintenance of law and order. Looking at the Anglo-American and Soviet models, one can see that there are important differences of opinion about the interlocking roles and powers of the executive, judicial, and legislative branches of the government. However, from the point of view of a long established tradition in democratic theory, these branches should have separate and coequal powers. How they will function in an integrated manner is a perennial ground of inquiry and theorizing on the part of political scientists. The development of political parties, interest groups, universal suffrage, and the processes of election, referendum, and recall constitute the minimum requirements for a democratic polity.

The economic goals are tied to the increments in national output, personal income, monetization of the economy, the manufacturing (including mining and processing) of goods, a trained labor force, state or private entrepreneurship, adequate financial and trade set-ups, and the provision of the distribution facilities. As we noted earlier, factory, firm, and machine serve as a lure for all modernizing countries, but most of them have to contend with cottage industries and non-mechanized agricultural production, if only because they can afford limited development of industrial facilities.

Education is an important social goal, but its extent and character are determined by other goals of political and economic modernization undertaken by a country. Education is always needed for developing the bureaucracy. Bureaucracy is a feature of all modernizing countries today, because bureaucracies are important for running the political and economic machineries. The other important functions of education are to provide individual citizens with jobs, opportunities for social mobility, informed communication with fellow citizens and power-holders and, of course, to facilitate their participation in the political system of the country. One should not forget the role of education in creating empathy and in making a more humane person out of the average citizen. We should also note that education has often been used for indoctrination and brainwashing in a totalitarian state.

The goals associated with cultural autonomy and the pursuit of artistic excellence, the last two items on our ideology list, are related to the socialization of a person to indigenous values at home, at school, and in the fairs and festivities that are common and prized occurrences in modernizing countries. There is a need in today's world to explore both one's own tradition as well as the traditions of other peoples and nations. Libraries, museums, art galleries, plays, movies, the mass media, as well as indigenous institutions of folk storytellers, singing bards, puppetry, and recreational as well as artistic pursuits and personal hobbies all need conservation as well as development. The roles of the writer and the artist are considered very crucial in modernizing nations, for their traditional pursuits of excellence as well as for their potential for creating revolutions in the minds of men.[11]

We turn next to the exploration of the strategies for implementing the goals enunciated above.

The strategies of modernization

We shall discuss the question of strategies in terms of a series of dilemmas posed in the actual development process of the modern as well as the modernizing countries. This will help us relate our discussion to real issues that have occurred in the past, and bring into focus any lesson that may be derived from the resolution of such issues. It will also afford us an opportunity for summarizing the essence of the theoretical analyses of modernization problems presented in the earlier chapters. (As we noted earlier, modernization is a dialectical process in which many elements interact.) We believe that the ideology of modernization when combined with goals, strategies, and comprehensive national plans provides the answer to the question, 'modernization for what?'

(i) *The revolutionary approach versus the evolutionary approach*

Much energy has been spent in describing the anatomy of a revolution[12] or laying out the causes and conditions for its success.[13] Despite these efforts, no one can predict when a revolution will occur. It seems that revolution is a unique event, which, once it takes place, historians and other social scientists can trace the reasons for, but the prediction of its occurrence will remain in doubt, if only because of the dialectic that obtains between self-fulfilling and self-falsifying prophecies.[14] If revolution is predicted, the forces may work in such a way that they bring about a revolution. This is self-fulfilling prophecy. On the other hand, the prediction of a revolution may spur the power-holders to avert it, in which case it will be a self-falsifying prophecy. Both occur in history. One should also consider the fact that unique events cannot be predicted. Therefore, it is impossible to state in advance why a revolution like the Cuban Revolution succeeded and the other so-called revolutions in Latin America aborted. The same may be said of the success of the Russian, Chinese, and Vietnamese Revolutions, and the failures of similar efforts in other South East Asian countries.

Whether a revolution succeeds or not, it certainly unhinges the power bases of the rulers and the elite class. If these remain exploitative and simply bolster their position more after each disturbance, there are bound to be further revolutions, in the beginning perhaps abortive, until one of them succeeds.

The evolutionary approach suggests that adequate leadership and selective cooperation with industrial countries may lead to modernization without the necessity of going through a revolution. However, the point we wish to make is that either with or without revolution, a country will have to embark on compehensive national planning for the resolution of the demands raised by the various sections of the populace. We noted the role of planning for both 'the gradualist' and 'the revolutionary' approaches to societal transformation in a preceding chapter. We will discuss planning again in a later section.

(ii) *Nationalism versus internationalism*

The worldwide movement for change in this century is couched in the language of nationalism. This nationalism is a different kind of movement than the nationalism of the eighteenth and nineteenth centuries. The national consciousness which increased in Europe after the French Revolution was rooted in common descent, language, territory, political entity, custom and tradition, and religion, as Hans Kohn has aptly pointed out.[15] However, the nationalism of the twentieth-century modernizing countries is the nationalism of political consciousness and of the social uplift of all sections of the people. There is of course a link between the two forms of nationalism inasmuch as the growth of nationalism anywhere and at any time depends on 'the process of integration of the masses of the people into a common political form.'[16] However, Rupert Emerson puts his finger on the nerve of present-day nationalism, when he speaks of its purposes in the context of Africa, as follows:[17]

> What is important for the present purpose is that the different types of organizations which the political leaders have brought into being and the different functions which they have performed have all contributed to the growth of *political consciousness.* It may equally be presumed that in doing so they have also contributed to the spread of *national integration* save where their focus has been implicitly or explicitly divisive because they rested upon a tribal, religious, or regional basis [italics added].

Emerson was emphasizing the role of associations in the absence of competing party systems in Africa, but his view of the emergent nationalism of the new era is well-expressed above and in his other writings.[18]

The emphasis on nationalism should not deflect attention from the gathering momentum of internationalism in the present century. There are actually three kinds of internationalism in the contemporary world. One is the concept of the world-wide proletarian revolution advanced by Marx and Engels and temporarily suspended in Russia by Stalin and subsequent leaders to work for 'the building of socialism in one state,' but constantly resurrected by Marxist socialists,[19] and by Mao Tse-tung. The other is the concept of internationalism espoused by the capitalist nations, which try to win the sympathy of modernizing nations to their ideology of the 'open society' through various kinds of aids: educational, scientific, as well as technological and military. The third kind of internationalism is spread by the United Nations and its specialized agencies (now over a hundred in number), which become the forum for debate of common issues facing all nations and which also provide international assistance. Besides these, there are regional associations like the Pan American Union, the Afro-Asian bloc, the European Economic Community, the Eastern European bloc, and other viable networks of bilateral and multi-national cooperation among the modern and the modernizing nations.

The thrust of internationalism is toward solving issues which affect more than one nation; the thrust of nationalism is toward the survival of the nation and the development of its own polity and economy. There have been sporadic efforts toward regional associations or federations of nations with a single political structure, but very few seem to have succeeded so far.[20] In fact, our prognosis is that both nationalism and internationalism will be viable movements for the rest of this century at least.

(iii) *Political development versus economic growth*

One of the most debated issues in the literature on modernization is which one should be given priority, political development or economic growth. We know that in the West economic growth came first and then political development (especially party rule, and the popular participation in the political process) followed as a consequence of it. In the Soviet countries, the leadership, after over-throwing the bourgeois class, worked energetically for economic growth so that the gains of the revolution could be stabilized, but in none of these countries has political development (in the sense of the choice of parties in the system of party rule, and the expression of deviant opinion in the political process) followed beyond the stage where it was, at the inception of the revolutionary regime.

A. F. K. Organski believes that political development should precede economic growth.[21] Daniel Lerner and others assert that economic growth must start before political development can follow.[22] S. N. Eisenstadt puts the issue tersely:[23]

> The interrelationship between economic and political develop-
> ment has proved to be rather complicated and paradoxical.
> Contrary to the rather naive assumption often found in the older
> literature that these two are always concomitant and reinforce
> one another, more recent evidence shows that, at least in
> somewhat later stages of modernization, they might sometimes
> run counter to each other.

Eisenstadt points to such facts as that the growing pressures from the people for more economic benefits under a liberal regime may impede economic growth, and similarly, that the special beneficiar-ies of rapid economic growth may try to obstruct the liberalization of the political framework.

No doubt evidences of both kinds are available in history. Often, a liberal regime unable to cope with economic demands gets weakened and overthrown by the military, as in the case of Indonesia, and the military regimes of Pakistan. A fast growing economy fails to liberalize the polity, as in the case of the oil-rich countries of the Middle East, or the military dictatorships of many modernizing Latin American countries. However, we do not agree with Eisenstadt that political and economic developments cannot occur concurrently. The key again lies in comprehensive national planning.

(iv) *Centralization versus decentralization*

This is an issue which occurs in many contexts as we noted in earlier chapters. In the political sphere, a new nation is faced with the problems of creating viable national organs of the state (for which some degree of centralization of power is necessary) and its subsidiaries and wings in the region, the province, the city, or the village. How much power should be allotted to each body and the kind of authority a superior body may have over a subordinate one are matters of great controversy. For instance, even now the debate goes on in India over whether the Republic of India should be treated as a federation or as a centralized union.[24] Despite the constitutional division of items over which the central legislature and the state legislatures may have concurrent or separate powers to legislate (as in the case of India), there are often acute conflicts of interest between the central and the state governments. In such a situation, the tendency to centralize more power, authority, and resources in the hands of the central government may speak for the viability of the regime, but not necessarily for the democracy of the system.

Similarly, economic resources when centralized in the hands of state industries and enterprises (public sector) limit the entrepreneurship of the capitalist forms of production and investment (private sector) but they may have the effect of distributing the gains of the economy to more people than the capitalist class and their associates usually envision. However, there are other ways of narrowing the income gap in a mixed economy, for instance, through taxation and fiscal as well as monetary policies. When economic centralization, either socialist (state ownership, management, and control) or capitalist (cartels and private monopolies), moves in the direction of crash programs of industrialization, it is generally at the cost of the resources and wealth of the rural sector. It usually creates great discrepancies between the urban and the rural way of life. Such dislocations can either cause apathy, or be the breeding ground for outbreaks, revolts, and, perhaps, revolution.

The impact of industrialization on the life of the community is an important problem to be considered in the context of centralization. In many modernizing countries, the educated, the rich, and the ambitious flock to the cities and the seats of political power, and the illiterate, the poor, and the fatalists remain in the rural areas to be exploited by them. In such a situation, community development programs get lip service compared to the development of national institutions and monuments. Again, we believe that national planning is the answer to the dilemma of centralization versus decentralization in a modernizing country.

(v) *Elitism versus democracy*

Both words, elitism and democracy, have to be explicated before we can discuss the dilemma of the situation. By elitism, we mean the guidance by the elite in political as well as managerial affairs. This often confers on the elite special prerogatives and leads to the formation of a special group to which effective entry is barred for a large section of the population. By democracy, we mean popular participation in political decision-making, in the disposition of wealth on an equalitarian basis, and in the guaranteeing of the freedoms of speech, thought, and action of individuals, and safeguards for the press, minority groups (racial, religious, or cultural), and other disadvantaged groups (like the elderly, women, and the poor).

It should be noted here that the leadership in a modernizing country always decries elitism and praises democracy, because that is the ethos of the new ideology of nationalism. However, often the leaders do not mean what they say.

Any modernizing country will need a bureaucracy (well-educated and trained personnel) and a 'knowledge elite' to advise the leaders, to formulate plans, and to implement them. Only a select percentage of people can fulfill these taks. Meritocracy will generally prevail here. What is important, however, is that equality of opportunity should exist for all qualified people to join these ranks. A stratum of intellectuals (as Lenin called them) is found even in a classless socity.

As distinguished from the bureaucratic and technical realms of the social system, the political realm must be open to all citizens and interest groups in a democracy. Political leadership cannot be the prerogative of the knowledge elite, the party elite, the bureaucratic elite, or the military elite. Full bargaining and coalitions must prevail in the political, social, and cultural realms. It is here that the role of the communities and ethnic groups in political participation takes on special importance.

As between elitism and democracy, there is no choice for a modernizing country except to opt for democracy (i.e. full popular participation) in all realms except where technical and procedural decisions are involved which need special competence. The work of the scientist, the bureaucrat, and the technician must go on in a somewhat privileged fashion to avoid undue non-task related distraction and to implement the general rule of efficiency, so long as these people are infused with the ideology of modernization formulated above. They need to be guided by the principles of equity and justice laid down in the comprehensive national plan devised by the leadership in full consultation with the masses.

National planning

We come now to the most important ingredient of modernization, viz. comprehensive national planning, without which any effort toward modernization is bound to fail. Planning is a word disliked in the capitalist countries, such as the United States. The following fact, as reported by John Kenneth Galbraith, would, therefore, come as a surprise to many:[25]

> If we take as the measure of the amount of planning the proportion of all current resources – gross national product – fully controlled and disposed of by the state, about 20 per cent of the American economy is planned. For India the comparable figure is 13-14 per cent.

And this was so in 1961 after ten years of the operation of India's two national plans! People in the United States usually think of planning as being associated with socialism or with the capitalistic sector, but not with their national government.

If national planning is socialistic in character, so be it. The weight of the arguments presented in the preceding analysis of modernization problems suggests that there is no escaping the need for comprehensive national planning for a modernizing country. However, what we wish to emphasize at this point is that every national plan has a political as well as an economic character. Often the political aspect is expressed in the vague jargon of 'democratic goals,' but its real character is revealed when one scrutinizes the economic consequences of the projects outlined in the plan. Sociologists and political scientists would do well to explore these hidden dimensions of the plan rather than take its opening words as providing the key to the plan.

The politics of planning is a fascinating subject of study. How groups vie in advancing the legitimacy of their claims, how one or more groups obtain hegemony over others, how the leadership behaves, how compromises are made and, finally, how the national plan is formulated, would provide a welcome lesson to modernizing countries. Unfortunately, not many studies are available on these processes. Most books are written on the economics of planning rather than on the politics of it. One needs to realize that there is more of a lesson in the politics of planning about the success or failure of the plan than in the rationality pursued in its economic structure. Lenin, the master planner, never forgot this important point. In a sense, his two essays, *What is to be Done* (written in 1902) and *Two Tactics of Social-Democracy in the Democratic Revolution,* written when the revolution broke out in Russia in 1905, laid the groundwork for the success of the Leninist strategy of action.[26]

The key to the success of a national plan is not so much in the hands of the planners or its executors as in the hands of the people, who must be convinced and impressed by the specific ideology (in the sense in which we use this term) of modernization. And the way to accomplish this was again articulated well by Lenin: 'We must "go among all classes of the population" as theoreticians, as propagandists, as agitators, and as organizers.'[27] The masses cannot be active unless someone activates them, but they cannot be activated unless the ideology impresses them and infuses them with revolutionary zeal.

If we move from the politics to the economics of planning, we must again realize that planning involves value judgments irrespective of what an economist or planner may say. Often the argument of the positivist scientist (an objectivity-professing economist) is that he is merely seeking the maximization of factors of production, so that 'self-sustaining growth' may take place in an economy. We have to reject this argument, because 'self-sustaining growth' of either the capitalist or the Soviet industrial system involves political decisions and choices of values, which are non-economic in nature. As the inveterate economist and planner Dudley Seers points out, ' "Development" is inevitably treated as a normative concept, as almost a synonym for improvement. To pretend otherwise is just to hide one's value judgments.'[28] We would like to add that economic necessities must be subjected to the screening of the ideological necessities of the modernizing nations.

If we accept the premise that all plans are value impregnated (i.e. either they can serve class interests or they can serve all individuals on an equitable basis), we can then examine the economic imperatives in a rational manner. For instance, resource-use must be maximized, rational accounting of production factors must be maintained, and entrepreneurship must be made available. Entrepreneurship has many meanings for the economist, as Bert F. Hoselitz points out: 'Some writers have identified entrepreneurship with the function of uncertainty bearing, others with the coordination of production resources, others with the introduction of innovation, and still others with the provision of capital [in a capitalist society].'[29] A nation should have no difficulty in putting the coordination of these factors in the hands of economic and technical experts if the ideology of modernization is acceptable to all sections of the population.

We have shown so far the necessity of formulating the ideological base of national planning with mass support and then leaving the coordination and factor calculation of economic variables in the hands of the economists. We would like to add now the fact that popular participation in the objectives of planning makes for a commitment which goes farther in the implementation of a plan than the exhortations of planning officials and bureaucratic

131

executors of the plan. In other words, some form of planning must start from below in the communities and in the regions and then should be coordinated on the national level.

This leads us directly to the role of the communities, the ethnic and the sub-cultural groups in the modernization of a country. These units should not be treated merely as the recipients of whatever benefits may be envisaged for them in the national plan. They should be considered to some extent as masters of their own destiny and, more importantly for the purposes of the success of the plan, as agents of change. A person, a group, or a community will not feel deprived or exploited if each has the opportunity to participate in the shaping of the plan. The mistakes committed by oneself are easier to live with than the failures inflicted on one by other people's decisions. We are not oblivious of the fact that competing demands will be made by individuals, groups, and communities. However, as we pointed out in our model of modernization, the interests must be cumulated by working out compromises democratically rather than by national leadership alone or by the economic technician.

One of the questions that is raised is whether a nation will disintegrate if divisive forces within it are encouraged. This is a question about national integration which we will go into later. But to exclude communities and ethnic groups from decision-making is to take either an authoritarian or an anemic view of the political process. Karl Deutsch, as we noted earlier, has provided an important insight into this matter. He thinks that groups of persons must be linked by complementary habits and facilities of communication. And he correctly points out that ' "Cultural autonomy" cannot be divorced from the personal, local, regional, or occupational autonomy of human beings.'[30] The neglect of village life in modernizing countries cannot be more eloquently described than in Deutsch's words:[31]

> In underdeveloped countries, nationalists often have been more successful in building parties rather than armies; armies rather than schools; schools rather than factories; and factories rather than fundamental changes in village life . . . In general they did not come to grips with the fundamental productive forces of their countries.

We are aware that the view of community autonomy we are presenting here may sound utopian and unrealistic to an economic planner, who may be in a hurry. Hurried solutions are never the best ones as both the modern and the modernizing nations have realized in the short history of the industrialization of the West or in the planning of the modernizing countries. There may be a race against time but the race for true modernization is lost already if economic improvement comes only with economic or political dictatorship. Dictatorship of the capitalist class or dictatorship of the Party (communist or any other) is no solution to the problems of modernity.

The true solution of modernization is in the nature of leadership (which incorporates the ideology which propels any leadership) available in a country. We should like to note that a modernizing country needs four kinds of leadership. In the economic field, it needs entrepreneurial leadership, especially the innovating kind. This can be created through training as David McClelland has shown;[32] also it should be noted here that latent entrepreneurship exists in all cultures as William McCord has indicated.[33] In the field of administration and management, a country needs the professional organizer (or the 'bureaucratic virtuoso,' as Merton calls him[34]) whose job is not merely to set up efficient organizations but to coordinate the activities of the 'diseconomies' and the 'economies' of administration. These two kinds of leadership need special aptitudes and more specialized training. The third kind of leadership is for the community, where one needs the 'cosmopolitan' rather than the 'local,' to use Merton's terms again, or the 'modern man,' a characterological type formulated by Alex Inkeles and described earlier. On the national level, a modernizing country needs value synthesizers and activists, who must coordinate as well as guide the actions of the professional specialists involved in national planning and the community leaders who guide the 'polities' of the communities, rural or urban, throughout the nation. The community leadership and the national leadership cannot be specialized to the point that it goes beyond the reach of the common man. If at all, the only special qualification needed for it should be that of a 'generalist,' who has an overview of all fields and perhaps no specialty of his own.

The question of integration of a nation depends so much on its leadership. We believe that four kinds of integration are needed for the viability of a nation. These are: (a) value integration, (b) role integration, (c) decision integration, and (d) social control integration. Value integration is a field in which the 'cosmopolitans' of the group, community, and the nation will have to play a crucial role. Role integration needs the guidance of experts in working out the interrelationships of the emerging 'modern roles' in society. The planners will have to give great attention and thought to this field. The decision integration is the set of procedures as well as interlocking leaderships from the village to the national level which makes the projects envisaged in a plan succeed. This cannot be laid out in a blueprint as role integration can, but has to be worked out empirically at each stage of the development and the unfolding of the plan. The role of the social scientist is crucial in assessing this. And, finally, social control integration will be in the hands of the legislators and the developing legal system of the land for purposes of its advanced planning but will rest in the hands of the executive branch, including the magistracy and the police, for the resolution of conflicts as they occur in the process of its implementation. These forms of integration cannot be discussed at any great length here.[35]

Some prognoses

Population

We will now present a general perspective and guidance on selected problems which affect all modernizing nations. One of the problems relates to population growth. The genetic, technological, and social researches in the field must be expedited to provide effective planned parenthood guidance for all countries of the world. If individuals in a nation can be persuaded to feel committed toward the national goals, one of which must be population control, and if social and psychological supports for family planning were available to couples of reproductive age, we have no doubt that the 'population explosion' could be contained. A civil service of family planners degenerates into a rule-enforcing bureaucracy. Perhaps 'barefoot doctors'[36] as found in the People's Republic of China, and the commitment of college and even of high school students will be more effective than family planning hospitals and special cadres of family planning officers. Most important of all is, of course, people's own conviction and commitment to it. From the opportunity to participate in *national plan making* may flow other decisions like voluntary birth control, which, as the planners know, needs great motivation and even greater continuous effort to succeed.

Education

Education is another field where the modernizing country needs to shape its own system to its specific needs. The Anglo-American system of education is expensive, burdensome, and even unrealistic for the needs of a country which has not joined the industrial ranks. Mass education should be geared to the imperatives of the national plan. No doubt, proficiency in the sciences, engineering, medicine, and other professions will be needed for which whoever may qualify should be recruited. But 'basic education' should deal with

134

social, agricultural, and environmental problems along with the inculcation of humanitarian values. Above all, a modernizing country needs the reinforcement of humaneness in the educational system. We must assume, however, that even an illiterate person is humane; a literate and academically educated person has merely the opportunity to increase the range of information and knowledge on which humaneness is based.

Education and vocation are often interlinked, but if our ideology of modernization is adopted, and especially if the principle of equality (including economic equality) and satisfaction of basic necessities – both emphasized in our model of modernization – prevail, the correlation of the level of education to income does not have to obtain. Of course, the kind of education needed for scientists and technologists will always be related to their vocations and professional tasks. Education, vocation, and income have been ladders of social mobility in both the capitalist and the Soviet countries, and we have no reason to believe that this process will stop in the modernizing countries under any form of planning. However, the discrimination based on lack of education must cease if the objectives stated in our model of modernization are followed.

The community

The community must receive proper attention in any comprehensive national planning. Too often the myth of the nation leads to inroads of the capitalist entrepreneur or business interests on the metropolis, the city, or the rural community,[37] where human bonds are destroyed under the euphemism of the 'profit-seeking man.' The profit-seeking man or the hedonist is more often the creation of a capitalist system than the creator of the capitalist system. Similarly, the *Kolkhozes* and the communes of the Soviet countries are artificial communities, which have now become viable. However, they are often kept under control through the Party ideology and its indoctrination programs; given a degree of freedom, as in Bulgaria and elsewhere, the people of such communities want to migrate to the cities.[38] The communities, natural or artificial, must be given an opportunity to determine their own fortunes and fates without economic or Party-determined ideological coercion. If national planning starts from the communities and gets cumulated as it reaches higher levels, we believe that the communities will settle down to the kind of life which most people desire there; they can live with the so-called material deprivations if these are voluntarily inflicted by themselves.

Ethnic pluralism

Ethnic and subcultural groups must be guaranteed their rights to maintain their own folkways and customs. Their integration in national life is one of the most controversial issues today both empirically and sociologically. We noted in an earlier chapter that no nation exists without some ethnic or subcultural diversity. The problem of their integration has been deemed to be either 'assimilative,' in the sense that they should adopt the values and attitudes of the majority group, or 'pluralistic,' which is a term for cultural separation but often economic dominance by the majority group both in the capitalist and the Soviet industrial systems. We cannot examine the intricacies of this situation here. We merely wish to state that economic discrimination is the root cause of social discrimination in all such situations and the principles of national planning being elaborated here have the best possibility of coping with the problems of the minority groups. Ethnic renaissance is nothing new in the decade of the 1970s; it is found as much in the modern industrial nations as in the modernizing nations of yesterday and today.

Family

The family of the modernizing country does not have to become nuclear in order for economic gains to follow. We make this assertion despite the strictures of scholars like Marion J. Levy, Jr., [39] and Bert F. Hoselitz.[40] The latter claims that 'It may even be argued that the abolition of certain aspects of the traditional joint family [in India] is necessary because with them the demands of the new economic order could not be adequately met.'[41] No empirical study has confirmed such views; also these scholars tend to minimize the costs of nucleation of the family structure.

Religion

The religion will no doubt go through some secularization process because society will experience the benefits of rationality, but no special ethics of any persuasion are going to be the motive force for change in the religious views and in the outlook of any group. The need for religious beliefs and rituals is personal and communal, and science, rationality, or national planning (of the kind we suggest here) is not going to supplant it.

The city and the country

The difference between the city and the country will not be effaced, and need not be effaced in a modernizing country. What is needed is to stop the exploitation of the countryside by the city in the name of 'progress.' It does not help very much, first to destroy the forest and its fauna and flora, to pollute the waters of rivers and lakes, and then to undertake programs of reforestation and the creation of animal preserves as well as the cleaning of dirty waters. If the waste as well as the destruction wrought by industrialism are heeded by the modernizing nations, their planning, and therefore, their future will be different and perhaps even better.

Democracy

Finally, we come to the most important, and perhaps highly controversial question, viz. the question of 'a guide for democracy.' Democracy as an ideal-type does not exist anywhere. It is for this reason that scholars like Robert A. Dahl think of specialized dimensions of it, such as the right of each citizen to participate in elections and the openness of each political office to public contestation, as constituting the key to democracy. Such a system Dahl calls 'polyarchy.'[42] It is not only of passing interest to note here that, as of 1969, Dahl counted only twenty-six nations of the world which had fully inclusive polyarchies; these included India, Israel, Jamaica, and Uruguay.[43] The United States and Switzerland were considered special cases because of restrictions on ethnic groups in the former and the inability of women to vote in the latter country. The ideal of democracy is often easier to preach than to practice.

One of the important goals of democracy is to shatter all efforts of special groups to practice 'tyranny over the minds of men.' From this emerges the basic rights of free speech for individuals and freedom of the press as well as the guarantees against harassment of all deviant opinions. Universalistic law, judicial trial for the accused, artistic freedom, freedom to teach professionally accepted knowledge in the classroom, freedom of religion, freedom of movement for individuals, and myriads of other freedoms and rights given to man in the evolutionary history of human civilization, and as compiled, for instance, in the Universal Declaration of Human Rights adopted by the United Nations and ratified by the majority of member states, seem to be the bulwarks of democracy.[44] Whether the right to private property should be a basic right of all individuals is open to question in view of the misuse of this right in history, which created some of the worst sufferings ever known.

137

Conclusion

This, then, is our view of modernization, and it should be considered as a humanistic manifesto for the modernizing nations. The answer to the question, 'modernization for what?' is in essence the answer provided in history (and pinpointed in this chapter) to man's progress toward individual freedoms, cultural autonomy, and the societal pursuit of welfare and excellence.

11 Epilogue

Imperatives of modernization

We have presented a comprehensive model of modernization in an earlier chapter. We believe that our model can be applied to all countries of the world. Thus the shortcomings of modernization in the so-called developed countries can also be ascertained with the help of our model.

It is a truism to state that the developing countries of today follow two routes to modernization. One is the route of capitalism, the other is that of socialism. However, the real implications of capitalism or socialism in the developmental process have nowhere been delineated as sharply as we purpose to do here.

We will first present the popular case – shall we say, the stereo-typical view of modernization. In it, we describe the romantic, the utopian, and the realistic images held by the people and the leaders of the world today. As we go on, we soon discover that two utopian images, viz. the capitalist and the socialist, are in a sense guiding lights for the modernization process of all countries. We therefore provide a careful delineation of the modelic implications of these two images. We call them the capitalist and the socialist models of modernization. These models are then used to highlight the empirical analysis of the developmental process of the United States, the Soviet Union, the People's Republic of China, Japan, and India. An overview of the modernization of these five countries is presented here also as a test of our model of modernization. We hope that the present analysis will be useful in guiding the future direction of the developed and the developing countries.

Public images of modernization

Modernization has two world-wide referents today: advanced

industrial capitalism and advanced industrial socialism. We can call the former the capitalist model, and the latter the socialist model. However, before we go into the intricacies of these models, it would be helpful to evaluate the public images (sometimes adopted by professionals also) of modernization. These we would call the romantic, the utopian, and the realistic images of modernization. After outlining these images, the theory and praxis of the capitalist and socialist models will be presented.

(i) *Romantic image*

From Plato and Aristotle to Hobbes, Locke, and Rousseau, and Gandhi in our own time, there have been many scholars who have tried to reconstruct society in their own images. However, it is generally agreed today that Plato's 'philosopher-king' is as untenable a concept for the ideal society (read modern society) as is Gandhi's *sarvodaya* ('the flowering of all'); Aristotle's neat division of society into monarchy, aristocracy, and constitutional government shows pitfalls, especially when one considers that he thought of democracy as a perversion of the constitutional form of government.

Hobbes's Leviathan has often turned into a tyrant, and Locke's state into an inhibiting force for the agents of social change. Rousseau's General Will remains unrealized in the body politic, and so does Gandhi's *ahimsā* (non-violence). However, despite these lessons of history, people have not given up trying to visualize an ideal society. Today, the romantic are undeterred in giving ideal society a new appelation, that of modern society.

The confident peoples of the West and the resurgent peoples of the Soviet East are proud of their heritages; and the longing gentry as well as the aroused peasantry of the Third World seem anxious to join them. Everyone has a vision of his own about modernity.

The dreams of the leaders of the Third World are fed by the ideas of some highly sophisticated specialists, viz. those who have dared to measure the modernity of society and of man. However, it is becoming increasingly clear that Daniel Lerner's 'modern society' and Alex Inkeles's 'modern man' are as much expressions of faith in the abilities of men and societies to modernize through evolutionary process as they are techniques of measuring modernity. David McClelland's 'need for Achievement' (*n*-A, as it is called) is often used as a potent concoction for the same purpose of arousing false hope. The intentions of these learned scholars have perhaps been misconstrued, although their field activities spanning nations have been partially instrumental in this misinterpretation of their views.

140

It is apparent that the counter cultures proliferating in the West in this century are no different than the Owenites and the Prudhonists of the past. They all conjure up an image of modernization which is highly romantic.

(ii) *Utopian image*

There are two utopian images of modernization which we shall call the capitalist and the socialist images. The public images of these two systems differ somewhat from their models developed by experts, as we will show later on. The capitalist image is construed as preserving the sanctity of private property, putting ownership of the means of production in capital-intensifying private or corporate hands, and a fluid class system in which labor can maximize personal gain and thus move up in the hierarchy in society. The philosophy of this system can be summed up in the well-known phrase, 'life, liberty, and the pursuit of happiness.' The larger politics of such a society is in the long run determined by the economic entrepreneurs and their ties with worldwide capitalism.

The socialist image of modernization presupposes that private property be controlled, if not abolished, that the means of production be socially owned as far as possible, that benefits from work be equalized, and that the labor, not the owner, determines the process of work and the emoluments flowing from it. Most cases of mixed economy fail to follow this route, because the ultimate philosophy of this system is the Marxist tenet, 'from each according to his capacity to each according to his need.' The politics of this society is determined by the leadership of the Communist Party and the proletariat as well as the evolving direction of world socialism.

(iii) *Realistic image*

The realistic image of modernization is shaped by the resources and social life of a country and the ideology of its leadership. The people in general want the quality of their life improved; for instance they seek satisfaction of basic necessities, such as food, clothing, housing, health, and education. They also need freedoms, such as protection of life and limb (security against violence and arbitrary arrest); freedom of speech (the right to dissent); freedom of movement (to travel or to emigrate at will); freedom of belief (to hold on to one's religious, ethnic, subcultural values); and, of course, freedom to receive impartial information. The rights of assembly, of a free press, and of non-fettered artistic and creative pursuits are also considered necessary for modernity.

How these can be achieved, what are the prerequisites, and what model a society should choose for its own development are some of the issues which baffle the developing countries of today.

The problem of determining what makes for modernization is very complex indeed. As we noted above, the public images do not conform with each other. Neither do they always provide realistic guidelines for policy decisions and actions. As far as models of modernization are concerned, it needs to be emphasized that the notion of model has been too frequently popularized and so may mean whatever one wants it to mean, given one's value preferences. However, social scientists have spent a great deal of time and energy in articulating the problems of model-building.

A model stipulates the causal understanding of a phenomenon under investigation. It also helps to interpret in advance the varying consequences of social actions, so that policy decisions can be made on a rational basis. It is with these ends in view that the following discussion of the models of modernization is presented.

Models of modernization

We noted earlier that the empirical model for modernization for any country today is advanced industrialism. In a sense, Max Weber and Karl Marx are the twin godfathers of the two chief models of advanced industrialism, viz. capitalism and socialism. Weber's ideas and analyses shape the developments in the advanced stages of the capitalist society, Marx's ideas and prescriptions guide the direction of the socialist society. The word model, as noted earlier, is used here in the sense of a theoretical construct.

(i) *The capitalist model*

(a) *Model of society* In order to understand the intricacies of the model of capitalist society, we want to explicate first Max Weber's view of society. Weber defined society in a nominalistic way. Men are involved in subjectively meaningful actions, which are called 'conduct' (or 'behavior'). The conduct is purposeful, value-directed, affectual, or traditional. 'Social relationship' exists when people take each other's conduct into account, which gives rise to a probability of action.

Social conduct and social relationship imply the idea of the existence of a legitimate order. The legitimacy is consensual. Thus, Weber's society is the creation of goal-seeking men, who produce a growth product, called 'society,' through rule-guided behavior. For Weber, society is the synthesis of individual conducts and social relationships. It is a whole whose parts have been aggregated in terms of the conjunctions (and disjunctions) of actions.

(b) *The capitalist framework for modernization*   Max Weber's view of society has been accepted by the scholars of the capitalist world, perhaps because it presents a healthy image for capitalist society and a working model for it. Weber's 'ideal-type' constructs, especially of bureaucracy, his emphasis on the rational working out of social processes, and his summation of discrete variables, e.g. market worth, social honor, and political power in the construct social stratification form the backbone of the functionalist school in sociology. This school has often been accused of giving aid to the maintenance of the status quo in capitalist societies.

For Weber, social processes can be understood by observing how societies change through their internal dynamism. In his framework, individuals and groups have to adjust to such changes in society or reap the consequences. Weber believed that the march of history is ultimately guided by rationality and freedom, although he warned against excessive bureaucratization in capitalist society.

In the realms of economics and politics Weber saw competing powers. He believed that interest aggregation goes on all the time in society; various groups always safeguard their prerogatives; and, in the end, societal power, which 'claims the *monopoly of the legitimate use of force* within a territory,'[1] i.e. the state, reconciles divergent and conflicting interests. He no doubt gave certain primacy to economic power. But he also noted that social as well as political statuses have a tendency to be transformed into economic power and vice versa.

According to Weber, the market is the model for the circulation of currency as well as of wealth, status, and power. In his framework, there will always be rulers and ruled, rich and poor, and high and low statuses in society. What are needed are some general and legal safeguards and protections against the exploitation of the disadvantaged by the rulers. Nothing could suit the philosophy of the capitalist society better.

The model for modernization in this framework could be restated in terms of the interlocking relationship of the following variables: market economy, free enterprise, profit motive, entrepreneurship, efficiency, support for science and technology, freedom of the labor force, and a rational legal system.

(ii) *The socialist model*

(a) *Model of society*   As with Max Weber, we will depict the view of society constructed by Karl Marx, the progenitor of the socialist

143

society. For Marx, society is not comprehended by rules of nominalism but of realism. According to him, society is an economic totality, not an aggregate, however organic that aggregate may be; it is a whole, the parts of which are in constant dynamic relationship with it. Society, up until and including the capitalist stage, has also suffered from an internal contradiction.

Society is made up of forces of production, which can be analysed in terms of the linkage of the means of production to the relations of production; Marx also makes the distinction between 'base' and 'super structure,' the former being the factors of production and the latter all other institutional systems. The population is divided in groups in terms of class relations, which are antagonistic; thus class cleavage is a necessary component of such a society. Class consciousness provides the dynamic for social change. According to Marx, the focus of attention in society should not be the myriads of discrete variables, used by the functionalists today, but only three realistic factors, viz. forces of production, class relations, and class consciousness.

(b) *The socialist framework for modernization*   For Karl Marx, the capitalist society is composed of two main classes, viz. the bourgeoisie who own the means of production, and the proletariat who have only labor power. Such a society develops contradictions, so it changes to a higher level of production and existence, viz. socialism. In socialist society, the ownership of the means of production is transferred from private hands to the state and classes are done away with. The socialist society brings the proletariat to power; the old conditions of production (for private gain) are abolished and class antagonism vanishes forever.

In the Marxist model of society, there is no aggregation of discrete 'interests' but the opposite of it. The accretion of acquisitive interests is disvalued in favor of the collective interest of the proletariat. This model conceives of economic equality of individuals as supplanting class-, status- and power-directed hegemony of the capitalists. It claims that, under socialism, individual freedoms will return; and in such a society there will no longer be the difference between the rulers and the ruled.

Marx stipulates that true democracy should bring about abolition of class prerogatives and the conduct of societal affairs in terms of self-regulation. One can see that here the axis of power is not the state, not the holders of capital but a self-managing community. The state, in so far as it exists, is not hegemonic and an instrument of bourgeois power, but is dictated by situational needs to abolish capital and to eliminate the bourgeoisie as a class. The state at best is a mechanism for the reacquisition of labor's freedoms as well as a vehicle of social control in the process of reorganization of power and societal values.

With the advent of communism, the state will 'wither away.' The guiding principle of such a society would be: 'from each according to his capacity, to each according to his need.' In the march of history, Marx wanted the workers to shake off false consciousness (especially the values of capitalism) and take to the path of class war. The call of his *Communist Manifesto* was: 'Working men of all countries, unite!' 'The proletarians have nothing to lose but their chains.'

The socialist model for modernization as laid down by Marx could be construed in the following terms: abolition of private ownership of the means of production, dictatorship of the proletariat, reorganization of labor for higher social production, planning, exhortation and group self-examination, non-accretion of stratum interests, societal pride, and labor freed from primordial bonds.

Some problematics

We should now mention some basic issues involved in the modernization process, whether one considers the capitalist or the socialist route to modernization. These issues are of two kinds. One concerns the condition of man, his health and happiness. The other concerns the condition of society, its strengths and its weaknesses, which help or hinder man's growth in it.

The first concern of modernization theory is for man. Marx was troubled by man's alienation under the capitalist system; Weber gave the state, especially the institution of law, a crucial role in guarding the interests of the individual. They both discussed other important issues, e.g. man's socialization process, his affiliations, the determination of his goals, as well as the shaping of an individual's needs and interests. Finally, the question of freedom was paramount in their minds. However, they approached these issues and questions from quite different standpoints, as might be clear from the preceding analysis.

The second concern of modernization theory is about the nature of society. What happens to family, economic growth, value system, processes of decision-making, and, most important, the reward system? How should kinship, production system, value orientations (religious as well as secular), and political institutions (in the past, the major societal decision-making and decision-enforcing body) be guided in the future?

We do not intend to go into a general discussion of these questions now, because they will engage our attention when we examine the modernization process of the five countries mentioned earlier. Instead, we want to pursue one basic problem of theorizing, viz. conceptualization, and see if any comparison of Marx and Weber is possible on an 'objective' basis. The following exercise in theorizing is not meant to answer the question, 'Who was right? Marx or Weber?' but to indicate that theorists are of necessity selective in their terms, their definitions, and their hypotheses. However, through explication, terms can be reconceptualized so as to incorporate important missing dimensions. In the end, it is the power of a concept to throw light on an empirical phenomenon that is important, not how well it fits a particular set of values.

Theorizing

Let us start with some concepts, which are basic to the understanding of human actions and society, no matter which framework one adopts. I have selected four of these concepts for discussion, because they directly relate to modernization. These concepts are: land, labor, capital, and management.

Land is soil and/or water-covered area with a geographic boundary; labor is the energy exerted by a human being to produce something; capital is what accumulates in the production process for further productive use, and management refers to the deployment of skills and knowledge, for organizing complex group activities. These are first-level definitions.

Land can increase or decrease in use, if knowledge is added to the production method; labor can similarly be more or less efficient in terms of skills imparted or neglected. Capital can increase to a certain point under competition, and management can be more resourceful if guided by scientific principles. These developmental conceptions of the four terms will perhaps be also universally accepted.

However, the moment one tries to relate these concepts to each other and form a theory out of them, disagreements occur. For instance, in the Marxian lexicon, one cannot think of labor without its 'use-value' and its 'surplus value,' or without making a distinction between 'socially necessary' labor and 'alienated' labor under capitalism. Similarly, for Marx, capital is the creation of a value by the addition of the 'surplus value' of labor, whereas for the non-Marxist economist, capital is the asset produced by the exchange of labor and the division in the production process of labor. Management in the form of government or bureaucracy was construed as the executive branch of the capitalist class by Marx, but it is necessary for rational decision-making in the Weberian theory. In other words, it is not only the conceptualization which

146

matters but the referents of terms which are linked together in an organic whole that are subject to debate. The referents become the bone of contention. Classes are nominal for Weber but real for Marx. That is still another bone of contention.

Society is viewed in terms of the interlocking relationship of its constituent concepts, which in the case of labor, capital, and management, as we have seen above, have different connotations in the Marxian theory and the Weberian theory. Not only the conceptualization of society, but the reality of society also has different dimensions. It is not fruitful to ignore any important dimension because it cannot be incorporated into one's theoretical framework.

There are some dimensions which are necessary for the comprehension of a phenomenon. We propose to show below how the phenomenon of the relationship between only two elements, viz. land and labor, is both empirically and logically different from its articulation proposed by Marx or others in the past. In fact, the ensuing exercise in explicating the concept of 'rights in property' (relating land to labor) is also meant to incorporate and advance beyond the Marxian and the functionalist interpretations of these rights as they occur in history and society.

Rights in property

In *The German Ideology* (originally published in 1832), Marx stipulated the following initial forms of property ownership: tribal ('basically nomadic'), Graeco-Roman, and feudal. He did not have then or even later a correct interpretation of the Asiatic mode of production. The *Grundrisse* (written in 1857) and *Das Kapital* (first volume published in 1867) carry his major references to India, whose villages were described by him as communes, which were also 'hereditary possessors' of land. He said: 'In the Asiatic form (at least, predominantly), the individual has no property but only possession; the real proprietor, proper is the commune – hence property only as *communal property* in land.'[2] He makes the assertion in spite of the fact that there were two opposed views on the matter,[3] and that he was familiar with them.[4] One view was that land was private property in India,[5] and the other was the one to which Marx subscribed.

Marx's assertion is meant to highlight the fact of the development of ownership of property from the communal (ownership by the gens of the tribe or by the village communes of India) to the feudal (proprietorship vested in the lord) to the capitalist (private ownership) stages. But the issue of ownership can be understood better if we relate the concept of property to those of land and labor.

Land (or any other natural resource) has a use for purposes of production. The relationship of man (or his labor) to land can be one of cultivator, tiller, hunter, or some other subsistence-level activity. It can also be in the form of other relationships, such as a worker, a share cropper, or hired laborer.

However, when it comes to appropriating the usufruct of the land, all manner of complications arise. First, if tools have been used, they must be manufactured by oneself or paid for by barter or compensatory labor. Then, if the cultivator is not the owner, he has to pay some compensation (rent or what have you) to the owner, who may be obliged to pass on part of it to those higher up in authority and power. We are already moving beyond the stage of primitive production.

In the historical evolution of society, both Marx and the non-Marxist social scientists have put emphasis on the complicated beginnings of property rights in ancient times. It has been shown that the individual and social rights in land get more rule-directed as society evolves from the settled-agricultural stage to the feudal and the capitalist stages. Presumably, under primitive production, ownership was not a problem at least in the juridical sense. But as soon as one shifts one's attention from the communal to the feudal and the capitalist stages of society, the question of ownership becomes pivotal.

However, ownership is not a unitary category. Let us explicate the involved phenomena. Ownership in land can have at least the following dimensions in terms of rights and privileges: managing rights (example, as *Kamatiya* or farm manager in north India in a patrimonial system), occupancy rights (for instance, to build a house on it), the absolute or limited right, conversion rights (to convert land into orchard, pond, etc.), improvement rights (to irrigate), exchange rights (to barter for another resource), transfer rights (to lease, to retrieve, or hold for someone), sale rights (to realize money value), and inheritance rights (to bequeath it to kin or to inherit it, if someone holding it dies). Each one of these rights in the land (or another natural resource) can often exist independently of the other rights (some have been mentioned in the study of India[6]), although it is evident that, as one moves up the scale, the rights become more inclusive.

As the mode of production advanced, other rights accrued in the land. In the feudal society, the categories of possessor and proprietor were latched on to those of the owner and its subcategories discussed above. Robert Patton, in his *The Principles of Asiatic Monarchies* (1801), made the distinction between 'possessory right' and 'proprietory right,' i.e. the monarch was the proprietor of the land and the peasant was only the possessor.[7]

Marx picked up this idea, although in the case of India, as we noted earlier, he was partial when he said that the village possessed the land. We can thus stipulate an additional dimension here. In a hypothetical situation, if the peasant is the owner, the village can be the possessor (in the sense of some rights subject to the check of village elders) and the monarch can be the proprietor.

In juridical terms, proprietorship includes the concept of dominion (suzerainty to sovereignty) rights of the feudal monarch or the modern nation-state, while possessorship defines only domain rights of the whole village or of the chieftain who holds the title (such as *Jagir* of Mughal times in India). The domain rights accrue under a grant or a settlement, or the permission of the overlord (the *zamindari* system of India under the British rule is one such example). However, ownership can imply all these rights from the dominion rights to the domain rights to the use of all the rights discussed earlier held together, or independently. Ownership can also mean only one of the several rights mentioned earlier, from management to sale to inheritance of property.

We analysed the determinants of the rights to property to prove a simple point. Marx felt that the capitalist mode of production, which multiplies these rights, is more alienating than anything else in history. He wanted to abolish these rights and that is what accounts for his disgust with private property.[8] It is true that Max Weber and other scholars took note of these historical developments, especially with regard to the feudal system of the West.[9] Max Weber even felt that the development of science and rationality helped in sorting out these issues and making them commensurate with the advancement in society. However, Marx and his followers believed that the team of lawyers and jurisprudents help only the cause of capital's hold over society and the exploitation of the labor by the bourgeoisie.

It should be noted that the analysis of rights in land presented here is a first step in understanding the complicated legal system of property rights under capitalism, as well as international rights of exchange and transfer in the present world. Weber believed in nation-states and so had faith in law, equity, and justice in the capitalist society. Marx believed in international socialism, so he wanted to put an end to the nightmare of bourgeois rights to property and labor's domination by capitalists in terms of these rights. We have presented the basic difference in capitalist perspective and the socialist perspective as sharply as we can.

Now that we have seen that the capitalist model of modernization implies the ordering of society on very different principles than the socialist model, one is left with the question of evaluating the relative strengths of these models in guiding the modernization process of the contemporary world. Much theoretical work needs to be done before a satisfactory answer to this question can be given. We know that the theorists in the capitalist world are more preoccupied with the problems of their own societies than dealing with the implications of Marxian theory. The same applies to the theorists of the Soviet socialist world. So, at this stage, we will not venture into providing our own answer to this question. We reserve that for a future occasion. Instead, we merely give here our impression of the individual strengths of the two models in terms of delineating the *Weltanschauungs* of the capitalist and the socialist societies. But before we do so, it is helpful to ask the vital question: in which direction is the world actually moving? Or, more pointedly: is the world going to adopt the socialist model or the capitalist model of modernization?

Alternatives

As we have pointed out, there are two alternatives to modernization available today: the capitalist system and the socialist system. Marx did not live to see the latter come into existence, and Weber barely witnessed its inception before his death. However, with the viability of both systems established in the contemporary world, the developing countries have a genuine choice today.

(i) *Two* Weltanschauungs

The *Weltanschauungs* of the capitalist and the socialist systems need to be comprehended. Under capitalism, private ownership of the means of production will continue forever, labor will sell its services in a market situation, the state will guarantee the accumulation of profit, and all private gains by individuals can be bequeathed to their heirs.

Under socialism, private ownership of the means of production is abolished, labor, as a class, determines the level of production; non-familial labor is not available for personal profit; and any private property, which can be converted into independent means of production, cannot be inherited.

It is clear that according to these criteria, only the Soviet countries and Cuba qualify as socialist countries. Other so-called socialist countries are more like capitalist countries because they cannot qualify on the important criterion of abolishing all private ownership of the means of production. This point is very significant, because it enters directly into the modernization efforts of any country.

(ii) *Social dimensions of modernization*

If we accept the above thesis and agree that capitalist and socialist systems are two very divergent ways of organizing social life, we can discuss the issues of equality, democracy, freedom, societal advancement, and individual fulfillment in a more detached and dispassionate way than the protagonists of these two systems have done in the past.

In the capitalist system, there is legal equality of persons, but no effort to equalize incomes. (In fact, the legal assignment of the status of person to a corporation complicates the matter very much). It is claimed there that democracy can be introduced and preserved only by republican institutions of government, e.g. multi-party system, universal franchise, rights of referendum and recall, and so forth. However, praise for this kind of participatory democracy does not always take into account voters' apathy, the strength of the capitalist hold on governmental policies and its equally powerful control of the mass media of communication.

(iii) *Democracy*

We would like to say a word here about democracy. At the minimum, it involves a form of government in which all people participate. In the West, it has been called 'government by the people.' In Ancient Greece, *demos* was the poorer people, so one can think easily of the rule of the poor over the rich or the proletariat over the bourgeoisie.

A democracy stipulates unfettered conditions of popular participation in the decision-making process affecting the whole society. The end result of this process must also be articulated, so that it can be compared with non-democratic rule. If only these specific criteria are kept in mind, the classless Soviet societies qualify as democracies as much as the class-based societies of the industrial West.

(iv) *Freedoms*

The issue of freedoms is sticky, to say the least. No doubt the freedoms of press, speech, assembly, and movement are seemingly more important in capitalist countries than in the Soviet countries. Our thesis is that the capitalist societies worked out these problems over at least two centuries, whereas the Soviet societies have had hardly thirty to sixty years to grapple with them. It is clear to us that the strength of Soviet Russia or the People's Republic of China is now so well established, that these countries can open their gates for free exchange of ideas with capitalist societies and can survive the test of the viability of their system. We know that the basic *Weltanschauung* of the capitalist society cannot be permitted to be challenged by the powers that be, and this equally holds true for the socialist society.

(v) *Progress*

As far as advancement of society and individual fulfillment is concerned, there are many issues to focus on. The neglect of poor people in health, education, employment, and the advancement of their children is not at all so evident in the Soviet countries as it is in the capitalist ones (with exceptions such as Sweden). Ghetto problems, the crime situation, and mental sickness in the capitalist countries are again equally acute; the Soviet countries do much better on these counts.

Recreation is available equally in both systems. The pursuit of excellence, whether in science or in the arts, goes on in the Soviet world as much as in the capitalist world. However there are important limits on intellectual freedom in the arts, literature, and social studies in the Soviet system.

We have carried a general discussion of societal modernization as far as we can. It would help to see now how five countries, viz. the United States, the Soviet Union, the People's Republic of China, Japan, and India fare today in terms of our own model of modernization. Such an analysis would also provide guidance for the future of these countries as well as others in the contemporary world.

Profiles in modernization

As we set out to present the profiles in modernization of five selected countries, it may be useful to recapitulate the main features of our own model of modernization. We indicated in our model discussed earlier that modernization is a process of directed change. Its goals are economic growth, political development, national autonomy, and social reconstruction. The reconstruction is based on the principles of equality, fraternity, enhancement of freedoms, and satisfaction of basic needs. The goals are articulated by individuals and cumulated by groups. In the short run, revolutionary methods can be used for implementing these goals. But in the long run, the goals must be self-sustaining. They require reaffirmation through consensus and democratic consent.

Let us examine the state and the stages of modernization of the five countries selected for analysis in terms of their general profiles. Their stage of modernization will be ascertained in terms of their approximation to the model depicted above. Their states of

modernity will be fathomed from their performance on selected
variables of political, economic, and demographic nature.

We will first present the crucial demographic and economic data
on all the five countries and then examine the significance of these
data in terms of the history of modernization of each country.

TABLE 1 *Population Profiles in 1978*

	United States	Soviet Union	People's Republic of China	Japan	India
Population mid-1978	218.4	261	930	114.4	634.7
Birth-rate	15	18	22	16	34
Death-rate	9	9	8	6	14
Rate of natural increase (annual %)	0.6	0.9	1.4	1	2
Infant mortality rate	15	28	65	9	129
Population under 15 years (%)	24	25	33	24	40
Population over 64 years (%)	11	9	6	8	3
Life expectancy at birth (years)	73	69	65	74	49
Literacy (%)	99	99	25	95	34
Urban population (%)	74	62	24	76	21
Projected labour force increase 1978-2000 (million)	26.6	20	136.9	12	155.6
Per capita gross national product (US$)	7,890	2,760	410	4,910	150

Source: 1978 World Population Data Sheet, Washington D. C., The Population
Reference Bureau, Inc. except for literacy data.

It should be noted that economists generally classify any country
with an annual GNP per capita income up to US $250 as a
low-income country, and with an income between $251 to $4,000 as
a middle-income country. The industrial countries have incomes of
$4,000+. In terms of demographic variables, the industrial coun-
tries have generally a birth-rate of 16 per thousand or less, a
death-rate of 13 per thousand or less, and a life expectancy of 70

153

years or more. The combination of these demographic variables often provides a better index of the modernity of a country than the incomes variable or any other set of variables.

United States

The United States had a population of 218.4 million in 1978 of which 74 per cent was classified as being urban. Its Gross National Product (GNP) per capita income was $7,890, which was the highest in the world if we leave out three tiny oil countries of the Middle East, viz. Kuwait, Qatar, and the United Arab Emirates. The birth-rate of the United States was 15 and the death-rate 9 per thousand. The infant mortality rate was 15 per thousand live births and life expectancy was 73 years. Twenty-four per cent of its population was below 15 years of age and 11 per cent was above 64 years, the normal age of retirement. If the 1978 rate of natural increase (0.6 per cent per year) holds, the United States will add 26.6 million people to its labor force by the year 2000. Almost 99 per cent of Americans are literate. It is clear that in terms of basic economic and demographic criteria, the United States is a modern country.

In political terms, the country won its independence after fighting a bloody war with the British in the eighteenth century, and it had to go through a civil war in the nineteenth century to maintain its integrity and the equalitarian values embodied in its Constitution. However, from the beginning, the American nation has operated on the principle of checks and balances, which does not permit any specific organ of the state to concentrate power in its own hands. Thus, the formation of the state was weak throughout the nineteenth century. With developments in science and technology and the growth of industrialism, however, the capital-owning class gradually started to concentrate economic power in its own hands, while the state began to appropriate more political power, especially after the Depression of 1929 and the Presidency of Franklin D. Roosevelt. Labor also began to show its muscle, more so after the Second World War.

Today, the largest employers in the country are the big steel industry, the automobile industry, and the newspapers, in that order. The American people are very proud of their free press. They cherish their political institutions, including their two-party system and their periodic elections to public offices based on the principles of consensus, referendum, and recall. The stereotypical image of the American polity is that it is run by the people, but actually the hand of big business in important decisions, especially with regard to the maintenance of capitalism, can be seen everywhere.

When Abraham Lincoln first ran for the Congress, all he spent was 75 cents (out of $200 donated by friends) for a barrel of cider with which he treated some farm hands. He returned the rest of the money to the contributors.[10] In 1978, two candidates from New York's 18th District together spent over $1 million in their campaigns. And most of it was their own money.[11] The way big business and big labor finances American elections today is no secret. The relationship between campaign financing of a candidate and policy-making if the candidate wins is a crucial area in which little investigation by scholars has been done.

It is clear from the direction taken by the American polity that no one is in a hurry to dismantle the major institutions of capitalism; this can be seen by examining the growth of the big national corporations as well as the multinational corporations. The checks by the government on monopolies, cartels, and unfair labor practices as well as consumer shortchanging are meant more to keep the capitalist system viable than really to give a fair deal to the weak and the downtrodden in the system.

In 1962, the top fifth of the American population owned 77 per cent of its personal wealth, which is three times more than the wealth of the remaining 80 per cent of the American population.[12] This was the picture of personal wealth distribution in the 1960s. As distinguished from wealth, which is what the capitalist class holds, the income distribution in 1978 was as follows (as gleaned from Internal Revenue Service statistics): The top 5 per cent of families had an income of $40,500 or more. The top 20 per cent earned incomes above $26,000. The next 20 per cent earned between $18,800 and $26,000. The lowest 20 per cent of families earned $7,900 or less. Thus the top 20 per cent of Americans earned more than three times as much as the bottom 20 per cent of the population.[13] The American dream is to move up the income hierarchy and go to the top. In this scramble for success, honor, and power, there can be little sympathy for equalization of incomes.

Equality is perceived in American society in other terms than economic. The American race is for equity, not equality. In the nineteenth century, the Civil War was fought to free the slaves; a universal franchise and the right of labor to organize were other issues that were also won. In the twentieth century, governmental support for farmers, older people (social security and medicare), minorities (civil rights legislation of the 1960s), and improvements in education, welfare, housing, and manpower have been to the forefront.

The New Deal under Franklin D. Roosevelt no doubt started regulatory agencies for business and commerce, but at no point have the competitive and profit-making rights of the capitalists been abridged or downgraded. The pace of industrial capitalism is now creating havoc for the lower class and the unskilled and this is a great challenge to the modernization process of America today. The challenge is exacerbated because some minority groups have a majority of their population in the underprivileged strata.

In sum, the United States is a modern country in terms of economic, demographic, and political variables. It is now attacking its social evils, such as prejudice, discrimination, problems of old age, health, and deviancy, as well as environmental pollution. However, it has to go a long way in these matters. The profit motive often puts a stranglehold on some of its humanitarian policies. The pace of technological change disrupts family, community, and even deeply held ethical values. In the race for power, wealth plays a key role. Only time will tell if the capitalist system will be able to conserve and advance the state of modernization that exists in the United States today.

Soviet Union

The Soviet Union had a population of 261 million in 1978. Its birth-rate was 18 per thousand, which was higher than that of the United States, Japan, and most other industrial countries of the world. Its death-rate was 9 per thousand. Sixty-two per cent of the population lived in urban areas which was less than that in Japan and the United States. Infant mortality in the Soviet Union was 28 per 1,000 live births, which was again much higher than in the United States and Japan. Twenty-five per cent of the population was below 15 years of age. At the current rate of increase of 0.9 per cent per year, the Soviet Union will add 20 million more to its labor force by the year 2000. The per capita GNP income was $2,760, which was more like that of middle-income-level countries, but living standards in the Soviet Union are not reflected in the dollar value because of artificial exchange rates and the socialist way of sharing amenities and production. The Soviet Union is the second most advanced industrial nation in the world by any standards.

The socialist revolution of 1917 transformed Russia from a backward autocratic state to the first socialist republic of which Karl Marx had dreamed. The Union of Soviet Socialist Republics abolished private ownership of the means of production, liquidated the bourgeois class, and integrated scores of ethnic groups into a republic of fifteen peoples. In keeping with the principles of scientific socialism, classes were abolished and the dictatorship of the proletariat was established. This was the first socialist state in history, so there were no blueprints, no past experiences to draw on. V. I. Lenin, the father of the nation, had to start from scratch. The toll in life, labor, and production was heavy in the beginning.

Lenin soon acknowledged the productive role of three strata of people, viz. the intelligentsia, the workers, and the peasants. But he would not trust the army, the bureaucracy, and the old guard. He abolished them and later on replaced them from the workers' ranks. Economic policies had to be framed somewhat on a pragmatic basis, with the important proviso that under no circumstances was capitalism to return to Russia. The policies of Stalin after Lenin's death were dictated equally with a view to keeping the Communist Party in command and to ensconcing himself in power. Purges were common, families and marriage ties were broken up, communities were isolated. Against great odds, the Soviet Union finally made the ascent to modernization.

If in the United States, the emphasis is on equity, in the Soviet Union, the operating principle is one of equality. Along with private wealth, unemployment was officially abolished by the Bolshevik Revolution. Every able-bodied person must work; only the old, the indigent, and children are to be supported by the state. Education is free and presumably everyone is literate. (Incidentally, no questions concerning the ability to read and write were asked in the 1970 census of the Soviet Union.) Its economic growth and social reconstruction, although first based on revolutionary methods of coercion and force, but starting in 1928 with the Five-Year National Plans, kept pace with the times. However, it has deployed more resources in building its military might, making it equal to, if not superior than the United States; this might have shortchanged the standard of living of an average Russian.

There have been ups and downs in Soviet Russia's planning. From the liquidation of the Kulaks on the land, to the conversion of all private agriculture into *kolkhozes* and communes, to the building of factories and crash programs for the utilization of its raw materials and resources, the Soviet Union has come a long way in the last sixty years.

It is true that discrepancies in wages and salaries still exist in Russia. However, they have been shortened as far as possible. In 1932, an engineer received over 2.5 times the wage of a manual worker; in 1972, this was decreased to 1.3 times.[14] The wages of the intellectual stratum (what is called the professional class in the West) are still higher. For instance, directors of research institutes get 500 to 700 rubles a month ($690-$966), whereas junior researchers get only 105 to 125 rubles ($145-$172).[15] Women constitute 54 per cent of the Soviet Union's population, and 54 per cent of them are in the labor force.[16]

It would be gratuitous to expect that even a socialist modernizing country, whose goal is industrialism, should not face some inequality in incomes. If nothing else, the producers have to contend with the problem of incentives. Faced with the issue of shortages in agriculture, the Soviet Union has permitted some private plots, whose produce is sold in the market. But such plots do not exceed 1 per cent of agricultural land,[17] and 90 per cent of them are farmed by women.[18]

Food, housing, health, and leisure are not commodities for profit in the Soviet Union as far as providing these basic necessities for all is concerned. However, agricultural surplus is used by the government toward reconstruction needs. It is also true that variations in the quality of health care, restaurants, country *dachas*, apartments, and vacation centers do exist. The party, the university, and the factory authorities have usually a better share of the valued goods and services.

The right of inheritance was abolished in 1918 in keeping with Marxist socialist principles, but some inheritance has been permitted. However, it cannot be compared with that in the capitalist countries, if only because the means of production cannot be privately owned. It is difficult to imagine that a society could have no social problems. Drinking is one such problem in the Soviet Union. About 10 to 15 per cent of the income of an average factory or office worker is spent on alcohol. It has now become such a problem that about 13,000 doctors and 55,000 assistants are engaged full time in combatting alcoholism.[19]

The race for equality is not an easy one. The Soviet leaders are aware of the discrepancies that still prevail. In one study, it was found that:[20]

> of every 100 secondary-school graduates coming from families of collective-farm members and state-farm workers, only 10 continued to study after completion of secondary school and 90 went to work, while of every 100 graduates coming from the families of urban non-manual persons, 82 continued their studies and only 15 went to work.

Although this study cites unequal opportunities (and/or motivation) in the system, it also shows that life is not as rigidly organized and programmed in Russia as some people would like to believe.

The question of human rights is another debated issue. The freedom of the dissidents to practice and propagandize anti-Soviet doctrines is severely curtailed. But not all freedom of expression concerning human rights is punished and its propagators jailed; one has only to look at Andrei D. Sakharov's 'Memorandum,' which was sent to Leonid Brezhnev in March 1971. However, the memorandum was not published in the Soviet Union.[21] Perhaps the Soviet authorities are still doubtful as to the consequences of permitting the liberties, which Sakharov is claiming on behalf of his compatriots. In our judgment, relaxation of rules about publications, travel, and creative endeavors in the arts is not going to shake the foundation or to compromise the strengths of the socialist society.

The Soviet Union is a viable society, where less inequality in wealth exists than in any capitalist society, despite its emphasis on industrialism. In terms of the economic (not the comparable dollar income but the buying capacity of the wages earned by the average Russian worker) and demographic variables, it is indeed a modern nation. In political terms, its Constitution and philosophy of life do not permit more than one party in the country. However, if one judges a country's polity by the participation of its people in the societal decision-making process, then in terms of both voting in elections as well as deliberating on its national Five-Year Plans,[22] the country shows strengths which are unmatched elsewhere.

The family today is a viable unit. Although the state preaches atheism (according to the Marxist tenet, 'religion is the opiate of the masses'), believers are permitted to practice their religious faiths and dogmas. The average Russian is less handicapped in terms of jobs and income than the average worker in a capitalist society, if only because inflation, recession, and depression do not plague the Russian economy. As the Russian polity matures and people compare the fruits of their revolution with those of other countries, it is possible that the leaders of the Soviet Union will open their roads wide to traffic in ideas, peoples, and commodities. Modernization is a continuing process which never stops for any country.

People's Republic of China

On October 1, 1949, Mao Tse-tung formally inaugurated the People's Republic of China, after years of grisly fighting with the armies of Chiang Kai-shek and the Kuomintang generals. Chou En-lai was named the head of the State Administrative Council. As Mao said:[23]

> If there is to be revolution, there must be a revolutionary party. Without a revolutionary party, without a party built on the Marxist-Leninist revolutionary theory and in the Marxist-Leninist revolutionary style, it is impossible to lead the working class and the broad masses of the people in defeating imperialism and its running dogs.

For almost three decades, these two leaders guided the destiny of the People's Republic of China (PRC), one through his ideological tenets and lectures and the other through his diplomatic and pragmatic policies. The initial help of the Soviet Union and the

159

earlier enmity of the United States has now been reversed, so that now the Soviet Union is the disliked partner and the United States, perhaps, a helpful ally in Communist China's race toward modernization.

After the 1953 Census of the PRC (when the population was reported to be 601.9 million including 12 million overseas Chinese and 7 million Taiwanese), not much information was available in the West about its demographic condition. However, from documents retrieved and brought to light recently, the following picture emerges.

In 1978, the estimated population of the People's Republic of China was 930 million. Its birth-rate was 22 per thousand (somewhat less than conjectured) and the death-rate was 8 per thousand. Its current rate of natural increase was 1.4 per cent which, if continued, will add an additional 136.9 million people to its labor force by the year 2000. Its urban population was 24 per cent, about which we will comment shortly. Thirty-three per cent of its population was below 15 years of age and 6 per cent above 64 years of age. Its life expectancy was 65 years and the infant mortality rate was 65 per thousand live births. Its rate of literacy was 25 per cent, which was less than any other country including India in our sample of five countries under review here. The per capita GNP income of the People's Republic of China was $410, which barely puts it among the middle income countries on the economic indicator. By all odds, the PRC is not yet an industrial country although it has sent its own satellite into space and has even detonated a hydrogen bomb.

We will examine the PRC's pace of modernization in terms of the unfolding policies of the Chinese Communist Party, declared by Mao to be 'the force at the core leading our cause forward.' During the first five years, the vast problems of a stagnating economy had to be taken care of as quickly as was necessary to build the strengths of the Party. On July 1, 1950, the decision was made to recruit one-third of industrial labor in China into the Communist Party within three to five years.[24] However, by the middle of 1953, there was a halt in recruiting rural party members and an emphasis on consolidating the then current membership. The attention of the Party moved toward increasing production.

Private enterprise and business were permitted to flourish for a while, although under the control of the government. Provisional regulations for private enterprise were announced a year after the formation of the People's Republic, and a readjustment policy toward business was announced two years later. The government was in no hurry to strangle private enterprise altogether, especially in the face of scarcity and famine conditions.

In administrative terms, first there was the 'Three-Anti' Campaign against corruption, waste, and bureaucracy in August 1951. Six months later, there was the 'Five-Anti' Campaign against bribery, theft of state property, tax evasion, theft of state economic secrets, and embezzlement in carrying out government contracts. For the illiterate masses, the slogans of the Party and the quotations from Chairman Mao were potent guides for action. Although the need for centralization of power in the Party was great, large areas of freedom were available to China's vastly spread out regions. Mao's statement on August 9, 1952, on the subject of autonomous regional government for minority groups assuaged the fears of many. The regional governments were allowed to control their own finance, security, militia, local language, arts, and culture.

In terms of production, the Ministry of Agriculture stated in 1952 that 35 million peasant families (40 per cent) were taking part in 6 million 'mutual aid teams' and 3,000 'production cooperatives'.[25] In October of the same year, the State Planning Board was set up. By the December of 1952, the First Five-Year Plan for industrial and agricultural development was in shape, which was to begin in 1953. In February 1953, Premier Chou En-lai reported to the Chinese People's Political Consultative Committee that it was intended to establish 2,000 state farms and 34,000 cooperatives with a membership of 141 million people.[26] These are mind-boggling figures.

However, the PRC cadres were up to the task. On February 7, 1953, Chairman Mao asked the Party to oppose bureaucratization among leading cadres and organs of the government. On February 13, agrarian reforms were ended and collectivization began. On April 17, the Government Administrative Council issued orders to stop the 'blind influx' of peasants into cities. The ability of the government to halt time and again the flow of agricultural labor to the cities has saved the People's Republic of China from overurbanization. It has also given an incentive to the people to work harder on the farms. By the end of 1953, basic level elections had taken place for 166 million people and secondary elections for People's Congresses were also completed for one-fifth of the population.[27]

On January 1, 1954, plans for heavy industry and railway construction were announced along with proposed increments in agricultural cooperatives from 15,000 to 35,000. The same month, the cadres were given a 40-weeks-a-year plan to improve their education. It was felt necessary that the less educated cadres should be given at least a senior primary or junior middle school education. Some were to receive higher education also.

On June 11, 1954, the New China News Agency (NCNA) stated

161

that there were 91,000 agricultural producer cooperatives in the PRC. (By September 30, 1958, NCNA announced again that 90.4 per cent of peasant households had joined the communes.) On July 13, 1954, the *People's Daily* reported that the All-China Federation of Cooperatives was to organize 5 million handicraft workers into cooperatives by 1957; the remaining millions would follow suit in the Second Five-Year Plan.

We have reviewed in detail the agricultural, handicraft, and industrial policies of the early years of the formation of the People's Republic of China in order to gauge the momentum of its race toward modernization. From the beginning of his tenure as Chairman of the Party to his death in 1976, Mao Tse-tung had two goals: one to set up a revolutionary socialist society, and the other, to keep the masses and the Communist Party together. In his own words: 'We must have faith in the masses and we must have faith in the party. These are two cardinal principles. If we doubt these principles, we shall accomplish nothing.'[28]

The events of 1958 called the 'Great Leap Forward,' and the events of the years 1966-70, which were started officially by Chou En-lai in a Peking rally on May 1, 1966, when he said that this was the beginning of the 'Great Proletarian Cultural Revolution,' should be considered in the light of the above two principles. No doubt, during these years, there were strikes, leading to break-downs in production, purges, rallies, and all around insecurity for men in power. But too much has been made about the political upheaval and little attention has been paid to the compulsion of an agricultural economy of the order of China trying to move into the modern age and abolish elitism at the same time.

The emphases on socio-economic change and class abolition are primary in these two movements. As early as 1954, the governmental provisioning system was replaced with a salary system 'in order to unify the wage system of workers in state organs.' Also, it was necessary to regulate the grain supply in urban and rural areas, leading to a nationwide rationing system. Not only were the governmental workers brought in line to give up their privilege, but in 1957, pork supply (a valued item in Chinese food) was made the same for cadres as for citizens.

The political education of the intelligentsia was necessary. In 1957, the State Council issued a directive that graduates of higher education should be screened for political reliability if they wanted to teach or to go on to graduate studies. They were also to be tempered by the experience of physical labor for some time in farm and factory before taking up their new posts. A policy of decentralization of enterprises was promulgated, giving increasing power to local authorities.

162

In September 1956, Mao Tse-tung was reconfirmed as Chairman of the Party in the Eighth National Congress (its first meeting since 1945), and in November he issued firm strictures on many points. He urged people to follow simple industrious living, to combat subjectivitism, sectarianism, and bureaucracy, and to oppose Han chauvinism regarding national minorities and 'great-nation' chauvinism in matters of international affairs.

The 'Great Leap Forward' did not succeed, perhaps because the time was not ripe, or perhaps because the leaders were in too much of a hurry. The shortfalls in agricultural production became a great handicap. The smelting of iron in backyard furnaces in order to improve steel production was discontinued in August 1959. It should be noted that the basic material from which agricultural implements have been made in China for the past 2,000 years has been iron. Although few localities mine iron, smelting by smiths in small villages has been a common practice in the past.[29] Thus this experiment was not as foolish as one might think. It had to be abandoned for reasons of efficiency.

In 1966, the Cultural Revolution was promulgated with the basic intention of uprooting the seeds of class formation in China. A rally in Shanghai on February 24, 1967, affirmed Mao's 'Three-in-one Combination,' which stated that revolutionary masses, revolutionary leading cadres, and the People's Liberation Army were the agents of change.[30] This faith in revolutionary change was symptomatic of what was happening during the entire period. The fates of leading personalities like Liu Shao-ch'i and Lin Piao are secondary to the drama of socialist reconstruction.

The 'intellectuals' in the universities were to be subjected to the demands of socialism as much as the cadres. *The New York Times* reported on October 13, 1968, that in Shanghai government officers had sent '40 per cent of the cadres to do manual work.'[31] Chiang Ching, the wife of Mao Tse-tung, who, since Mao's death, lives in disgrace as a member of 'the gang of four,' was praised on October 16, 1969, for her 'model revolutionary plays.'[32]

In 1970, the Cultural Revolution was officially brought to an end. By August 1971, full control had been established over twenty-five of the twenty-nine provinces of the PRC with the help of the army. Schools and colleges started functioning on all levels and weaknesses in the curriculum were remedied. Science, mathematics, and languages began to receive primary attention.

In 1971, salaries for a peasant on a commune began at 24.5 yuan (or $10) per month, those of a young army general or experienced technician were $100 per month. Rents for one- or two-room apartments were $1 to $3 per month. Vegetables sold from 1.5 to 2 cents per lb., rice 7 cents per lb., meat was 20 to 40 cents per lb., eggs 30 cents per dozen and milk 10 cents per quart. Each person had 6 yards of cloth per year. City workers spent one-third of their income on food. The ubiquitous bicycle cost 35 to 45 dollars.[33] Some workers were permitted to own small plots of land and even sell their produce in a limited free market.

The isolation of China from the mainstream of world traffic ended with the visit of the American President, Richard M. Nixon, in 1972. Since then, China has almost been an open book. So we will not comment on political happenings any more. Instead, we will concentrate on developments in its social institutions.

The Chinese family today does not suffer any more from the abuses of the past. On April 30, 1950, the Marriage Law was passed, which banned arranged and child marriage, sale of children, concubinage, polygamy, discrimination against illegitimacy, and interference with the rights of a widow to remarry. These measures are strictly enforced. Now, women have equal rights with men in work, equal status at home and outside, equality in holding property and in the matter of divorce. They also have the right to retain their maiden names. The 'bare-foot doctors' have improved health care in the rural areas and rural sanitary conditions are far superior to any found in the developing or even some of the developed countries of the world. The Party preaches atheism but devoutly religious persons of any faith are permitted to carry on their worship as they please.

The People's Republic of China is not yet a modern country in terms of economic and demographic variables, but it is certainly a fast developing country. It is perhaps the only country which has equalized living conditions in the urban and rural areas. As with other socialist countries, it permits only one party, but its policies of decentralization and political education and discussion in the communes go a long way in meeting popular wishes. The Party no doubt sets the pace though. In 1961, on the fortieth anniversary of the Communist Party of China, the party membership was 17 million. Eighty per cent of members had joined the party since the founding of the People's Republic of China in 1949.

It is clear that the power struggles within the leadership in Communist China have not come to an end. One should remember that the People's Republic of China has existed for only thirty years compared to the Soviet Union's existence of sixty years. The present struggle highlighted in the newspapers in November 1978, may ease out either Hua Kuo-feng, the Chairman and Prime Minister, or Teng Hsiao-ping, the Deputy Prime Minister, from their offices, or it may be merely a realignment of forces, but it will not subvert the socialist system. The People's Republic of China has gone too far to turn away from socialism. The call for modernization chanted by Teng is crucial though. But it is no different than the directive on 'walking on two legs' given to the PRC as reported in *Hung Chi* on June 8, 1970:[34]

> the simultaneous development of industry and agriculture and that of heavy and light industry, with priority given to the development of heavy industry; simultaneous development of industries run by central authorities and of local industries; simultaneous development of large, medium, and small industries and the simultaneous application of foreign and indigenous methods of production under centralized leadership.

As Mao Tse-tung, the father of the People's Republic of China, said at one time, 'We stand for self-reliance. We hope for foreign aid but cannot be dependent on it.'[35] The new Chinese leaders would not be able to supplant the wisdom of Mao Tse-tung's faith in the people and the people's determination to win out against all odds. There may be hard times ahead for the People's Republic of China, but it is poised for great leaps in modernization.

Japan

Japan is a maritime nation, whose main strength lies in its entrepreneurship and its ancient cultural values. In 1978, its population was 114.4 million, concentrated within only 372,000 square kilometers of land. It is the seventh most populous country in the world; the other six countries having more population are the four countries whose profiles we are presenting here and Indonesia and Brazil. Japan's birth-rate was 16 per thousand and death-rate 6 per thousand. At the current rate of natural increase of 1 per cent per year, it will add 12 million more people to the labor force by the year 2000. Its infant mortality rate was 9 per thousand live births, which was not only the lowest of the countries we are discussing here, but the lowest in the world except Iceland. Its life expectancy was 74 years.

Seventy-six per cent of the Japanese lived in cities. Its rate of literacy was 95 per cent. Twenty-four per cent of the Japanese population were below 15 years of age and 8 per cent above 64 years. The per capita GNP income of Japan was $4,910. By all accounts, Japan is a modern country.

The modernization of Japan has taken place in an evolutionary way; its accomplishment is unique outside the orbit of the Western industrial nations. How was it achieved? The forces of development gained momentum in the second half of the Tokugawa period, which lasted from 1603 to 1868. During this period, there was honest and efficient administration in many provinces. Capital formation was easy because merchant families were permitted to acquire fortunes and pass them on to their heirs, unlike the *samurai* class which had to spend all its acquired wealth. By 1868, the population was still about 80 per cent rural. However, male literacy was 40 to 50 per cent,[36] and even rural literacy was 25 per cent.[37] A survey of cultivated land had already been carried out by Japan in 1876; agricultural inputs and methods had increased production in the last years of the Tokugawa period.

With the Meiji Restoration, the oligarchs came to power and they ousted the Shogunate and other feudal lords. The new men of power introduced land reforms and elevated the merchant class to higher levels of economic, but not political, power. However, agriculture did not receive the same attention as commerce and industry. The extension of the commercial, industrial, and military activities of Japan continued through the annexation of Taiwan in 1895 and Korea (which became a protectorate in 1905) in 1910. The Russo-Japanese War of 1904-5 and the invasion of China in 1937, were other landmarks in Japan's military pursuits, which ended with its defeat in the Second World War in 1946.

The occupation government under General Douglas MacArthur gave Japan a new constitution, under which the elected Diet and Cabinet were made supreme, a new Bill of Rights was enforced, labor unions were encouraged and land reforms were carried out. The curricular content of public schools was made democratic and the universities were expanded. Special rights were given to women: for instance, to inherit property and join coeducational schools. Both a free press and political parties were encouraged. Shintoism was disestablished as a state religion and the divinity as well as the power of the Emperor was curtailed.

It is true that in 1946, Japan was a beaten nation, floundering in rags. But the country pulled itself up by its bootstraps, so to say. Once the Allies were convinced that the war-making power of Japan was done away with, the power of the zaibatsu (financial oligarchy) came back quickly into its own despite the 'zaibatsu-busting' policy of the occupation regime. Political leadership passed into conservative hands, so that even a former war criminal could become Prime Minister.

The skills, which industrial labor gained during the ascendency of the military in the Meiji period, were quickly used for a different national purpose. It should be noted, however, that Japan's industrialization was well on its way during the inter-war years. A 'dual' economy had developed whereby agricultural and traditional industries were revived along old lines of small-scale labor-intensive methods. On the other hand, a modern sector was developed using all the knowledge of scientific techniques of production and organization.[38] Although this general practice was adopted throughout the Meiji period, it gained new momentum in the 1970s. For instance, the 'sunset' industries, such as cotton textiles and soap, receive little attention from the planners today; instead, the 'sunrise' industries receive premium help and protection. Such industries are computers, aircraft, electronic goods, housing, nuclear power, and oceanography. Needless to say, the Japanese production of cars, trucks, color television sets, and synthetic rubber and chemicals have flooded the international market recently.

What lies behind this drive for world leadership in industrial production? A combination of factors: first, the various conservative governments that have been in power since 1948 (with one brief exception); second, the 'administrative guidance' of business by government; and, finally, the will and the discipline of the Japanese people themselves.

However, the explosive growth in the Japanese economy does not match its pace of modernization in other areas. It is estimated that almost 95 per cent of Japan's leaders in government, business, industry, and banking come from only six leading universities. Many cases of suicide are reported among people who fail to gain admission into Toyko University. In the major industrial establishments, there is a patrimonial system by which employees are not dismissed in the lean season, often referred to as 'paternalism-life time commitment,' and in return they agree not to seek another job in a competitive firm.[39] The obedience to authority and seniority in Japan is more like that in a traditional than a modern society. Because of increased incomes, the Japanese are no doubt spending more now on travel and recreation. But they suffer from substandard housing, inadequate sewage disposal, and bad roads.

The family is as strong as ever, although Japan may be moving away from the 'stem' family system of the past to the nuclear family system. Often the parents of the wife rather than the husband reside in a wage-earner's house. The obligations of *on* and *giri*, which Ruth Benedict talked about in her famous book, *The Chrysanthemum and the Sword*,[40] have no doubt gone through some change but the debt to the nation and the parents continues.

The Japanese feel that they work for a 'national family' or the 'Rising Sun family,' as it used to be called. The 'team spirit' in the factories and the firms is quite strong. In fact, Chie Nakane, in her book, *Japanese Society*,[41] claims that the Japanese, besides being guided by the 'attributes' of ascribed and achieved status, are chiefly governed by a 'frame,' which is 'a particular relationship which binds a set of individuals into one group.' This 'frame' may

167

account for the 'team spirit.' James G. Abegglen calls it 'a rephrasing' of feudal loyalties, commitments, rewards, and methods of leadership in the setting of modern industry.[42]

Opinion is divided today on whether Japan has changed its traditional values of hierarchy, loyalty to authority, and attitude of isolation from the world. The method of Japanese modernization suggests that old leaders and old values are still in the saddle. The capitalist class is riding the waves with the help of the government and the conservative leaning of the parties in power. Authoritarianism rather than individualism guides the organizational and behavioral standards of the Japanese society. Whether this will eventually succumb to more democratic and competitive values as in other capitalist countries is hard to say.

There are strong socialist parties in Japan and a stronger socialist following in the labor unions. But this socialism is not enough to move the Japanese polity in the direction of even experimenting with a mixed economy. So long as Japan is not subjected to any international barriers of trade and traffic, it will keep prospering. But ultimately an island nation, short of natural resources, must contend with the problem of self-sufficiency and the removal of 'dualism' in its industrial policy.

Eventually, the Japanese people will demand more equalitarian standards and better living conditions from their government and employers. More than 50 per cent of Japanese women are employed now in non-domestic work. The real test of Japanese modernization will come, however, when increasing incomes[43] will make the workers seek expanding facilities for education and greater social mobility in the class hierarchy. The present elitism in governmental and business bureaucracies will have to give in as universities turn out graduates and political parties put up candidates who are not satisfied with the status quo. Japan's ability to handle that situation will determine whether modernization has pierced its classical veil and influenced the roots of its ancient culture.

India

India is the only country in our sample which has a 'mixed economy' based on the so-called 'socialistic pattern of society.' In 1978, India's population was 634.7 million, second only to that of the People's Republic of China in the world. Its birth-rate was 34 per thousand and its death-rate 14 per thousand. Its infant mortality rate was 129 per 1,000 live births. Such birth-rates, death-rates and infant mortality rates put India clearly in the category of non-developed countries; these rates are higher than those of the other four countries discussed earlier. Forty per cent of India's population were below 15 years of age and only 3 per cent above 64 years. At the current rate of natural increase of 2 per cent per year, India will add 155.6 million more people to its labor force by the year 2000. Life expectancy in India was 49 years and its rate of literacy 34 per cent, which was higher than the People's Republic of China's rate of literacy of 25 per cent. Twenty-one per cent of India's population lived in cities as compared to 24 per cent in the People's Republic of China. India's per capita GNP income was $150, which put it squarely in the category of low-income countries. India was not a modern country yet, although it had made important advances since its independence from the British in 1947.

Let us look closely at Indian conditions. If one wants to be optimistic, one could say that India has maintained successfully a parliamentary form of government where the leadership has been elected by ballot (based on adult suffrage) in six general elections since 1952. It has promulgated six Five-Year and three One-Year National Plans since 1951. Its general growth-rate since 1950 has been 3.5 per cent per year. It has doubled food production from 55 million tons in 1950 to 120 million tons in late 1970s. It increased its irrigated lands from 28 million acres in 1950 to 85 million acres in 1970.[44]

India gained in literacy from 17 per cent in 1951 to 34 per cent in 1978. Primary education is now free in India and compulsory in most of the states. In 1900, there were 16,000 college students; today, there are 3 million college students studying in 100 universities and 4,500 colleges. India's manpower engaged in scientific research and development was third in the world in middle 1970s. India has carried out an atomic explosion and sent its own satellite into space. It is considered the tenth ranking country in the world in terms of industrial output. However, it is not an industrial country as yet.

The problem of India lies with its primarily massive population base and its rate of increase in the recent past. Although India was one of the first countries in the world to start family planning in 1952, success has been limited. In family planning, the 1950s were the decade of pilot projects and the clinical approach (giving family planning advice to those seeking it); the 1960s became associated with community extension, i.e. providing information to communities, educating people, and seeking group support. In 1965, a major push was made in favor of Lippes Loop and other intrauterine devices (IUD's). Also services were provided through auxiliary nurse-midwives, health assistants, and multipurpose workers.

By 1975, 16 per cent of 102 million married couples in the reproductive age group (15 to 44 years) were protected by contraceptives.[45] Today, the 'cafeteria approach,' started in 1965, prevails. People shop for their own method, whether it is condom, diaphragm, jelly, or foam tablets, all available at the Public Health Center (PHC). There were 5,288 such centers in 1974. In addition, the pill has been in use since 1967, and the government has distributed condoms (*nirodh*) at cost in all states. The government was spending Rupees 1 billion per year ($1 = Rupees 8 approximately) on family planning in 1976.

The results of family planning have not been appreciable because India started with a base population of 361 million in 1951 and cut its death-rate quickly because of health measures and hygienic protection. Birth-rates take much longer to control unless massive abortions are used, as they were in Japan after the Second World War. State-backed abortion in India is a recent development.

India's rural population of 79 per cent live in over 567,000 villages. Seventy per cent of the population engage in agriculture. Although India started a community development scheme in the early 1950s and introduced the Panchayati Raj (Local Self Government) in 1959, the power of the village *panchayats* (assemblies) was limited. The governmental developmental schemes were no doubt carried out through them as well as through the Community Development Blocks, of which there were 4,894 in 1972. Despite these schemes, India remained a poor and populous country.

The feudal hold of the landholders was slackened by the abolition of the *zamindari* system (introduced by the British), when 20 million farmers received direct tenancy of the land. However, production was a different matter. Despite the ceilings on land (an individual family could own from 9.1 to 60 acres), production was controlled by the big landlords, who wanted to keep agricultural labor in bondage through usury, debts, and other methods of servitude.[46] There was still bonded labor in seventeen states in 1976.

In 1971, there were 5 million workers employed in factories, and, in 1972, a total of 6.9 million were registered as seeking employment. This was presumably the laboring class. The educated group was faring no better. In the middle of 1978, the government estimated that 700,000 college graduates were looking for work and their number was increasing by 150,000 a year.[47] India is, to all intents and purposes, a capitalist country, and cannot solve its problems of unemployment, food, health, and housing as can socialist countries like the People's Republic of China or the Soviet Union. K. N. Raj, the Indian economist, estimated that in 1976 about 10 million people were actively seeking work, as gleaned from the applicants on the live registers of the employment exchanges.[48] We suspect that about one-third may be at least high-school graduates, because the drop-out rate from colleges was about 1 million per year during this period. K. N. Raj also states that only the top 5 per cent of India's population could be categorized as 'middle class.'[49] To this, one needs to add the statistics that about 41 per cent of India's urban population and 48 per cent of its rural population are classified as below the poverty line (poverty being defined calorically in this case). The stark conditions of the Indian masses could not be depicted more sharply.

Looked at in another way, India is a solvent country. Its foreign exchange reserves, depleted earlier by costly oil imports, had gone up to $5 billion in 1978,[50] thanks to massive remittances from Indians living abroad to their families and relatives at home. India is able to acquire capital from abroad. In 1968, its loans stood at $1 billion; in 1978, they were $8.5 billion. Its pace of development can be seen from the fact that in 1978, one out of eight jobs was in the export sector, and one out of three acres of land was used for export produce. It was able to create food grain reserves to guard against famine and disasters. The Green Revolution had brought in increased yields in wheat and rice, but it had also created inequities along the way. For instance, in the state of Punjab, where the Green Revolution created massive yields, only 10 to 20 per cent of households reaped its benefits; there was a widening gap between the rich and the poor.[51]

The nationalization of insurance, banking, and wholesale trade in food grains has no doubt given the government leverage over some deployment of resources. But the control by the business class of the economy is substantial, and so is its influence on elections through campaign financing[52] and newspaper proprietorship. India has a free press like the United States and Japan, but like these two countries, the capitalist class has an uncanny hold on a vast sector of the press. In the case of India, the radio and television media are under the control of the government as in the Soviet Union and the People's Republic of China.

The Indian polity has recently extricated itself from drifting in the direction of dictatorship under Indira Gandhi's period of emergency, but the compulsion of poverty joined with the popular demand for higher levels of living may present important obstacles in the way of its future modernization. India considers itself as midway between the capitalist route and the socialist route to modernization. But, in our judgment, it is squarely in the camp of capitalism, so long as the capitalist class can keep its profits and maintain its hold on the press and the purse strings of the parties, as well as negotiate independent deals with multinational corporations.

India's pace of modernization will depend on the political will of its leaders and the strategies of its business class. Unlike Japan, India's political leadership is fragmented and its capitalist class shortsighted. Also, the Indian bureaucracy is trained in the British tradition of 'wait and see,' rather than the developmental leadership of the United States. Indian youth is restless but has no vision. The old guard holding political power today is more given to gamesmanship than to a vision of a new India. A second level of leadership is emerging, though more in politics and finance than in the bureaucracy or in the educational institutions. The latter is burdened with bureaucrats at present.

The future of India's modernization lies in the hands of the political, bureaucratic, business, and educational elites. If they work together with determination, they can pull the country out of its present morass. If not, then either military dictatorship or a socialist revolution may be in the offing. The challenges of massive population growth and growing unemployment leave very few alternatives for modernization in the contemporary world.

Concluding remarks

It may be helpful to highlight the main points we have emphasized in this essay. Modernization must take into account the economic, political, and demographic variables. It is a process of cultural change, which for the Third World has often implied Americanization, Europeanization, or Sovietization. Some authors emphasize total value change in terms of what obtains in these countries, others think of diffusion or selective borrowing, still others adhere to the idea of indigenous growth in any one of these directions. At the core of such a change is the concept of industrialism, which, with its accoutrements, is called modernization.

The process through which value change takes place has been referred to as comprising one or more of these phenomena: economic growth, political modernization, eclecticism, nativism. The interlocking relationships of economic growth and political modernization have been presented earlier in the case of five countries, viz. the United States, the Soviet Union, the People's Republic of China, Japan, and India. We noted that Japan and India have been eclectic in some respects, while advancing toward the goal of industrialization and institutional modernization. We have rejected the thesis that temporary stagnation of the economy, as in the early years in the Soviet Union or from 1958 to 1962 in the People's Republic of China, was an anti-modern process because the leadership was engaged in its own struggle on the political front. We also referred to the Sovietization of agriculture and production as well as the reshuffling of the elites in the two Soviet countries at various periods as helping the socialist model of modernization, which we articulated earlier.

We indicated the strengths and weaknesses of the socialist system as well as the capitalist system of modernization; they are both viable models for the Third World countries. What is important to keep in mind is the condition of man in these societies and the freedoms which he enjoys given the natural constraints of each system.

We ran into a problem about democracy. There is no agreed-upon meaning of this term.[53] However, we noted that if democracy implies popular input in major societal decisions and necessary safeguards against arbitrary decisions by the policy-makers, then both systems of modernization qualify as democracy. Some freedoms are more restricted in one system than another, but given the viability of each system, there are natural pressures in each to open the gates for free traffic in ideas and thought. It is the shortsightedness of leaders which occasionally puts barriers in the way of the fulfillment of human rights and basic freedoms.

Finally, we would like to close with a comparison of the five countries under review here by showing how they have performed on selected items of growth during the last decade-and-a-half. It will also give us an understanding of their modernization efforts.

TABLE 2 *Performance on Growth Indices*

		United States	Soviet Union	People's Republic of China	Japan	India
GNP per capita average annual growth (%)	1960-76	2.3	3.8	5.2	7.9	1.3
Index of per capita food production 1965-7 = 100	Av. 1974-6	114	113	108	107	107
Energy Average annual growth of production (%)	1960-75	2.9	5.7	4.6	-3.9	4.1
Per capita consumption (kilograms of coal equivalent)	1975	10,999	5,546	693	3,622	221

Source: World Development Report, 1978, Washington, D.C.: The World Bank, August, 1978.

It can be seen that in terms of GNP per capita growth-rate and providing food and energy production and consumption, none of the countries in our sample has stagnated in recent years. The rates of GNP per capita average annual growth for Japan and the People's Republic of China have been ahead of other countries, and India's has been the slowest. In food production, all the five countries are doing fairly well, with the United States doing better than the others, and the Soviet Union a close second to the United States.

In terms of energy production, the Soviet Union, the People's Republic of China, and India are far ahead. The United States has been rather slow despite its proved oil reserve of 29,500 million barrels.[54] Japan's energy production has actually decreased in the fifteen-year period under review. It should be noted though that Japan imports all its oil and has no known reserves. The per capita consumption of energy is highest in the United States, the Soviet Union and Japan, in that order, which speaks for the industrial development and urbanization of these countries. The People's Republic of China and India have low energy consumption. But both have great potential for increasing it, because the People's Republic of China has proved oil reserves of 20,000 million barrels and India has 3,000 million barrels. The Soviet Union also has a proved oil reserve of 75,000 million barrels, which is two and a half times as large as that of the United States.[55] There can be no doubt that all five countries can accelerate their pace of economic growth; only, in Japan's case, the price of energy has to be paid for by savings and/or exports.

Modernization is a challenge, which none of the five countries discussed above will fail to live up to. For the rest of the world, these countries are the landmarks, either as goals or as vantage comparison points. The debate on modernization must move forward from the hackneyed realm of ethno-centric values to the many demands and pressures of today. The future direction of modernization can be gauged from a realistic evaluation of the experience of these five countries. However, it bears repeating that, in the capitalist model, one starts with the assumption that inequalities in income will always exist, so that modernization can deal only with the specific problems of equity, justice, and freedom in advancing economic growth. In the socialist model, equalization of income takes precedence over the preservation of private property or advancement of economic growth. There, modernization works faster for the poor and the impoverished, but freedoms take longer to achieve. For the first time in history, the modernizing countries have a choice between these two viable models or any variant thereof.

Notes

1 General perspective

1 The concept of 'paradigm' has been used in a technical sense by Thomas S. Kuhn in his book, *The Structure of Scientific Revolutions,* University of Chicago Press, 1970 (2nd edition). However, the scientific paradigm he has in mind has about two dozen different referents. Robert K. Merton uses 'formal paradigms' to expose 'the array of assumptions, concepts and basic propositions employed in a sociological analysis.' See Robert K. Merton, *Social Theory and Social Structure,* Chicago: Free Press, 1957 (rev. edition), p. 13. The concept of 'model' has been elucidated by Baidya Nath Varma in 'The Role of Concepts and Models in Social Science,' in the book edited by him, *A New Survey of the Social Sciences,* New York: Asia Publishing House, 1962.

In the present book, we use the concept of paradigm in the sense of an analytical framework, and the concept of model as a more specialized schema within it. The weaknesses of social science models in approximating the criteria of natural sciences are well known. They have also been discussed in this book at several places.

2 William McCord, *The Springtime of Freedom: The Evolution of Developing Societies,* New York: Oxford University Press, 1965,

3 Simon Kuznets, among others, has claimed that in the last fifty years, the 'gap' between industrial and modernizing nations has increased both absolutely and in terms of per capita income. See Simon Kuznets, 'Quantitative Aspects of the Economic Growth of Nations,' in *Economic Development and Cultural Change,* vol. V, no. 1, October 1956, pp. 1-23.

4 The term 'behavioral science' was coined about 1949 by a group of scientists at the University of Chicago. It referred to the biological and social sciences. Later the Ford Foundation adopted and popularized this term among scholars. See James G. Miller, 'Toward a General Theory for the Behavioral Sciences', *American Psychologist,* September 1955, reprinted in Leonard D. White (ed.), *The State of the Social Sciences,* University of Chicago Press, 1956, and Ford Foundation Annual Reports.

5 We will use the terms 'modernity' and 'modernization' interchangeably in this book.

6 Horace M. Kallen, 'Modernism,' in Edwin R.A. Seligman (editor-in-chief), *Encyclopedia of the Social Sciences,* New York: Macmillan Company, 1937, p. 566.

7 *Ibid.*

8   Some denotations of 'rationality' in Max Weber's works are as follows: (a) rejection of non-utilitarian yardsticks, (b) belief in valid canon, (c) rejecting traditional bonds, (d) faith in *naturalis ratio,* (e) systematic arrangement, (f) formal method, (g) distinction between valid norms and empirical givens, (h) logical consistency, (i) historical development of a phenomenon, (j) teleological consistency, (k) this-worldly attitude, (l) a belief in man's prosperity and long life on earth, (m) rules of experience as the basis of guidance of action, (n) systematization, (o) systematic use of means, (p) lack of dependence on ecstatic experience, (q) sublimation of emotional drive, (r) casuistry: definitional as well as analytical, as in legal thought, (s) value-rationality, (t) purposive rationality, (u) normative control, (v) goal-directed action, (w) hierarchy of controls, and (x) motivational commitment.

    Among others, see the following English translations of Max Weber: *The Protestant Ethic and the Spirit of Capitalism,* New York: Charles Scribner's Sons, 1958; *From Max Weber: Essays in Sociology,* New York: Oxford University Press, 1946; *The Religion of China: Confucianism and Taoism,* Glencoe, Illinois: The Free Press, 1951; *The Religion of India: The Sociology of Hinduism and Buddhism,* Chicago: Free Press, 1958; and *Max Weber on Law in Economy and Society,* Cambridge, Mass.: Harvard University Press, 1954.

9   Baidya Nath Varma has made the distinction between 'means-end' schema which applies to technological efficiency and 'ritual-end' schema, which applies to value utilitarian efficiency. See his 'The Role of Concepts and Models in Social Sciences,' *op.cit.,* p. 175.

10   We are referring here to the ways in which values are combined. Tradition has as much logic as modernity, which is often forgotten by writers who espouse modernity.

11   Emile Durkheim, *The Division of Labor in Society,* Chicago: Free Press, 1933.

12   Emile Durkheim, *The Elementary Forms of the Religious Life,* New York: Collier Books, 1961.

13   Howard Becker, 'Current Sacred-Secular Theory and Its Development,' in Howard Becker and Alvin Boskoff (eds), *Modern Sociological Theory in Continuity and Change,* New York: Dryden Press, 1957, pp. 133-86.

14   Baidya Nath Varma, 'Hinduism and India's Development,' in Mario D. Zamora, J. Michael Mahar and Henry Orenstein (eds), *Theories in Culture,* Quezon City, Philippines: Kayumanggi Publishers, 1971, pp. 135-44. See, also in this context, the provocative work of Annemarie de Waal Malefijt, *Religion and Culture,* New York: Macmillan Company, 1968, chs 12 and 13.

15   Robert K. Merton, *Social Theory and Social Structure,* New York: Free Press, 1968, pp. 368-84.

16   Karen Horney, *The Neurotic Personality of Our Time,* New York: Norton, 1937.

17   Leon A. Festinger, *A Theory of Cognitive Dissonance,* Stanford University Press, 1957.

18   Baidya Nath Varma, 'Hinduism and India's Development,' *op.cit.*

19   Manning Nash, 'The Multiple Society in Economic Development: Mexico and Guatemala,' *American Anthropologist,* vol. 59, October 1957, pp. 825-33.

20   'Polyarchies are regimes that have been substantially popularized and liberalized, that is, highly inclusive [popular right to participate in elections and office] and extensively open to public contestation [of offices].' Robert A. Dahl, *Polyarchy: Participation and Opposition,* New Haven: Yale University Press, 1971, p. 8.

21   Feliks Gross, 'Ethnic Identity and Ethnic Politics,' a paper presented at the Columbia University Faculty Seminar on Cultural Pluralism, December 13, 1973 (mimeographed).

2 The paradigm and the problematics of modernization

1 Kroeber, A.L. and Clyde Kluckhohn, *Culture: A Critical Review of Concepts and Definitions,* New York: Vintage Books, 1963 [1952].
2 Heilbroner, Robert L., *The Great Ascent: The Struggle for Economic Development in Our Time,* New York: Harper & Row, 1963, pp. 20-22.
3 *Ibid,* p. 53.
4 Daniel Lerner, 'Modernization: Social Aspects' in David L. Sills (ed.), *International Encyclopedia of the Social Sciences,* New York: Crowell Collier & Macmillan, 1967.
5 *Ibid.*
6 Daniel Lerner, *The Passing of Traditional Society: Modernizing the Middle East,* Chicago: Free Press, 1958.
7 *Ibid.,* pp. 43-75.
8 *Ibid.,* p. 46.
9 *Ibid.,* p. 45.
10 Manning Nash, 'Social Pre-requisites to Economic Growth in Latin America and South East Asia,' in *Economic Development and Cultural Change,* vol. XIII, no. 3, April 1964, p. 226.
11 The issues of convergences and divergences (related to what I have called cultural monism and cultural relativism) of national cultural systems with the modern polity of the West came up frequently in the book review section of the *American Anthropologist* during the period April 1969 to June 1970, when the journal had a subsection titled 'modernization'. It has been widely discussed in the anthropological literature.
12 See National Resources Committee, 'The Process of Urbanization: Underlying Forces and Emerging Trends,' in Paul K. Hatt and Albert J. Reiss, Jr, *Cities and Society,* Chicago: Free Press, 1951, pp. 64-77.
13 A very provocative approach to some of the dilemmas of modern societies was formulated by Henry Pratt Fairchild in his book, *Versus: Reflections of a Sociologist,* New York: Philosophical Library, 1950. See also the excellent work of Robert S. Lynd, *Knowledge for What?,* Princeton University Press, 1948.
14 Daniel Lerner, *The Passing of Traditional Society: Modernizing the Middle East, op.cit.*
15 Among others, see Lloyd I. Rudolph and Susanne H. Rudolph, *The Modernity of Tradition: Political Development in India,* University of Chicago Press, 1967; Joseph R. Gusfield, 'Tradition and Modernity: Misplaced Polarities in the Study of Social Change,' *The American Journal of Sociology,* vol. 72, no. 4, January 1967, pp. 351-62; Albert O. Hirschman, *Development Projects Observed,* Washington, D.C.: Brookings Institution, 1967; and Albert O. Hirschman, *A Bias for Hope: Essays on Development and Latin America,* New Haven: Yale University Press, 1971.
16 See Baidya Nath Varma, 'Beyond Max Weber,' in *Indian Journal of Social Research,* vol. XI, no. 1, pp. 65-7.
17 The concept of 'marginal man' was developed by Robert E. Park in *Race and Culture,* Chicago: Free Press, 1950, pp. 345-92; see also E. V. Stonequist, *The Marginal Man: A Study in Personality and Culture Conflict,* New York: Scribner, 1937.
18 For a perspective on some of these issues, see Kenneth Keniston, *Youth and Dissent,* New York: Harcourt Brace, 1971, and Helen Scott Nearing, *Living the Good Life,* New York: Schoeken, 1971. Also George Fischer, *Ways to Self Rule: Beyond Marxism and Anarchism,* Hicksville, New York: Exposition Press, 1978.

3 The ideological theories of modernization

1 Max Weber, *The Protestant Ethic and the Spirit of Capitalism*, New York: Charles Scribner's Sons, 1958. The controversy on the topic has been adequately summed up in *The Protestant Ethic and Modernization: A Comparative View*, S.N. Eisenstadt (ed.), New York: Basic Books, 1968.

2 Reinhard Bendix, *Nation-Building and Citizenship: Studies of Our Changing Social Order*, New York: John Wiley 1964, p. 2.

3 *Ibid.*, pp. 2-4.

4 David Riesman, *et al.*, *The Lonely Crowd*, New York: Doubleday, 1955, ch. 5.

5 Neil J. Smelser and Seymour Martin Lipset, 'Social Structure, Mobility and Development,' in *Social Structure and Mobility in Economic Development*, Chicago: Aldine, 1966, pp. 42-5.

6 See, in this context, Friedrich Engels's 'Manifesto of the Communist Party: Preface to the English Edition of 1888,' in Marx, Engels, Lenin, *The Essential Left*, London: George Allen & Unwin, pp. 9-13.

7 V. I. Lenin, 'What is to be Done?: Burning Questions of Our Movement,' and 'State and Revolution,' in James E. Connor (ed.), *Lenin on Politics and Revolution*, New York: Pegasus, 1968.

8 See, among others, the classic work of Alexis de Tocqueville, *Democracy in America*, 2 vols, New York: Alfred A. Knopf, 1945.

9 The role of the Castro regime in Cuba has been assessed in many different ways. Barbara Ward feels that Cuba was relatively advanced in many respects before Castro came to power. See Barbara Ward, *The Rich Nations and the Poor Nations*, New York: W.W. Norton, 1962, p. 132. However, Kalman H. Silvert, a careful student of Latin American politics says that

> many bits of evidence suggest that Castro's Cuba is functioning in certain respects like a modern nation-state ... The military as well as political confidence vested until very recently in the Cuban militia, and even the present process of military professionalization, all smack of modern ways of weaving the military into the social fabric. The power of the government to withstand blockade, cultural and political isolation, the work of exiles in sabotage and attempted invasion, drought, hurricane, and massive technical inefficacy coupled with uninformed political experimentation implies a strength which can only be based in important measure on a high degree of consensus from certain groups and a special kind of opposition from others.

See Kalman H. Silvert, *The Conflict Society: Reaction and Revolution in Latin America*, New York: American Universities Field Staff, 1966, p. 234. Silvert's analysis seems realistic and is borne out by the later progress of Cuba. Claude Regin, in filing 'A Report on Castro's Island, Fifteen Years Later,' says, 'Many independent observers agree that despite 15 years of shortages and rationing, a majority of Cubans would vote for him if he were to stand in a free and democratic election.' in *The New York Times*, January 27, 1974.

10 Karl Marx and Friedrich Engels stipulate ten important measures which must be taken in the most advanced countries in 'Manifesto of the Communist Party,' reprinted in Marx, Engels, Lenin, *The Essential Left*, *op.cit.*, p. 35.

11 Claude Regin, 'A Report on Castro's Island, Fifteen Years Later,' *op.cit.*

12 Gómez Millas's presentation as quoted in K. H. Silvert (ed.), *Discussion at Bellagio*, New York: American Universities Field Staff, 1964, pp. 34-7.

13 Sylvia G. Haim (ed.), *Arab Nationalism: An Anthology*, Berkeley: University of California Press, 1962. See also, Manfred Halpern, *The Politics of Social Change in the Middle East and North Africa*, Princeton University Press, 1963,

and Gabriel Baer, *Studies in the Social History of Modern Egypt,* University of Chicago Press, 1969.

14 Gustave E. von Grunebaum (ed.), *Unity and Variety in Muslim Civilization,* University of Chicago Press, 1955, p. 12ff; see also Gustave E. von Grunebaum, 'Problems of Muslim Nationalism,' in R.N. Frye (ed.), *Islam and the West,* The Hague: Mouton, 1959.

15 Rupert Emerson, *From Empire to Nation,* Boston: Beacon Press, 1962, ch. X.

16 Julius K. Nyerere, 'Ujamaa,' in William H. Friedland and Carl G. Rosberg, Jr. (eds), *African Socialism,* Stanford University Press, 1964.

17 *Ibid.*

18 'Decade of Independence: Black Africa Finds Slow Going Trying to Make It Alone,' in *U.S. News & World Report,* December 31, 1973.

19 Tom Mboya, *Freedom and After,* Boston: Little, Brown, 1963, as quoted in K.H. Silvert, *Discussion at Bellagio, op.cit.,* p. 159.

20 Margaret W. Fisher and Joan V. Bondurant, *Indian Approaches to a Socialist Society,* Berkeley: University of California, Indian Press Digests-Monograph Series, No. 2, July 1956, pp. 35-105.

21 *Ibid.,* p. 40.

22 Jayaprakash Narayan, 'The Nature of the Revolutionary Situation around the World,' an address delivered to the national conference, 'The United States in a Revolutionary World,' at Princeton University, April 1968 (mimeographed), p. 5. A later source indicates that by 'May 1969 the number of Gramdan villages rose to over 100,000, that is one-fifth of all India's villages have opted for Gramdan.' See Erica Linton, *Gramdan—Revolution by Persuasion,* Nonviolence in Action Series, London: Friends Peace and International Relations Committee p. 8, n.d.

23 Erica Linton, *Gramdan–Revolution by Persuasion, ibid.,* p. 1.

24 See, in this connection, Robert Nisbet, *Social Change and History: Aspects of the Western Theory of Development,* New York: Oxford University Press, 1969, ch. 6.

25 Karl Marx and Friedrich Engels, 'Manifesto of the Communist Party,' *op.cit.,* p. 47.

26 W. W. Rostow, *The Stages of Economic Growth: A Non-Communist Manifesto,* Cambridge University Press, 1960.

27 Robert Nisbet, 'Ethnocentrism and the Comparative Method,' in A. R. Desai (ed.), *Essays on Modernization of Underdeveloped Countries,* 2 vols, New York: Humanities Press, 1972, pp. 95-114.

28 Satish K. Arora, 'Political Development: Policy Constraints and Value Preferences,' in A. R. Desai (ed.), *Essays on Modernization of Underdeveloped Countries, op.cit.;* several other essays in this volume repeat the same theme with somewhat similar arguments. See also A. R. Desai, *Recent Trends in Indian Nationalism,* Bombay: Popular Book Depot, 1960. This argument has been joined by others, such as Yogendra Singh, 'Traditional Culture Pattern of India and Industrial Change,' in A. B. Shah and C. R. M. Rao (eds), *Tradition and Modernity in India,* Bombay: Monaktalas, 1965, pp. 47-69; R.N. Saksena, 'Modernization and Development Trends in India,' *Sociological Bulletin* (Journal of the Indian Sociological Society), vol. 21, no. 2, September 1972, pp. 91-102; Ramkrishna Mukherjee, 'Indian Sociology: Historical Development and Present Problems,' *Sociological Bulletin,* vol. 22, no. 1, March 1973, pp. 29-58. M. N. Srinivas has developed his thought in a series of essays in M. N. Srinivas, *Social Change in Modern India,* Berkeley: University of California Press, 1966.

4 On the theory and the methodology of modernization studies

1 Max Weber, *The Methodology of the Social Sciences,* Chicago: Free Press, 1949, pp. 89-92.

2 Daya Krishna, 'Some Reflections on the Concept of Political Development as Represented in the Writings of Some American Political Scientists of the Sixties,' East-West Center, University of Hawaii (mimeographed).
3 Talcott Parsons and Edward A. Shils, 'Values, Motives, and Systems of Action,' in Talcott Parsons and Edward A. Shils (eds), *Toward A General Theory of Action*, Cambridge, Mass.: Harvard University Press, 1951, pp. 76-9.
4 Gabriel A. Almond, 'Introduction: A Functional Approach to Comparative Politics,' in Gabriel A. Almond and James S. Coleman (eds), *The Politics of the Developing Areas*, Princeton University Press, 1960, pp. 3-64.
5 *Ibid.*
6 David Easton, *The Political System*, New York: Alfred A. Knopf, 1953.
7 Karl W. Deutsch, *Nationalism and Social Communication*, Cambridge, Mass., MIT Press, 1966.
8 Hans L. Zetterberg, *On Theory and Verification in Sociology*, Totowa, New Jersey: Bedminster Press, 1963.
9 *Ibid.*, ch. 1.
10 Paul A. Baran, *The Political Economy of Growth*, New York: Modern Reader Paperbacks, 1968; also see, George Novack. *Democracy and Revolution*, New York: Pathfinder Press, 1971.
11 Hans L. Zetterberg, *On Theory and Verification in Sociology, op.cit.*, p. 17.
12 K.H. Silvert, (ed.) *Expectant Peoples: Nationalism and Development*, New York: Random House, Vintage Books, 1963.
13 Lucien W. Pye, *Politics, Personality, and Nation Building: Burma's Search for Identity*, New Haven: Yale University Press, 1962.
14 S. N. Eisenstadt, *Modernization: Protest and Change*, Englewood Cliffs: Prentice-Hall, 1966.
15 Fred W. Riggs, ' "Agraria and Industria": Toward a Typology of Comparative Administration,' in William J. Siffin (ed.), *Toward the Comparative Study of Public Administration*, Bloomington: Indiana University Press, 1959.

5 The sociological theories of modernization

1 Auguste Comte, *The Positive Philosophy*, freely translated and condensed by Harriet Martineau, London: George Bell, 1896.
2 Herbert Spencer, *The Principles of Sociology*, New York: D. Appleton, 1898.
3 Ferdinand Tönnies, *Community and Society (Gemeinschaft und Gesellschaft)*, translated by Charles P. Loomis, East Lansing: Michigan State University Press, 1957.
4 Sir Henry Sumner Maine, *Ancient Law*, New York: Henry Holt, 1885.
5 Howard Becker, 'Current Sacred-Secular Theory and Its Development,' in Howard Becker and Alvin Boskoff (eds), *Modern Sociological Theory in Continuity and Change*, New York: Dryden Press, 1957, pp. 133-85.
6 Robert Redfield, 'The Folk Society,' *The American Journal of Sociology*, vol. 52, January 1947.
7 An excellent exposition is available in Maurice Dobb, *Economic Growth and Underdeveloped Countries*, New York: International Publishers, 1963.
8 For a succinct discussion of Weber's views, see Talcott Parsons, *The System of Modern Societies*, Englewood Cliffs: Prentice-Hall, 1971, p. 2ff.
9 S. N. Eisenstadt (ed.), *The Protestant Ethic and Modernization: A Comparative View*, New York: Basic Books, 1968.
10 Talcott Parsons, *The Structure of Social Action*, 2 vols, New York: Free Press, 1968 [1937]. Parsons said, 'Spencer is dead. But who killed him and how?'
11 Talcott Parsons, *Societies: Evolutionary and Comparative Perspectives*, Englewood Cliffs: Prentice-Hall, 1966, p. 2.

12 *Ibid.*, p. 26.
13 Talcott Parsons, *Structure and Process in Modern Societies,* Chicago: Free Press, 1960, p. 103.
14 *Ibid.*, p. 162; see also Talcott Parsons, *The System of Modern Societies,* Englewood Cliffs: Prentice-Hall, 1971, pp. 114-15.
15 *Ibid.*, pp. 94-8.
16 Talcott Parsons and Edward A. Shils, 'Values, Motives, and Systems of Action,' in Talcott Parsons and Edward A. Shils (eds), *Toward a General Theory of Action,* Cambrige, Mass.: Harvard University Press, 1951, pp. 76-88. Parsons first identified the pattern variable 'Achievement-Ascription,' which was later changed to 'Performance-Quality.' See Talcott Parsons, 'Pattern Variables Revisited,' *American Sociological Review,* vol. 25, no. 4, August 1960, pp. 467-83.
17 Talcott Parsons, *Societies: Evolutionary and Comparative Perspectives, op.cit.,* pp. 18-21.
18 Talcott Parsons, 'Pattern Variables Revisited,' *American Sociological Review, op.cit.*
19 Talcott Parsons, *Societies: Evolutionary and Comparative Perspectives, op.cit.,* pp. 22-7.
20 Marion J. Levy, Jr, *Modernization and the Structure of Societies: A Setting for International Relations,* Princeton University Press, 1966, pp. 9-15.
21 *Ibid.*, p. 56.
22 *Ibid.*, p. 17.
23 Amitai Etzioni, *The Active Society: A Theory of Societal and Political Process,* New York: Free Press, 1971 [1968], p. 74.
24 *Ibid.*, p. 225.
25 *Ibid.*, p. 430.
26 David Easton, *Varieties of Political Theory,* Englewood Cliffs: Prentice-Hall, 1966, p. 152.
27 Amitai Etzioni, *The Active Society, op.cit.,* p. vii.
28 Talcott Parsons, *The System of Modern Societies, op.cit.,* p. 143.
29 Daniel Bell, *The Coming of Post-Industrial Society: A Venture in Social Forecasting,* New York: Basic Books, 1973, p. 52.
30 *Ibid.*, pp. 424-33.
31 Talcott Parsons, *The System of Modern Societies, op.cit.,* pp. 114-16.
32 Daniel Bell, *The Coming of Post-Industrial Society, op.cit.,* p. 433.
33 Herbert Gans, *More Equality,* New York: Pantheon Books, 1974.
34 S..M. Miller and Pamela Roby, *The Future of Inequality,* New York: Basic Books, 1970.
35 Arthur B. Shostak, *et al., Privilege in America: An End to Inequality?* Englewood Cliffs: Prentice-Hall, 1973. This book contains a competent recent annotated bibliography.
36 Among his other works, see Seymour Martin Lipset, *The First New Nation: The United States in Historical and Comparative Perspective,* Garden City, New York: Doubleday, 1967 [1963]; *Political Man and the Social Bases of Politics,* Garden City, New York: Doubleday, 1960; *Revolution and Counterrevolution: Change and Persistence in Social Structures,* Garden City, New York: Doubleday, 1970, (rev. edition [1963, 1968]).
37 Seymour Martin Lipset, *The First New Nation, op. cit.*
38 Talcott Parsons, 'Social Structure and Political Orientation,' *World Politics,* vol. 13, October 1960, p. 114.
39 Seymour Martin Lipset, *Political Man, op.cit.,* ch. 1, and Seymour Martin Lipset, *The First New Nation, op.cit.,* part III.
40 Seymour Martin Lipset, *Political Man, op.cit.,* p. 46.
41 Seymour Martin Lipset, *Revolution and Counterrevolution, op.cit.,* p. 265.

42 *Ibid.*, p. 243.
43 *Ibid.*, p. 232.
44 *Ibid.*, p. 237.
45 *Ibid.*, p. 24.
46 Joseph Bensman and Arthur J. Vidich, *The New American Society: The Revolution of the Middle Class*, Chicago: Quadrangle Books, 1971, pp. 23-5.
47 *Ibid.*, ch. 9.
48 *Ibid.*, p. 27.
49 *Ibid.*, pp. 264-5.
50 *Ibid.*, pp. 274-84.
51 *Ibid.*, p. 275.
52 Albert O. Hirschman, *A Bias for Hope: Essays on Development and Latin America*, New Haven: Yale University Press, 1971.

    The following remark of the Indian economist sums up the situation very well: 'The style that is most likely to suit the decade of the seventies is not one of intervention or even involvement but of duty done without too much fuss or subsequent bother. . . . The poorer countries are in a mood to call it a day if aid gives the slightest suspicion of intervention.'

    See I. G. Patel, 'Aid Relations for the Seventies,' in Barbara Ward *et al.*, (eds), *The Widening Gap*, New York: Columbia University Press, 1971, pp. 307-8.
53 José Ortega y Gasset, *The Revolt of the Masses*, New York: W. W. Norton, 1932, p. 11.
54 Bernard Rosenberg, 'Mass Culture in America,' in Bernard Rosenberg and David Manning White (eds), *Mass Culture: The Popular Arts in America*, Chicago: Free Press, 1957, p. 4.
55 *Ibid.*
56 *Ibid.*, p. 5.
57 *Ibid.*
58 Leo Marx, 'Notes on the Culture of the New Capitalism,' *Monthly Review*, vol. II, nos 3 and 4, July-August 1959, p. iii.
59 Among others, an early statement was by Herbert Blumer, 'The Mass, the Public, and Public Opinion,' in Alfred McClung Lee (ed.), *New Outline of the Principles of Sociology*, New York: Barnes & Noble, 1946, pp. 185-93.
60 Harold L. Wilensky, 'Mass Society and Mass Culture: Interdependence or Independence?' *American Sociological Review*, vol. 29, no. 2, April 1964, pp. 173-97.
61 William Kornhauser, *The Politics of Mass Society*, Chicago: Free Press, 1959, ch. 13; see also Paul F. Lazarsfeld and Robert K. Merton, 'Mass Communication, Popular Taste and Organized Social Action,' in Lyman Bryson (ed.), *The Communication of Ideas*, New York: Harper, 1948, pp. 95-118.
62 Bernard Berelson, 'The State of Communication Research,' *Public Opinion Quarterly*, vol. 23., no. 1, Spring 1959.
63 Lucien W. Pye (ed.), *Communications and Political Development*, Princeton University Press, 1963.
64 Lucien W. Pye, 'Introduction,' in *ibid.* p. 4.
65 *Ibid.*
66 Daniel Lerner, 'Toward A Communication Theory of Modernization: A Set of Considerations,' in Lucien W. Pye (ed.), *Communications and Political Development, op.cit.*, p. 348.
67 Robert K. Merton, 'Patterns of Influence: A Study of Interpersonal Influence and of Communications Behavior in a Local Community,' in Paul F. Lazarsfeld and Frank N. Stanton (eds), *Communications Research 1948-49*, New York: Harper, 1949, pp. 180-219.

68 Among others, the usefulness of the application of these concepts for ana-lysing social change in India was demonstrated by Baidya Nath Varma, 'General Comments Concerning Research on India,' in Baidya Nath Varma (ed.), *Contemporary India,* New York: Asia Publishing House, 1965, pp. 342-52.

69 S. N. Eisenstadt, *Modernization, Diversity, and Growth,* Bloomington: Indiana University, Department of Government, 1953; and S. N. Eisenstadt, *Modern-ization: Protest and Change,* Englewood Cliffs: Prentice-Hall, 1966. See also S. N. Eisenstadt, *Tradition, Change, and Modernity,* New York: John Wiley, 1973.

70 S.N. Eisenstadt, *Modernization: Protest and Change, op.cit.,* pp. 129-61.

71 *Ibid.,* p. 141.

72 Shanti Tangri, 'Urbanization, Political Stability, and Economic Growth,' in Roy Turner (ed.), *India's Urban Future,* Berkeley: University of California Press, 1962, pp. 192-212.

73 Neil J. Smelser, 'Mechanisms of Change and Adjustment to Change,' in Bert F. Hoselitz and Wilbert E. Moore (eds), *Industrialization and Society,* The Hague: UNESCO-Mouton, 1963, pp. 32-48.

74 *Ibid.,* p. 47.

75 *Ibid.* A more careful presentation of the relationship of education to economic growth is presented, however, by Neil J. Smelser and Seymour Martin Lipset, 'Social Structure, Mobility and Development,' in Neil J. Smelser and Seymour Martin Lipset (eds), *Social Structure and Mobility in Economic Development,* Chicago: Aldine, 1966, pp. 29-42.

76 Neil J. Smelser, 'Mechanisms of Change and Adjustment to Change,' in Bert F. Hoselitz and Wilbert E. Moore (eds), *Industrialization and Society, op.cit.,* p. 42.

77 Edward Shils, *The Intellectual and the Powers and Other Essays,* University of Chicago Press, 1972.

78 Edward Shils, *The Intellectual Between Tradition and Modernity: The Indian Situation,* The Hague: Mouton, 1961, p. 9.

79 *Ibid.*

80 Seymour Martin Lipset and Reinhard Bendix, *Social Mobility in Industrial Society,* Berkeley: University of California Press, 1960 [1959].

81 *Ibid.,* p. 25.

82 *Ibid.*

83 Arthur L. Stinchcombe provides a needed corrective to the Lipset and Bendix study: 'The exceedingly high rate of property mobility which characterized American rural social structures when the national ideology was being formed apparently escapes their attention.' *Vide* footnote 4 in Arthur L. Stinchcombe, 'Agricultural Enterprise and Rural Class Relations,' *The American Journal of Sociology,* vol. 67, September 1961, pp. 165-76.

84 Robert N. Bellah, 'Religious Evolution,' *American Sociological Review,* vol. 29, no. 3, June 1964, p. 374.

85 Talcott Parsons, *Societies: Evolutionary and Comparative Perspectives, op.cit.*

86 Robert N. Bellah, *Tokugawa Religion,* Chicago: Free Press, 1957.

87 See the commentaries (especially the differences in perspectives) by Denis Brogan, Leo Pfeffer, and John R. Whitney, on Robert N. Bellah, 'Civil Religion in America,' in Donald R. Cutler (ed.), *The Religious Situation: 1968,* Boston: Beacon Press, 1968, pp. 331-93.

88 William J. Goode, 'Industrialization and Family Change,' in Bert F. Hoselitz and Wilbert E. Moore (eds), *Industrialization and Society, op.cit.,* p. 238.

89 William J. Goode, *World Revolution and Family Patterns,* New York: Free Press, 1970 [1963], p. xiii.

90 *Ibid.,* pp. xvi-xvii.

91 *Ibid.*

92 William J. Goode, 'Industrialization and Family Change,' in Bert F. Hoselitz and Wilbert E. Moore (eds), *Industrialization and Society, op.cit.,* p. 251.

93 William Peterson, *Population,* New York: Macmillan Company, 1969, 2nd edition, ch. 1.

94 For a competent global report, see Bernard Berelson, *et al.* (eds), *Family Planning and Population Programs: A Review of World Developments,* University of Chicago Press, 1969 [1966].

95 *Ibid.,* part 5 (summary).

96 Kingsley Davis, 'Population Policy: Will Current Programs Succeed?' *Science,* no. 158, pp. 730-9; and Ronald Freedman (ed.), *Population: The Vital Revolution,* Garden City, New York: Doubleday, 1964.

6 The economic and political theories of modernization

1 Simon Kuznets, *Six Lectures on Economic Growth,* Chicago: Free Press, 1959, pp. 13-15.

2 William Petersen, *Population,* New York: Macmillan Company, 1969.

3 Paul A. Samuelson, *Economics,* New York: McGraw-Hill, 1973, 9th edition, p. 767.

4 We computed the data given in the 1973 World Population Data Sheet of the Population Reference Bureau, Inc., Washington, D.C., for the countries listed in Samuelson. Unfortunately, detailed data for some countries were not available there. So we settled on the data given by *U.S. News and World Report,* December 17, 1973, which is incorporated here. Our own data on limited countries are quite harmonious with the ones reported here.

5 Hans W. Singer, 'Social Development: Key Growth Sector, Philosophy, Plans, and First Results of the UN Research Institute,' *International Development Review,* vol. vii, no. 1, March 1965, pp. 3-8.

6 Walt W. Rostow, *The Stages of Economic Growth: A Non-Communist Manifesto,* Cambridge University Press, 1960, ch. 2.

7 Adolf A. Berle, tr., a review of W. W. Rostow, *The Stages of Economic Growth,* in *The Saturday Review,* vol. 43, part 2, July 9, 1960, pp. 18-19.

8 Simon Kuznets, 'Notes on the Take-Off,' paper presented at the International Economic Association's Conference at Konstanz in September 1960, on 'The Economics of Take-Off into Sustained Growth,' and reprinted in Paul A. Samuelson (ed.), *Readings in Economics,* New York: McGraw-Hill, 1973, 7th edition, pp. 262-5.

9 *Ibid.,* p. 264.

10 Walt W. Rostow (ed.), *The Economics of Take-Off into Sustained Growth,* proceedings of a conference held by the International Economic Association, New York: St Martin's Press, 1963.

11 R. F. Harrod, *Towards a Dynamic Economics,* London: Macmillan, 1948. Most of the discussion of the theories of economic growth in this subsection, unless otherwise indicated, is based on the excellent review of Benjamin Higgins, *Economic Development: Problems, Principles, and Policies,* New York: W. W. Norton, 1959.

12 Benjamin Higgins, *Economic Development, op.cit.,* p. 145.

13 Harvey Leibenstein, *Economic Backwardness and Economic Growth,* New York: John Wiley, 1957, as interpreted by Benjamin Higgins, *Economic Development, op. cit.,* pp. 388-94.

14 Ragnar Nurkse, *Problems of Capital Formation in Underdeveloped Countries,* New York: Oxford University Press, 1973, ch. 1, as quoted in Benjamin Higgins, *Economic Development, op. cit.,* p. 397.

15 Gunnar Myrdal, *Economic Theory and Underdeveloped Regions,* London: Duckworth 1957, see also Benjamin Higgins, *Economic Development, op.cit.,* pp. 350-3.

16 Hans Singer, 'The Distribution of Gains Between Investing and Borrowing Countries,' *American Review Papers and Proceedings*, May 1950, and Hans Singer, 'The Concept of Balanced Growth and Economic Development: Theory and Facts,' University of Texas Conference on Economic Development, April 1958; Benjamin Higgins, *Economic Development, op.cit.*, pp. 386-74 and pp. 398-401. See also, Albert O. Hirschman, *The Strategy of Economic Growth*, New York, 1958; and Benjamin Higgins, *Economic Development, op.cit.*, pp. 401-8.

17 Among his books, see Bert F. Hoselitz (ed.), *The Progress of Underdeveloped Areas*, University of Chicago Press, 1952; Bert F. Hoselitz, *Sociological Aspects of Economic Growth*, Chicago: Free Press, 1960; Bert F. Hoselitz, *et al.* (eds), *Theories of Economic Growth*, Chicago: Free Press, 1960; and Bert F. Hoselitz and Wilbert E. Moore (eds), *Industrialization and Society*, The Hague: UNESCO-Mouton, 1963.

18 Bert F. Hoselitz, 'The City, the Factory, and Economic Growth,' *American Economic Review*, vol. 45, May 1955, pp. 166-84, reprinted in Paul K. Hatt, Jr; and Albert J. Reiss, Jr, *Cities and Society, op.cit.*, pp. 537-54.

19 Bert F. Hoselitz, 'Main Concepts in the Analysis of the Social Implications of Technical Change,' in Bert F. Hoselitz and Wilbert E. Moore (eds), *Industrialization and Society, op.cit.*, pp. 11-31.

20 Everett E. Hagen, *On the Theory of Social Change: How Economic Growth Begins*, Homewood, Illinois: Dorsey Press, 1962, pp. 121-2.

21 Edward Shils, *The Intellectual Between Tradition and Modernity: The Indian Situation*, The Hague: Mouton, 1961, p. 10.

22 David E. Apter, *The Politics of Modernization*, University of Chicago Press, 1965, p. 43.

23 Milton Singer, 'Changing Craft Traditions in India,' in Wilbert E. Moore and Arnold S. Feldman (eds), *Labor Commitment and Social Change in Developing Areas*, New York: Social Science Research Council, 1960, pp. 258-76.

24 Milton B. Singer, 'Shame Cultures and Guilt Cultures,' in Gerhart Piers and Milton Singer (eds), *Shame and Guilt: A Psychological and Cultural Study*, Springfield, Illinois: Charles C. Thomas, 1953; and Milton Singer, 'Cultural Values in India's Economic Development,' *The Annals of the American Academy of Political and Social Science*, vol. 305, May 1956, pp. 81-91; see also, Milton Singer, 'The Indian Joint Family,' in Milton Singer and Bernard S. Cohn (eds), *Structure and Change in Indian Society*, Chicago: Aldine, 1968, pp. 423-52.

25 See, among others, Vikas Misra, *Hinduism and Economic Growth*, London: Oxford University Press, 1962, and L. P. Vidyarthi (ed.), *Aspects of Religion in Indian Society*, Meerut, India: Kedar Nath Ram Nath, 1961.

26 Dudley Seers, 'The Meaning of Development,' *International Development Review*, Presidential Address by Dudley Seers at the Society for International Development 11th World Congress in New Delhi, November, 1969, reprinted, abridged, in Norman T. Uphoff and Warren F. Johnson (eds), *The Political Economy of Development: Theoretical and Empirical Contributions*, Berkeley: University of California Press, 1972, pp. 123-9.

27 'Development Myths,' in *Bulletin*, Institute of Development Studies, University of Sussex, vol. 1, no. 4, May 1969, p. 16.

28 *Ibid.*, p. 17.

29 *Ibid.*, p. 24.

30 See, among others, Heinz Eulau, *The Behavioral Persuasion in Politics*, New York: Random House, 1963, and Robert T. Holt and John E. Turner, 'The Methodology of Comparative Research,' in Robert T. Holt and John E. Turner (eds), *The Methodology of Comparative Research*, New York: Free Press, 1972, pp. 1-20.

31 Herbert H. Hyman, *Political Socialization,* Chicago: Free Press, 1959. Later studies have worked out some of the problems in political socialization.

32 Edward Shils, *Political Development in the New States,* New York: Humanities Press, n.d.

33 T. B. Bottomore, *Sociology: A Guide to Problems and Literature,* Englewood Cliffs: Prentice-Hall, 1963, p. 150.

34 S. N. Eisenstadt, *The Political Systems of Empires,* New York: Free Press, 1963, pp. 134 ff.

35 F. X. Sutton, 'Social Theory and Comparative Politics,' in David E. Apter and H. Eckstein (eds), *Comparative Politics,* New York: Free Press, 1963, pp. 67-81. According to Sutton, 'Agraria' is constituted of ascriptive, particularistic, and diffuse interactions, stable groups with limited spatial mobility, little occupational differentiation and a 'deferential' stratification system. Compared to the 'Agraria,' the 'Industria' has achievement-oriented, universalistic, and specific norms, high horizontal and vertical mobility, well-developed occupational system, an egalitarian class system and interest-oriented associations. These criteria are directly related to the 'pattern variables' schema of Parsons, discussed above in the text.

36 Joseph LaPalombara, 'Bureaucracy and Political Development: Notes, Queries, and Dilemmas,' in Joseph LaPalombara (ed.), *Bureaucracy and Political Development,* Princeton University Press, 1963, p. 37.

37 Joseph A. Schumpeter, *The Theory of Economic Development,* Cambridge, Mass.: Harvard University Press, 1934, p. 64.

38 See H. V. Wiseman, *Political Systems: Some Sociological Approaches,* New York: Frederick A. Praeger, 1966; Gabriel A. Almond, 'Introduction: A Functional Approach to Comparative Politics,' in Gabriel A. Almond and James S. Coleman (eds), *The Politics of the Developing Areas,* Princeton University Press, 1960, pp. 3-64; and Robert T. Holt and John M. Richardson, Jr, 'Competing Paradigms in Comparative Politics,' in Robert T. Holt and John E. Turner (eds), *The Methodology of Comparative Research, op.cit.,* pp. 21-71.

39 Harold D. Lasswell, *Politics: Who Gets What, When, How,* New York: McGraw-Hill, 1936.

40 Gabriel A. Almond, 'Introduction: A Functional Approach to Comparative Politics,' in Gabriel A. Almond and James S. Coleman (eds), *The Politics of the Developing Areas, op.cit.*

41 *Ibid.,* p. 17.

42 *Ibid.,* p. 35.

43 Fred W. Riggs, 'The Comparison of Whole Political Systems,' in Robert T. Holt and John E. Turner (eds), *The Methodology of Comparative Research, op.cit.,* pp. 75-149.

44 *Ibid.,* pp. 91 ff.

45 Robert T. Holt and John E. Turner, 'The Methodology of Comparative Research,' in Robert T. Holt and John E. Turner (eds), *The Methodology of Comparative Research, op.cit.*

46 Robert T. Holt and John M. Richardson, Jr, 'Competing Paradigms in Comparative Politics,' in Robert T. Holt and John E. Turner (eds), *The Methodology of Comparative Research, op.cit.*

47 *Ibid.,* pp. 51-8.

48 *Ibid.,* p. 70.

49 Gabriel A. Almond and James S. Coleman (eds), *The Politics of the Developing Areas, op.cit.*

50 David E. Apter, 'System, Process and the Politics of Economic Development,' in Bert F. Hoselitz and Wilbert E. Moore (eds), *Industrialization and Society, op. cit.,* pp. 135-58.

51 David E. Apter, 'Political Systems and Developmental Change,' in Robert

T. Holt and John E. Turner (eds), *The Methodology of Comparative Research, op.cit.,* p. 153.

52 *Ibid.,* p. 157.

53 Robert T. Holt and John M. Richardson, Jr, 'Competing Paradigms in Comparative Politics,' in Robert T. Holt and John E. Turner (eds), *The Methodology of Comparative Research, op.cit.,* pp. 41-5; see, especially, David Easton, *The Political System,* New York: Alfred A. Knopf, 1953, and David Easton, *Varieties of Political Theory,* Englewood Cliffs: Prentice-Hall, 1966.

54 Karl W. Deutsch, *The Nerves of Government: Models of Communication and Control,* New York: Free Press, 1963.

55 *Ibid.*

56 Karl W. Deutsch, *Nationalism and Social Communication, An Inquiry into the Foundations of Nationality,* Cambridge, Mass.: MIT Press, 1966 [1953].

57 Joseph LaPalombara, 'Parsimony and Empiricism in Comparative Politics: An Anti-Scholastic View,' in Robert T. Holt and John E. Turner (eds), *The Methodology of Comparative Research, op.cit.,* p. 379 (fn. 10).

58 Rupert Emerson, *From Empire to Nation: The Rise to Self-Assertion of Asian and African Peoples,* Boston: Beacon Press, 1962 [1960], p. 89.

59 Daniel Lerner, *The Passing of Traditional Society,* Chicago: Free Press, 1958.

60 Gabriel A. Almond, 'Introduction: A Functional Approach to Comparative Politics,' in Gabriel A. Almond and James S. Coleman (eds), *The Politics of the Developing Areas, op.cit.*

61 A. B. Lewis, 'Local Self-Goverment: a Key to National Economic Advancement and Political Stability,' *Philippine Journal of Public Administration,* vol. II, no. 1, 1958, pp. 54-7.

62 Seymour Martin Lipset, *Political Man: The Social Bases of Politics,* Garden City, New York: Doubleday, 1960, ch. 2; Daniel Lerner, 'Modernizing Styles of Life: A Theory,' ch. 2 in Daniel Lerner, *The Passing of Traditional Society, op.cit.;* and James S. Coleman, 'Conclusion: The Political Systems of the Developing Areas,' in Gabriel A. Almond and James S. Coleman (eds), *The Politics of the Developing Areas, op.cit.,* pp. 532-76.

63 James S. Coleman, 'Conclusion: The Political Systems of the Developing Areas,' in Gabriel A. Almond and James S. Coleman (eds), *The Politics of the Developing Areas, op.cit.*

64 Rupert Emerson hints in this direction, when he says: 'One must look elsewhere than to nationalism to decide even such over-all questions as whether a free enterprise system or Communism, liberal democracy or centralized authoritarianism, is most fitting and the vast majority of lesser decisions must also be taken primarily on other than nationalist grounds.' Rupert Emerson, 'Nationalism and Political Development,' *Journal of Politics,* vol. 22, February 1960, pp. 3-28, reprinted in Jason L. Finkle and Richard W. Gable (eds), *Political Development and Social Change,* New York: John Wiley, 1966, p. 172. See also Philip E. Jacob (ed.), *Values and the Active Community,* New York: Free Press, 1971

7 The anthropological theories of modernization

1 For an evolutionary view, see Morton H. Fried, *The Evolution of Political Society: An Essay in Political Anthropology,* New York: Random House, 1967. For a behavioralist view, see Ronald Cohen, 'The Political System,' in Raoul Naroll and Ronald Cohen (eds), *A Handbook of Method in Cultural Anthropology,* New York: Columbia University Press, 1973, pp. 484-99, and Ronald Cohen, 'Political Anthropology,' in John J. Honigmann (ed.), *Handbook of Social and Cultural Anthropology,* Chicago: Rand McNally, 1973, pp. 861-81. On law, see Laura Nadar and Barbara Yngvesson, 'On Studying the Ethnography of Law

and Its Consequences,' in John J. Honigmann (ed.), *Handbook of Social and Cultural Anthropology, op.cit.,* pp. 883-921.

2 Among others, see George Dalton, 'The Economic System,' in Raoul Naroll and Ronald Cohen (eds), *A Handbook of Method in Cultural Anthropology, op.cit.,* pp. 454-83, and Scott Cook, 'Economic Anthropology: Problems in Theory, Method, and Analysis,' in John J. Honigmann (ed.), *Handbook of Social and Cultural Anthropology, op.cit.,* pp. 795-860.

3 James L. Peacock and A. Thomas Kirsch, *The Human Direction: An Evolutionary Approach to Social and Cultural Anthropology,* New York: Appleton-Century-Crofts, 1973, ch. 2.

4 Clifford Geertz, *Peddlers and Princes: Social Change and Economic Modernization in Two Indonesian Towns,* University of Chicago Press, 1963.

5 *Ibid.,* pp. 147-57.

6 Leslie White, 'Energy and the Evolution of Culture,' *American Anthropologist,* vol. 45, 1943, pp. 335-56, and Leslie White, *The Evolution of Culture,* New York: McGraw-Hill, 1959.

7 Julian H. Steward, 'Evolution and Process,' in A. L. Kroeber (ed.), *Anthropology Today,* University of Chicago Press, 1953, pp. 313-26, and Julian H. Steward, *Theory of Culture Change: The Methodology of Multilinear Evolution,* Urbana: University of Illinois Press, 1955 [1951].

8 Robert L. Carneiro, 'The Four Faces of Evolution,' in John J. Honigmann (ed.), *Handbook of Social and Cultural Anthropology, op.cit.,* pp. 89-110.

9 *Ibid.,* p. 104.

10 *Ibid.*

11 Raoul Naroll, 'A Preliminary Index of Social Development,' *American Anthropologist,* vol. 58, 1956, pp. 687-715.

12 Robert L. Carneiro, 'Ascertaining, Testing, and Interpreting Sequences of Cultural Development,' *Southwestern Journal of Anthropology,* vol. 24, 1968, pp. 354-74.

13 Robert Redfield, 'The Folk Society,' *The American Journal of Sociology,* vol. LII, 1947, reprinted in Richard Sennett (ed.), *Classic Essays on the Culture of Cities,* New York: Appleton-Century-Crofts, 1969, p. 180.

14 See Horace Miner, 'The Folk-Urban Continuum,' *American Sociological Review,* vol. 17, October 1952, pp. 529-37, reprinted in Paul K. Hatt and Albert J. Reiss, Jr (eds), *Cities and Society,* Chicago: Free Press, 1951, pp. 22-34.

15 Oscar Lewis, *Life in a Mexican Village, Tepoztlan Restudied,* Urbana: University of Illinois Press, 1951.

16 *Ibid.,* p. 344.

17 Robert Redfield, *The Little Community* and *Peasant Society and Culture,* University of Chicago Press, 1960, p. 136 (of *The Little Community*).

18 *Ibid.,* p. 137.

19 Oscar Lewis, *Life in a Mexican Village, op.cit.,* p. 432.

20 Robert Redfield, *Peasant Society and Culture,* University of Chicago Press, 1956, pp. 40-1.

21 *Ibid.*

22 *Ibid.,* and Robert Redfield and Milton Singer, 'The Cultural Role of Cities,' *Economic Development and Cultural Change,* vol. III, 1954.

23 Eric R. Wolf, *Peasants,* Englewood Cliffs: Prentice-Hall, 1966.

24 *Ibid.,* p. 2.

25 *Ibid.,* pp. 3-4.

26 *Ibid.,* p. 50 ff.

27 Gideon Sjoberg, 'Folk and "Feudal" Societies,' *The American Journal of Sociology,* vol. 58, November 1952, pp. 231-9, reprinted in Jason L. Finkle and Richard W. Gable (eds), *Political Development and Social Change,* New York: John Wiley, 1966, pp. 45-53.

28 This distinction has been made by Edwin Eames and Judith Goode, 'Urban

Anthropology: A Critical Survey,' in Baidya Nath Varma (ed.), *The New Social Science*, Westport, Conn.: Greenwood Press, 1976.

29 Among others, see Horace Miner, *The Primitive City of Timbuctoo*, Princeton University Press, 1953; Horace Miner, *St. Denis, A French Canadian Parish*, University of Chicago Press, 1939.

30 Robert Redfield and Milton Singer, 'The Cultural Role of Cities,' *Economic Development and Cultural Change*, vol. III, 1954, reprinted in Richard Sennett (ed.), *Classic Essays on the Culture of Cities, op.cit.*, pp. 206-33.

31 Among others, see W. Lloyd Warner and Paul S. Lunt, *The Social Life of a Modern Community*, New Haven: Yale University Press, 1941, and W. Lloyd Warner and Paul S. Lunt, *The Status System of a Modern Community*, New Haven: Yale University Press, 1942.

32 W. Mangin, *Peasants in Cities*, New York: Houghton Mifflin, 1970, and R. Spencer (ed.), *Migration and Anthropology*, Seattle: University of Washington Press, 1970; also Owen M. Lynch, 'The Politics of Untouchability—A Case from Agra, India,' in Milton Singer and Bernard S. Cohn (eds), *Structure and Change in Indian Society*, Chicago: Aldine, 1968, pp. 209-40.

33 Oscar Lewis, *Five Families: Mexican Studies in the Culture of Poverty*, New York: Basic Books, 1959.

34 Kenneth Little, *West African Urbanization: A Study of Voluntary Associations in Social Change*, Cambridge University Press, 1965; and Aidan Southall (ed.), *Urban Anthropology: Cross-Cultural Studies of Urbanization*, New York: Oxford University Press, 1973.

35 Elliot Liebow, *Tally's Corner: A Study of Negro Streetcorner Men*, Boston: Little, Brown, 1967.

36 J. Spradley, *You Owe Yourself a Drunk*, Boston: Little, Brown, 1970.

37 Oscar Lewis, *Five Families, op.cit.*

38 Oscar Lewis, *The Children of Sanchez*, New York: Random House, 1961; and Oscar Lewis, *La Vida: A Puerto Rican Family in the Culture of Poverty—San Juan and New York*, New York: Random House, 1966.

39 Oscar Lewis, *La Vida, op.cit.*

40 Oscar Lewis, 'The Culture of Poverty,' *Scientific American*, vol. 215, 1966, pp. 19-25.

41 Oscar Lewis, *La Vida, op.cit.*, p. xlv.

42 *Ibid.*

43 Anthony Leeds, 'The Concept of the "Culture of Poverty": Conceptual, Logical, and Empirical Problems, with Perspectives from Brazil and Peru,' in Eleanor Burke Leacock (ed.), *The Culture of Poverty: A Critique*, New York: Simon & Schuster, 1971, p. 239.

44 Michael Harrington, *The Other America: Poverty in the United States*, New York: Macmillan Company, 1962, pp. 16-17.

45 Charles A. Valentine, 'The "Culture of Poverty": Its Scientific Significance and Its Implications for Action,' in Eleanor Burke Leacock (ed.), *The Culture of Poverty: A Critique, op.cit.*, p. 194.

46 Charles Dickens, *Sketches by Boz, illustrative of everyday life and everyday people*, New York: Oxford University Press, 1957; see also John D. and Mollie Hardwick, *The Charles Dickens Encyclopedia*, London: Osprey, 1973.

47 Frank Bonilla, 'Rio's Favelas: The Rural Slum Within the City,' in W. Mangin (ed.), *Peasants in Cities, op.cit.*, p. 81.

48 Eleanor Burke Leacock (ed.), *The Culture of Poverty: A Critique, op.cit.*, p. 34.

49 Oscar Lewis's review of Charles A. Valentine, *Culture and Poverty: Critique and Counter-Proposals*, University of Chicago Press, 1968, in *Current Anthropology*, vol. 10, nos. 2-3, 1969, p. 192.

50 See, among others, Edward C. Banfield, *The Unheavenly City: The Nature and Future of Our Urban Crisis*, Boston: Little, Brown, 1968.

51 Robert Redfield, *The Little Community, op.cit.:* p. 4.
52 *Ibid.,* p. 5.
53 Ferdinand Tönnies, *Community and Society (Gemeinschaft und Gesellschaft),* translated by Charles P. Loomis, East Lansing: University of Michigan Press, 1957.
54 Raymond Firth, *Elements of Social Organization,* Boston: Beacon Press, 1963, pp. 27-8.
55 Conrad M. Arensberg, 'The Community-Study Method,' *The American Journal of Sociology,* vol. 60, no. 2, 1954, pp. 109-24.
56 Conrad M. Arensberg, 'The Community as Object and as Sample,' *American Anthropologist,* vol. 63, no. 2, part I, 1961, pp. 241-64.
57 Conrad M. Arensberg and Solon T. Kimball, 'Community Studfi: Retrospect and Prospect,' *American Journal of Sociology,* vol. 73, no. 6, 1968, pp. 691-705.
58 *Ibid.*
59 Conrad M. Arensberg, 'The Community-Study Method,' *op.cit.*
60 Conrad M. Arensberg, 'American Communities,' *American Anthropologist,* vol. 57, no. 6, 1955, pp. 1143-60.
61 Conrad M. Arensberg and Solon T. Kimball, 'Metropolis and Social Class,' in Conrad M. Arensberg and Solon T. Kimball, *Culture and Community,* New York: Harcourt, Brace & World, 1965, ch. 9.
62 Anthony Leeds, 'Locality Power in Relation to Supralocal Power Institutions,' in Aidan Southall (ed.), *Urban Anthropology, op.cit.,* pp. 15-41.
63 *Ibid.,* p. 26.
64 *Ibid.,* p. 20.
65 *Ibid.,* pp. 24 ff.
66 Lewis Henry Morgan, *Ancient Society,* edited by Eleanor B. Leacock, Cleveland, Ohio: World Publishing, 1963, pp. 6 ff.
67 Robert M. MacIver, *The Web of Government,* New York: Macmillan Company, 1947, p. 158.
68 I. Schapera, *Government and Politics in Tribal Societies,* New York: Schocken, 1967 [1956], p. 5.
69 *Ibid.*
70 Gabriel A. Almond and James S. Coleman (eds), *The Politics of the Developing Areas,* Princeton University Press, 1960.
71 Ronald Cohen, 'Political Anthropology,' *op.cit.*
72 Morton H. Fried, *The Evolution of Political Society, op.cit.,* p. xi.
73 *Ibid.,* p. 229.
74 *Ibid.*
75 *Ibid.,* p. 230.
76 *Ibid.,* p. 235.
77 Meyer Fortes and E. E. Evans-Pritchard, *African Political Systems,* London: Oxford University Press, 1940, pp. 5 ff.
78 Leo Kuper and Marion G. Smith (eds), *Pluralism in Africa,* Berkeley: University of California Press, 1969.
79 Pierre L. Van den Berghe, 'Pluralism,' in John J. Honigmann (ed.), *Handbook of Social and Cultural Anthropology, op.cit.,* p. 965.
80 W. F. Ogburn and A. A. Goldenweiser (eds), *The Social Sciences and Their Interrelations,* Boston: Houghton Mifflin, 1927.
81 N. S. B. Gras, 'Anthropology and Economics,' in W. F. Ogburn and A. A. Goldenweiser (eds), *The Social Sciences and Their Interrelations, op.cit.,* p. 10.
82 *Ibid.,* p. 22.
83 Karl Polanyi, *et al,* (eds), *Trade and Market in the Early Empires,* Chicago: Free Press, 1957.
84 *Ibid.,* p. 240.
85 *Ibid.,* pp. 250-6.

86 See the excellent article by Scott Cook, 'Economic Anthropology: Problems in Theory, Method, and Analysis,' in John J. Honigmann (ed.), *Handbook of Social and Cultural Anthropology, op.cit.,* pp. 795-860.

87 Edward E. LeClair, 'Economic Theory and Economic Anthropology,' *American Anthropologist,* vol. 64, 1962, p. 1186.

88 Georg Simmel, *The Sociology of Georg Simmel,* translated and edited by Kurt H. Wolff, Chicago: Free Press, 1950.

89 Ludwig von Bertalanffy, 'The Theory of Open Systems in Physics and Biology,' *Science,* vol. CXI, 1950.

90 Marshall Sahlins, 'Economic Anthropology and Anthropological Economics,' *Social Science Information,* vol. 8, no. 5, 1973, pp. 13-33, as reprinted in Morton H. Fried (ed.), *Explorations in Anthropology: Readings in Culture, Man, and Nature,* New York: Thomas Y. Crowell, 1973, p. 277.

91 Raymond Firth, *Primitive Polynesian Economy,* London: Routledge & Kegan Paul, 1939; Raymond Firth, *Malay Fishermen: Their Peasant Economy,* London: Routledge & Kegan Paul, 1946; Raymond Firth and Basil S. Yamey (eds), *Capital, Saving and Credit in Peasant Societies,* Chicago: Aldine, 1964.

92 Sol Tax, *Penny Capitalism,* University of Chicago Press, 1953.

93 Eric R. Wolf, 'Types of Latin American Peasantry: A Preliminary Discussion,' *American Anthropologist,* vol. LVII, no. 3, 1955; and Eric R. Wolf, 'Closed Corporate Peasant Communities in Mesoamerica and Central Java,' *Southwestern Journal of Anthropology,* vol. XIII, no. 1, 1957.

94 Among his works, see George Dalton, 'Economic Theory and Primitive Society,' *American Anthropologist,* vol. 63, 1961, pp. 1-25; 'Bibliographical Essay,' in George Dalton (ed.), *Tribal and Peasant Economies: Reading in Economic Anthropology,* New York: Natural History Press, 1967; and 'The Economic System,' in Raoul Naroll and Ronald Cohen (eds), *A Handbook of Method in Cultural Anthropology, op.cit.,* pp. 454-83.

95 George Dalton, 'The Economic System,' *op.cit.,* p. 459.

96 *Ibid.,* pp. 469-74.

97 Manning Nash, 'The Multiple Society in Economic Development: Mexico and Guatemala,' *American Anthropologist,* vol. 59, October 1957, pp. 825-33, as reprinted in Jason L. Finkle and Richard W. Gable (eds), *Political Development and Social Change, op.cit.,* pp. 506-13.

98 Julius H. Boeke, *Oriental Economics,* New York: Institute of Pacific Relations, 1947, and J. H. Boeke, *Economics and Economic Policy of Dual Societies,* New York: Institute of Pacific Relations, 1953.

99 J. S. Furnivall, *Netherlands India: A Study of Plural Economy,* Cambridge University Press, 1939; and J. S. Furnivall, *Colonial Policy and Practice: A Comparative Study of Burma and Netherlands India,* Cambridge University Press, 1948.

100 Manning Nash, 'The Multiple Society in Economic Development: Mexico and Guatemala,' *op.cit.,* p. 507.

101 *Ibid.*

102 Arthur L. Stinchcombe, 'Agricultural Enterprise and Rural Class Relations,' *The American Journal of Sociology,* vol. 67, pp. 165-76, September 1961; reprinted in Jason L. Finkle and Richard W. Gable (eds), *Political Development and Social Change,* 2nd edn, New York: John Wiley, 1971, pp. 359-71.

103 See John Friedmann, 'On the Contradictions between City and Countryside,' *Comparative Urban Research,* Vol. VI, no. 1, 1978.

8   The activistic theories of modernization

1 Edward Shils, 'On the Comparative Study of the New States,' in Clifford Geertz (ed.), *Old Societies and New States,* New York: Free Press, 1963, pp. 22-3.

2 *Ibid.*
3 Gunnar Myrdal, *Rich Lands and Poor,* New York: Harper, 1957, chs 1-3.
4 Gunnar Myrdal, *Asian Drama: An Inquiry into the Poverty of Nations,* 3 vols, New York: Pantheon, 1968, p. 35.
5 *Ibid.,* pp. 53 ff; see also Gunnar Myrdal, *Value in Social Theory: A Selection of Essays on Methodology,* edited by Paul Streeten, New York: Harper, 1958.
6 Gunnar Myrdal, *Asian Drama, op.cit.,* pp. 57-67.
7 Gunnar Myrdal, *An American Dilemma,* New York: Harper, 1944.
8 Romesh Thapar, 'Prof. Myrdal's Inquiry into Poverty in Asia,' *India News,* September 6, 1968.
9 Beatrice Webb, *Our Partnership,* Longmans Green, 1948 [1894], pp. 117-18.
10 W. Arthur Lewis, *The Principles of Economic Planning,* Washington, D.C.: Public Affairs Press, 1951, p. 11.
11 W. Arthur Lewis, *The Theory of Economic Growth,* London: George Allen & Unwin, 1955; W. Arthur Lewis, 'Economic Development with Unlimited Supplies of Labour,' *The Manchester School of Economic and Social Studies,* May 1954.
12 W. Arthur Lewis, *The Principles of Economic Planning, op.cit.,* p. 14.
13 *Ibid.,* p. 19.
14 Ernest Mandel, 'Economics of the Transition Period,' in Pierre Frank, George Novack and Ernest Mandel, *Key Problems of the Transition from Capitalism to Socialism,* New York: Pathfinder Press, 1969, p. 44.
15 W. Arthur Lewis, *The Principles of Economic Planning, op.cit.,* chs 8-9.
16 Benjamin Higgins, *Economic Development: Problems, Principles and Politics,* New York: W.W. Norton, 1959, p. 294.
17 David C. McClelland, 'Community Development and the Nature of Human Motivation: Some Implications of Recent Research,' paper presented at the Conference on Community Development and National Change. MIT, CIS, December 1957 (mimeographed).
18 David C. McClelland, *The Achieving Society,* Princeton, New Jersey: D. Van Nostrand, 1961.
19 David C. McClelland, 'Community Development and the Nature of Human Motivation: Some Implications of Recent Research,' *op.cit.*
20 David C. McClelland, *The Achieving Society, op.cit.,* ch. 6.
21 David C. McClelland, 'Motivational Trends in Society,' a module, Morristown, N.J: General Learning Press, 1971, p. 7.
22 *Ibid.,* p. 9.
23 David C. McClelland, *The Achieving Society, op.cit.,* ch. 2; and David C. McClelland, 'Motivational Trends in Society,' *op.cit.,* p. 16.
24 David C. McClelland, 'Motivational Trends in Society,' *op.cit.,* pp. 16-17; and David C. McClelland and David G. Winter, *Motivating Economic Achievement,* New York: Free Press, 1969, chs 1-2.
25 David C. McClelland and David G. Winter, *Motivating Economic Achievement, op.cit.,* p. 213.
26 David C. McClelland, 'Motivational Trends in Society,' *op.cit.,* p. 17.
27 *Ibid.,* p. 12.
28 Everett E. Hagen, *On the Theory of Social Change: How Economic Growth Begins,* Homewood, Ill.: Dorsey Press, 1962, p. 30.
29 *Ibid.,* p. 86.
30 *Ibid.,* p. 87.
31 Everett E. Hagen, as quoted in Benjamin Higgins, *Economic Development, op.cit.,* p. 307.
32 *Ibid.*
33 Alex Inkeles, 'The Modernization of Man,' in Myron Weiner (ed.), *Modernization,* New York: Basic Books, 1966, pp. 138-50.

34 Alex Inkeles, 'The OM Scale: A Comparative Socio-Psychological Measure of Individual Modernity,' *Sociometry*, vol. 29, no. 4, December 1966, pp. 353-77.

35 Edward Shils, 'The Intellectuals in the Political Development of the New States,' *World Politics*, vol. XII, no. 3, April 1960, pp. 329-68, reprinted in John H. Kautsky (ed.), *Political Change in Underdeveloped Countries: Nationalism and Communism*, New York: Dryden Press, 1955.

36 Lucien W. Pye, 'Armies in the Process of Political Modernization,' *Archives Européennes de sociologie*, vol. 2, 1961, pp. 82-92, reprinted in Jason L. Finkle and Richard W. Gable (eds), *Political Development and Social Change*, New York: John Wiley, 1966, pp. 380-3.

37 *Ibid.*, p. 381.

38 *Ibid.*

39 *Ibid.*, p. 384.

40 Gino Germani and Kalman H. Silvert, 'Politics, Social Structure and Military Intervention in Latin America,' *Archives Européennes de sociologie*, vol. 2, 1961, pp. 62-81, reprinted as 'Politics and Military Intervention in Latin America,' in Jason L. Finkle and Richard W. Gable (eds), *Political Development and Social Change, op.cit.*, pp. 397-401.

41 *Ibid.*

42 Edward Shils, 'The Military in the Political Development of the New States,' in John J. Johnson (ed.), *The Role of the Military in Underdeveloped Countries*, Princeton University Press, 1962, p. 39.

43 *Ibid.*, p. 58.

44 Morris Janowitz, 'Introduction: Organizing Multiple Goals: War Making and Arms Control,' in Morris Janowitz (ed.), *The New Military: Changing Patterns of Organization*, New York: John Wiley, 1967 [1964], p. 28.

45 *Ibid.*, pp. 28-9.

46 Moshe Lissak, 'Selected Literature of Revolutions and Coups d'Etat in the Developing Countries,' in Morris Janowitz (ed.), *The New Military, op.cit.*, p. 342.

47 *Ibid.*, p. 343.

48 Morris Janowitz, 'Introduction to the Paperback Edition,' in Morris Janowitz (ed.), *The New Military, op.cit.*

49 *Ibid.*

50 Max Weber, *The Theory of Social and Economic Organization*, New York: Oxford University Press, 1947, pp. 329-40.

51 Robert K. Merton, 'Bureaucratic Structure and Personality,' *Social Forces*, vol. XVII, 1940, pp. 560-8, reprinted with minor modifications in Robert K. Merton, *et al.* (eds), *Reader in Bureaucracy*, Chicago: Free Press, 1952, p. 363.

52 Karl Marx, in a letter to Kugelmann, reprinted in *Karl Marx and Friedrich Engels, Correspondence, 1846-1895*, New York: International Publishers, 1936, p. 309.

53 J. Donald Kingsley, *Representative Bureaucracy*, Yellow Springs, Ohio: Antioch Press, 1944, pp. 42-77.

54 J. Donald Kingsley, 'Bureaucracy and Political Development, with Particular Reference to Nigeria,' in Joseph LaPalombara (ed.), *Bureaucracy and Political Development, op.cit.*, pp. 316-17.

55 Ralph Braibanti, 'Public Bureaucracy and Judiciary in Pakistan,' in Joseph LaPalombara (ed.), *Bureaucracy and Political Development, op.cit.*, pp. 360-440.

56 S. C. Dube, 'Bureaucracy and Nation Building in Transitional Societies,' *International Social Science Journal*, vol. 16, 1964, pp. 229-36, reprinted in Jason L. Finkle and Richard W. Gable (eds), *Political Development and Social Change, op.cit.*, p. 403.

57 *Ibid.*, p. 406.

58 *Ibid.*, p. 407.

59 *Ibid*, pp. 407-8; see also S. C. Dube, *India's Changing Village: Human Factors of Community Development*, London: Routledge & Kegan Paul, 1958. An insight into the problems of the new bureaucracy of the Community Development Administration has been provided in Narmadeshwar Prasad, *Change Strategy in a Developing Society: India*, Meerut, India: Meenakshi Prakashan, 1970, ch. 8.

60 Fred W. Riggs, 'Bureaucrats and Political Development: A Paradoxical View,' in Joseph LaPalombara (ed.), *Bureaucracy and Political Development, op.cit.*, pp. 120-67.

61 *Ibid.*, pp. 121 ff.

62 Abraham Lincoln, as quoted in Leo Huberman, 'The ABC of Socialism,' in Leo Huberman and Paul M. Sweezy (eds), *Introduction to Socialism*, New York: Modern Reader Paperbacks, 1968, p. 80.

63 Karl Marx and Friedrich Engels, 'Manifesto of the Communist Party,' in Marx Engels, Lenin, *The Essential Left: Four Classic Texts on the Principles of Socialism*, London: George Allen & Unwin, 1961, p. 36.

64 Friedrich Engels, 'Socialism: Utopian and Scientific,' translated by Edward Aveling, in Marx, Engels, Lenin, *The Essential Left, op.cit.*, p. 146.

65 Friedrich Engels, 'Manifesto of the Communist Party: Preface to the English Edition of 1888,' in Marx, Engels, Lenin, *The Essential Left, op.cit.*, p. 12.

66 *Ibid.*

67 V. I. Ulianov (N. Lenin), 'The State and Revolution,' in Marx, Engels, Lenin, *The Essential Left, op.cit.*, p. 162.

68 Irving Louis Horowitz, *Three Worlds of Development: The Theory and Practice of International Stratification*, New York: Oxford University Press, 1966, p. 152.

69 Milovan Djilas, *The New Class: An Analysis of the Communist System*, New York: Frederick A. Praeger, 1957, p. 171.

70 *Ibid.*, pp. 78 ff.

71 V. I. Lenin, *Collected Works*, vol. X, New York: International Publishers, 1936.

72 Stalin, *Foundations of Leninism*, New York: International Publishers, 1939.

73 Milovan Djilas, *The New Class, op.cit.*, p. 38.

74 *Ibid.*, p. 39.

75 Reported to us by a Polish sociologist in private conversation.

76 Leo Huberman, 'The ABC of Socialism,' *op.cit.*, p. 69.

77 M. N. Rutkevich, 'V. I. Lenin and Problems of Development of Intelligentsia,' in *Transactions of the Seventh World Congress of Sociology*, held at Varna, September 14-19, 1970, Sofia: The Bulgarian Academy of Sciences Publishing House, 1973, vol. V, p. 165.

78 Barrington Moore, Jr, *Social Origins of Dictatorship and Democracy: Lord and Peasant in the Making of the Modern World*, Boston: Beacon Press, 1967.

79 *Ibid.*, pp. xiv-xvi.

80 *Ibid.*

81 *Ibid.*, p. 453.

82 Eric R. Wolff, 'On Peasant Rebellions,' *International Social Science Journal*, vol. 21, no. 2, 1969, pp. 286-94, reprinted in Morton H. Fried (ed.), *Explorations in Anthropology, op.cit.*, pp. 367-72; see also Eric R. Wolff, *Peasant Wars of the Twentieth Century*, New York: Harper & Row, 1969.

83 Eric R. Wolff, 'On Peasant Rebellions,' *op.cit.*, p. 371.

84 V. I. Lenin, *Collected Works*, vol. 22, Moscow, 1963-9, p. 144, as quoted in V. G. Afanasiev, 'V. I. Lenin on Scientific Administration of Socialist Society,' in *Transactions of the Seventh World Congress of Sociology, op.cit.*, p. 102.

85 *Ibid.*, p. 103.

9 Modernization theories: a summation

1 See H. Myint, *Economic Theory and the Underdeveloped Countries*, New York: Oxford University Press, 1971, pp. 24 ff.

2 J. H. Boeke, *Economics and Economic Policy of Dual Societies,* New York: Institute of Pacific Relations, 1953.

3 H. Myint, *Economic Theory and the Underdeveloped Countries, op.cit.,* pp. 315 ff.

4 The word *panchayat* has two meanings in the context of Indian justice. One refers to the governmentally recognized body of the village assembly or the socially recognized body of the caste assembly, which have their special jurisdictional functions. The other meaning of the *panchayat* incorporates any locally assembled body of judges, who administer decisions in the case of aggrieved parties, who accuse each other of some wrongdoing.

5 The data on Indian education are compiled from various sources, including *India: A Reference Annual, 1976,* New Delhi: Publications Division, Ministry of Information and Broadcasting, Government of India, 1971, and S. C. Mallik (ed.) *Management and Organization of Indian Universities,* Simla, India: Indian Institute of Advanced Study, 1971.

6 H. Myint, *Economic Theory and the Underdeveloped Countries, op.cit.,* pp. 244-5.

7 W. Arthur Lewis, 'Education and Economic Development,' *Social and Economic Studies,* June 1961, p. 116.

8 Robert K. Merton, 'Social Structure and Anomie,' in *Social Theory and Social Structure,* New York: Free Press, 1968, pp. 131-60.

10 Modernization for what?

1 Lucien W. Pye, 'Introduction,' in Lucien W. Pye and Sidney Verba (eds), *Political Culture and Political Development,* Princeton University Press, 1965, p. 3.

2 Barrington Moore, Jr, *Social Origins of Dictatorship and Democracy: Lord and Peasant in the Making of the Modern World,* Boston: Beacon Press, 1966, p. 160.

3 *Ibid.,* p. 20; see also, Max Beloff, *The Age of Absolutism: 1660-1815,* London: Hutchinson, 1954; H. S. Bennett, *Life on the English Manor,* Cambridge University Press, 1962; and D. Thomson, *England in the Nineteenth Century,* London: Pelican Books, 1950.

4 Barrington Moore, Jr, *Social Origins of Dictatorship and Democracy, op.cit.,* p. 109; see also Marc Bloch, *French Rural History,* London: Routledge & Kegan Paul, 1966; and D. Thomson, *Europe Since Napoleon,* New York: Alfred A. Knopf, 1962.

5 Barrington Moore, Jr, *Social Origins of Dictatorship and Democracy, op.cit.,* pp. 112-13.

6 *Ibid.,* p. 144.

7 Robert A. Dahl, *Polyarchy: Participation and Opposition,* New Haven: Yale University Press, 1971, p. 45.

8 Seymour Martin Lipset, *The First New Nation: The United States in Historical and Comparative Perspective,* Garden City, New York: Doubleday, 1960, ch. 2.

9 Joseph LaPalombara and Myron Weiner, 'The Origin and Development of Political Parties,' in Joseph LaPalombara and Myron Weiner (eds), *Political Parties and Political Development,* Princeton University Press, 1966, p. 19.

10 Bert F. Hoselitz, *Sociological Aspects of Economic Growth,* Chicago: Free Press, 1960, p. 68.

11 A glimpse of the modern scene in arts and letters is provided in André Malraux, *Anti-Memoirs,* translated by Terence Kilmartin, New York: Holt, Rinehart & Winston, 1968.

12 Crane Brinton, *The Anatomy of Revolution,* New York: W. W. Norton, 1938.

13 James C. Davies, 'Toward a Theory of Revolution,' *American Sociological Review,* vol. 27, February 1962, pp. 5-19.

14 The intricate relationships of social beliefs and their impact on social reality have been explored by Robert K. Merton, 'The Self-fulfilling Prophecy,' in Robert K. Merton, *Social Theory and Social Structure,* New York: Free Press, 1968, pp. 421-36; see also Robert Bierstedt, *The Social Order,* New York: McGraw-Hill, 1970, pp. 482 ff.

15 Hans Kohn, *The Idea of Nationalism: A Study in its Origins and Background,* New York: Macmillan Company, 1961 [1944], pp. 11-18.

16 *Ibid.,* p. 4.

17 Rupert Emerson, 'Parties and National Integration in Africa,' in Joseph L. LaPalombara and Myron Weiner (eds), *Political Parties and Political Development, op.cit.,* p. 262.

18 Rupert Emerson, 'Nationalism and Political Development,' *Journal of Politics, op.cit.,* pp. 3-28, reprinted in Jason L. Finkle and Richard W. Gable (eds), *Political Development and Social Change,* New York: John Wiley, 1966, pp. 157-73; and Rupert Emerson, *From Empire to Nation, op.cit.*

19 See the resolution on the 'Dynamics of World Revolution Today,' adopted by the Reunification Congress of the Fourth International, June 1963. Its implications are discussed by George Novack in 'The Uneven Development of the World Revolutionary Process,' in Ernest Mandel (ed.), *Fifty Years of World Revolution: An International Symposium,* New York: Pathfinder Press, 1968, and reprinted in George Novack, *Understanding History: Marxist Essays,* New York: Pathfinder Press, 1972, pp. 138 ff.

20 See Benjamin B. Cohen (editor-in-chief), *The Worldmark Encyclopedia of the Nations,* New York: Harper, 1960. An interesting theoretical study of 'The European Community' is provided in Robert S. Wood, 'Integration Theories,' *European Community,* no. 174, March 1974, pp. 17-19.

21 A. F. K. Organski, *The Stages of Political Development,* New York: Alfred A. Knopf, 1965.

22 Daniel Lerner, *The Passing of Traditional Society: Modernizing the Middle East,* New York: Free Press, 1958.

23 S. N. Eisenstadt, *Modernization: Protest and Change,* Englewood Cliffs: Prentice-Hall, 1966, pp. 144-7.

24 See Ishwar Chandra Saxena, 'The Doctrine of Precedent in India: A Study of Some of its Aspects,' in G. S. Sharma (ed.), *Essays in Indian Jurisprudence,* Lucknow and Delhi: Eastern Book Company, 1964, pp. 110-36; and J. Duncan M. Derrett, *Religion, Law and the State in India,* New York: Free Press, 1968.

25 John Kenneth Galbraith, *Economic Development in Perspective,* Cambridge, Mass.: Harvard University Press, 1962, p. 33.

26 See James E. Connor (ed.), *Lenin on Politics and Revolution,* New York: Pegasus, 1968.

27 V. I. Lenin, 'What is to be Done,' in James E. Connor (ed.), *Lenin on Politics and Revolution, op.cit.,* p. 55.

28 Dudley Seers, 'The Meaning of Development,' Communication Series no. 44, Sussex: Institute of Development Studies at the University of Sussex, p. 2 (mimeographed), n.d.

29 Bert F. Hoselitz, 'Enterpreneurship and Economic Growth,' *The American Journal of Economics and Sociology,* vol. 12, no. 1, October 1952, pp. 97-110, reprinted in Bert F. Hoselitz, *Sociological Aspects of Economic Growth, op.cit.,* p. 140.

30 Karl W. Deutsch, *Nationalism and Social Communication: An Inquiry into the Formation of Nationality,* Cambridge Mass.: MIT Press, 1966, p. 106.

31 *Ibid.,* p. 192.

32 David C. McClelland and David G. Winter, *Motivating Economic Achievement,* New York: Free Press, 1969, chs 3-6.

33 William McCord, *The Springtime of Freedom: The Evolution of Developing Societies,* New York, Oxford University Press, 1965, p. 143.

34 Robert K. Merton, 'Bureaucratic Structure and Personality,' in *Social Theory and Social Structure, op.cit.*

35 We are developing this framework in a separate theoretical study of national integration. Clifford Geertz has tried to wrestle with the problems of 'the reduction of primordial sentiments to civil order,' because 'the new states are abnormally susceptible to serious dissatisfaction based on primordial attachments.' See Clifford Geertz, 'The Integrative Revolution,' in Clifford Geertz (ed.), *Old Societies and New States,* New York, Free Press, 1963, pp. 105-57. McKim Marriott has a provocative thesis on the selection from preexisting cultural situations of the appropriate level of civilization on which the national policy can be based. See McKim Marriott, 'Cultural Policy in the New States,' in Clifford Geertz (ed.), *Old Societies and New States, op. cit.,* pp. 27-56. Myron Weiner provides a definition for integration and identifies some of the problems of political development in terms of national integration, territorial integration, value integration, and elite-mass integration. See Myron Weiner, 'Political Integration and Political Development,' in *The Annals of the American Academy of Political and Social Science,* vol. 358, March 1965, pp. 52-64, reprinted in Jason L. Finkle and Richard W. Gable (eds), *Political Development and Social Change, op.cit.,* pp. 551-62. W. Howard Wriggins shows how there is always the growing awareness of differences among groups after independence, which has both economic and political consequences for the stability of the nation. See W. Howard Wriggins, 'Impediments to Unity in New Nations: The Case of Ceylon,' *American Political Science Review,* vol. 55, June 1961, pp. 313-20, reprinted in Jason L. Finkle and Richard W. Gable (eds.), *Political Development and Social Change, op.cit.,* pp. 563-72.

36 'China: Population in the People's Republic,' *Population Bulletin,* vol. 27, no. 6, December 1971, p. 22.

37 Milton Kotler, *Neighborhood Government: The Local Foundations of Political Life,* New York: Bobbs-Merrill, 1969, chs 1-2.

38 See the sociological survey 'on town and village' (1967) in Bulgaria as reported in R. Vassilev, M. Draganov, and S. Mikhailov, *Sociology in Bulgaria,* Sofia: Bulgarian Academy of Sciences, Institute of Sociology, 1970.

39 Marion J. Levy, Jr, 'Some Sources of Vulnerability of the Structures of Relatively Non-Industrialized Societies to those of Highly Industrialized Societies,' in Bert F. Hoselitz (ed.), *The Progress of Underdeveloped Areas,* University of Chicago Press, 1952.

40 Bert F. Hoselitz, 'Social Structure and Economic Growth,' in his *Sociological Aspects of Economic Growth, op.cit.*

41 *Ibid.,* pp. 45-6.

42 Robert A. Dahl, *Polyarchy, op.cit.*

43 *Ibid.,* p. 248.

44 *Yearbook of the United Nations, 1975,* vol. 29, New York: Office of Public Information, United Nations, 1975.

11 Epilogue

1 Max Weber, 'Politics as a Vocation,' in H. H. Gerth and C. Wright Mills (eds), *From Max Weber, Essays in Sociology,* New York: Oxford University Press, 1946, p. 78.

2 Karl Marx, *Grundrisse,* translated by Martin Nicolaus, New York: Random House, 1974, p. 484.

3 Mark Wilks and several others maintained that land was privately owned in India. See Mark Wilks, *Historical Sketches of the South of India,* London: Longman, Hurst, Rees & Orne, 1810. On the other hand, Hugh Murray, among others, advanced the opposite argument that land was communally possessed in

NOTES TO PAGES 147-59

India. See Hugh Murray, *Historical and Descriptive Account of British India,* Edinburgh: Oliver & Boyd, 1832.

4 See Marx's *Exzerpte.* Also Lawrence Krader, *The Ethnological Notebooks of Marx,* The Hague: Von Gorcum, 1973, and Norman Levine, 'The Myth of the Asiatic Restoration,' *The Journal of Asian Studies,* vol. XXXVII, November 1977, pp. 73-85.

5 Mark Wilks, *Historical Sketches of the South of India, op.cit.* See also Richard Jones, *Essay on the Distribution of Wealth,* London: John Murray, 1831, which Marx had read.

6 See, among others, Walter C. Neale, *Economic Change and Reform in Uttar Pradesh, 1800-1955,* New Haven and London: Yale University Press, 1962.

7 Robert Patton, *The Principles of Asiatic Monarchies,* London: J. Debrett, 1801, p. 175.

8 The importance of law for private property can be gauged by the fact that, in 1978, there were 400.000 lawyers in the United States with another 100,000 students in colleges studying law. In the same year, there were only 3,500 lawyers in the People's Republic of China. I am grateful to Professor Victor H. Li of Stanford University Law School for this information.

9 Max Weber's interest in documenting developments in law started with his doctoral dissertation written in 1889. See Anthony Giddens, *Capitalism and Modern Social Theory: An Analysis of Marx, Durkheim and Max Weber,* Cambridge University Press, 1971, pp. 120-4. Also Max Rheinstein (ed.), *Max Weber on Law in Economy and Society,* New York: Simon & Schuster, 1967. For Max Weber's analysis of the interlocking relationship between land and labor, see Max Weber, *The Theory of Social and Economic Organization,* translated by A. M. Henderson and Talcott Parsons, New York: Free Press, 1964 [1947], pp. 238-50.

10 F. Orekhov, 'Dollar Democracy,' in Paul Hollander (ed.), *American and Soviet Society: A Reader in Comparative Sociology and Perception,* Englewood Cliffs: Prentice-Hall, 1969, p. 81.

11 Anthony Lewis in *The New York Times,* November 15, 1978. In presenting the profiles of the five countries, we will use the latest reports from the press, although the statistics have been carefully checked in terms of trends from past empirical studies on these countries.

12 A study conducted by Letitia Upton and Nancy Lyons of the Cambridge Institute as reported by Tom Wicker in *The New York Times* in 1971.

13 Data reported by *The Christian Science Monitor,* eastern edition, October 3, 1978. In 1974, the richest 20 per cent of families received 41 per cent of the total income and the poorest 20 per cent received only 5 per cent. *U.S. Bureau of Census,* Current Population Reports, series P-60, No. 101, 1976, p. 37.

14 Data reported by David K. Shipler from Moscow in *The New York Times,* November 6, 1977, on the occasion of the sixtieth anniversary of the founding of the Union of Soviet Socialist Republics.

15 *Ibid.*

16 *U.S. News & World Report, 1970.*

17 David K. Shipler, *The New York Times, op.cit.*

18 *U.S. News & World Report, op.cit.*

19 *U.S. News & World Report,* September 26, 1977.

20 V. N. Shubkin, 'Molodezh vstupaet v zhizn' ('Youth Enters Life'), *Voprosy filosofii,* vol. 19, no. 5 (May 1965), pp. 57-70. Translated in *Soviet Sociology,* vol. IV, no. 3 (Winter 1965), pp. 3-15.

21 Andrei D. Sakharov, 'The Sakharov Memorandum,' published in *The New York Times,* August 18, 1972.

22 'Tens of millions of people took part in the discussion of the directives of the five-year plan of the economic development of the USSR in 1966-70.' V. G.

198

Afanasiev, 'V. I. Lenin on Scientific Administration of Socialist Society,' in *Transactions of the Seventh World Congress of Sociology,* Sofia: The Bulgarian Academy of Sciences Publishing House, 1973, p. 103.

23 Mao Tse-tung, 'Revolutionary Forces of the World Unite, Fight Against Imperialist Aggression!' (November 1948), in *Selected Works,* vol IV., p. 284, reprinted in *Quotations From Chairman Mao Tse-tung,* Peking: Foreign Language Press, 1974, pp. 1-2.

24 The data on the People's Republic of China have been compiled from several sources. Wherever possible, they have been checked with Peter Cheng, *A Chronology of the People's Republic of China,* Totowa, N.J.: Littlefield, Adams, 1972.

25 *Ibid.*

26 *Ibid.*

27 *Ibid.*

28 Mao Tse-tung, 'On the Question of Agricultural Cooperation,' July 31, 1955, *Selected Works,* 3rd ed., p. 7., reprinted in *Quotations From Mao Tse-tung, op.cit.,* p. 3.

29 Morton H. Fried, *Centripetal and Centrifugal Tendencies in Chinese Society,* mimeographed, pp. 3-4.

30 Peter Cheng, *A Chronology of the People's Republic of China, op.cit.*

31 *Ibid.*

32 *Ibid.*

33 *Time* Magazine, May 3, 1971.

34 Peter Cheng, *A Chronology of the People's Republic of China, op.cit.*

35 Mao Tse-tung, 'We Must Learn to do Economic Work,' January 10, 1945, *Selected Works,* vol. III, p. 241. reprinted in *Quotations From Mao Tse-tung, op.cit.,* p. 194.

36 Herbert Passin, *Society and Education in Japan,* New York: Teachers' College, Columbia University 1965, p. 47.

37 J. I. Nakamura, 'Incentives, Productivity Gaps, and Agricultural Growth Rates in Prewar Japan, Taiwan, and Korea,' (mimeographed), p. 10.

38 E. S. Crawcour, 'The Modern Economy,' in Arthur E. Tiedemann (ed.), *An Introduction to Japanese Civilization,* New York: Columbia University Press, 1974, p. 492.

39 See James G. Abegglen, *The Japanese Factory,* Chicago: Free Press, 1958. This is one of the most debated issues in literature today. The occurrence of patrimonialism in some major and other small industries is not in doubt, but whether it has links with a past culture, or whether this practice is a temporary adjustment to the shift toward massive industrialization, is a question which has not quite been settled. See, among others, Kazuo Okochi, Bernard Karsh, and Solomon B. Levine (eds.), *Workers and Employers in Japan: The Japanese Employment Relations System,* Princeton University Press, 1974.

40 Ruth Benedict, *The Chrysanthemum and the Sword,* Boston: Houghton Mifflin, 1946.

41 Chie Nakane, *Japanese Society,* Berkeley: University of California Press, 1970.

42 James G. Abegglen, *The Japanese Factory, op.cit.*

43 The average rate of savings per household in Japan during the late 1970s was 10 to 15 per cent, which is also what an average factory or office worker in the Soviet Union spent on liquor.

44 The data on India have been compiled from various authoritative sources. A check has also been made with *India: A Reference Annual,* published every year by the Research and Reference Division, Ministry of Information and Broadcasting, Government of India.

45 *Ibid.* Also see Pravin Visaria and Anrudh K. Jain, *India* (Country Profiles Publication), New York: Population Council, May 1976; and Ravi Gulhati,

India's Population Policy: History and Future, World Bank Staff Working Paper no. 265, Washington, D.C.: World Bank, 1977.

46 See Pradhan H. Prasad, 'Essentials of Development in India,' *L.B.S. National Academy of Administration Journal,* vol. XIX, no. 2, Summer 1974, pp. 241-72.

47 William Borders in *The New York Times,* May 28, 1978.

48 K. N. Raj, 'The Economic Situation,' in *Economic and Political Weekly,* July 3, 1976, p. 995.

49 *Ibid.*

50 William Borders in *The New York Times International Economic Survey,* February 5, 1978.

51 Pradhan H. Prasad, 'Essentials of Development in India,' *op.cit.,* and Wolf Ladejinsky, 'The Green Revolution in Bihar—The Kosi Area: A Field Trip' and 'The Green Revolution in Punjab: A Field Trip', both reprinted from the *Economic and Political Weekly,* vol. IV, no. 39, September 27, 1969, and vol. IV, no. 26, June 28, 1969, in *ADC reprint,* no. 28, June 1976, New York: Agricultural Development Council, 1976.

52 In the 1971 general elections, the Congress Party in India reportedly spent 480,000 rupees per constituency when the law allowed maximum expenditure of 35,000 rupees per candidate. See W. H. Morris-Jones, 'India Elects for Change and Stability,' pp. 723-4, as mentioned in Robert L. Hardgrave, Jr, *India: Government and Politics in a Developing Nation,* New York: Harcourt Brace Jovanovich, 2nd edition, 1975, p. 194. In the race for the party presidency leading to the Prime Ministership in Japan in 1978, 'according to Asahi, large amounts are being spent once again, with individual payments going up to 300,000 yen, or more than $1,500.' Reported by Henry Scott-Stokes from Toyko in *The New York Times,* November 26, 1978.

53 See Richard McKeon (ed.), *Democracy in a World of Tensions,* University of Chicago Press, 1951.

54 Anthony J. Parisi, 'Who's Got the Oil, and Who Does the Counting?' in *The New York Times,* November 19, 1978.

55 *Ibid.*

Select bibliography

The literature on modernization is vast and increasing. The items listed below have been cited or used for this work.

ALMOND, GABRIEL A., 'Introduction: A Functional Approach to Comparative Politics,' in GABRIEL A. ALMOND and JAMES S. COLEMAN (eds), *The Politics of the Developing Areas,* Princeton University Press, 1960.

ALMOND, GABRIEL A. and JAMES C. COLEMAN (eds), *The Politics of the Developing Areas,* Princeton University Press, 1960.

ALMOND, GABRIEL A. and SIDNEY VERBA, *The Civic Culture: Political Attitudes and Democracy in Five Nations,* Boston: Little Brown, 1965.

ANSHEN, RUTH NANDA (ed.), *Mid-East: World-Center Yesterday, Today, and Tomorrow,* New York: Harper, 1956.

APTER, DAVID E., *The Politics of Modernization,* University of Chicago Press, 1965.

ARENSBERG, CONRAD M., 'American Communities,' *American Anthropologist,* vol. 57, no. 6, 1955, pp. 1143-60.

ARENSBERG, CONRAD M., 'The Community as Object and as Sample,' *American Anthropologist,* vol. 63, no. 2, part I, 1961, pp. 241-64.

ARENSBERG, CONRAD M., 'The Community Study Method,' *The American Journal of Sociology,* vol. 60, no. 2, 1954, pp. 109-24.

ARENSBERG, CONRAD M. and SOLON T. KIMBALL, 'Community Study: Retrospect and Prospect,' *The American Journal of Sociology,* vol. 73, no. 6, May 1968, pp. 671-705.

ARENSBERG, CONRAD M. and SOLON T. KIMBALL, *Culture and Community,* New York: Harcourt, Brace & World, 1965.

ARENSBERG, CONRAD M. and SOLON T. KIMBALL, 'Metropolis and Social Class,' in CONRAD M. ARENSBERG and SOLON T. KIMBALL, *Culture and Community,* New York: Harcourt, Brace & World, 1965.

ARORA, SATISH K. and HAROLD D. LASSWELL, *Political Communication: The Public Language of Political Elites in India and the United States,* New York: Holt, Rinehart & Winston, 1969.

BAER, GABRIEL, *Studies in the Social History of Modern Egypt,* University of Chicago Press, 1969.

BANFIELD, EDWARD C., *The Unheavenly City: The Nature and Future of Our Urban Crisis,* Boston: Little, Brown, 1968.

BANKS, ARTHUR and ROBERT TEXTOR, *A Cross Polity Survey,* Cambridge, Mass.: MIT Press, 1963.

201

BARAN, PAUL A., *The Political Economy of Growth*, New York: Modern Reader Paperbacks, 1968.

BARRINGER, HERBERT R. *et al.* (eds), *Social Change in Developing Areas*, Cambridge, Mass.: Schenkman, 1965.

BECKER, HOWARD and ALVIN BOSKOFF (eds), *Modern Sociological Theory in Continuity and Change*, New York: Dryden Press, 1957.

BELL, DANIEL, *The Coming of Post-Industrial Society: A Venture in Social Forecasting*, New York: Basic Books, 1973.

BELLAH, ROBERT N., 'Civil Religion in America,' in Donald R. Cutler (ed.), *The Religious Situation, 1968*, Boston: Beacon Press, 1968.

BELLAH, ROBERT N., 'Religious Evolution,' *American Sociological Review*, vol. 29, no. 3, June 1964.

BELLAH, ROBERT N., *Tokugawa Religion*, Chicago: Free Press, 1957.

BELOFF, MAX, *The Age of Absolutism: 1660-1815*, London: Hutchinson, 1954.

BENDIX, REINHARD, *Nation-Building and Citizenship: Studies of Our Changing Social Order*, New York: John Wiley, 1964.

BENNETT, H.S., *Life on the English Manor*, Cambridge University Press, 1962.

BENSMAN, JOSEPH and ARTHUR J. VIDICH, *The New American Society: The Revolution of the Middle Class*, Chicago: Quadrangle Books, 1971.

BEQIRAJ, MEHMET, *Peasantry in Revolution*, Ithaca, New York: Center for International Studies, Cornell University, 1966.

BERLE, ADOLF A., A Review of W.W. Rostow, *The Stages of Economic Growth*, in *Saturday Review*, vol. 43, part 2, July 9, 1960, pp. 18-19.

BIERSTEDT, ROBERT, *The Social Order*, New York: McGraw-Hill, 1970.

BLOCH, MARC, *Feudal Society*, London: Routledge & Kegan Paul, 1961.

BLOCH, MARC, *French Rural History*, London: Routledge & Kegan Paul, 1966.

BOEKE, J. H., *Economics and Economic Policy of Dual Societies*, New York: Institute of Pacific Relations, 1953.

BOEKE, JULIUS H., *Oriental Economics*, New York: Institute of Pacific Relations, 1947.

BOEKE, JULIUS H., *The Structure of Netherlands Indian Economy*, New York: Institute of Pacific Relations, 1942.

BOTTOMORE, T.B., *Sociology: A Guide to Problems and Literature*, Englewood Cliffs: Prentice-Hall, 1963.

BRAIBANTI, RALPH and JOSEPH T. SPENGLER (eds), *Administration and Economic Development in India*, North Carolina: Duke University Press, 1963.

BRAIBANTI, RALPH and JOSEPH T. SPENGLER (eds), *Tradition, Value and Socio-Economic Development*, North Carolina: Duke University Press, 1961.

BRINTON, CRANE, *The Anatomy of Revolution*, New York: W. W. Norton, 1938.

BRYSON, LYMAN (ed.), *The Communication of Ideas*, New York: Harper, 1948.

BRZEZINSKI, ZBIGNIEW and SAMUEL P. HUNTINGTON, *Political Power: USA/USSR*, New York: Viking Press, 1965.

CARNEIRO, ROBERT L., 'Ascertaining, Testing, and Interpreting Sequences of Cultural Development,' *Southwestern Journal of Anthropology*, vol. 24, 1968, pp. 354-74.

'China: Population in the People's Republic,' *Population Bulletin*, vol. 27, no. 6, December 1971.

COHEN, BENJAMIN B. (ed.), *The Worldmark Encyclopedia of the Nations*, New York: Harper, 1960.

COHEN, RONALD, 'Political Anthropology,' in John J. Honigmann (ed.), *Handbook of Social and Cultural Anthropology*, Chicago: Rand McNally, 1973.

COHEN, RONALD, 'The Political System,' in RAOUL NAROLL and RONALD COHEN (eds), *A Handbook of Method in Cultural Anthropology*, New York: Columbia University Press, 1973.

COHEN, R. and J. MIDDLETON (eds), *Comparative Political System: Studies in the Politics of Pre-Industrial Societies,* New York: Natural History Press, 1967.

COMTE, AUGUSTE, *The Positive Philosophy,* freely translated and condensed by Harriet Martineau, London: George Bell & Sons, 1896.

CONNOR, JAMES E. (ed.), *Lenin on Politics and Revolution,* New York: Pegasus, 1968.

COOK, SCOTT, 'Economic Anthropology: Problems in Theory, Method, and Analysis,' in JOHN J. HONIGMANN (ed.), *Handbook of Social and Cultural Anthropology,* Chicago: Rand McNally, 1973.

CUTLER, DONALD R. (ed.), *The Religious Situation: 1968,* Boston: Beacon Press, 1968.

DAHL, ROBERT A., *Polyarchy: Participation and Opposition,* New Haven: Yale University Press, 1971.

DAHL, ROBERT A. (ed.), *Regimes and Opposition,* New Haven: Yale University Press, 1971.

DALTON, GEORGE, 'The Economic System,' in RAOUL NAROLL and RONALD COHEN (eds.), *A Handbook of Method in Cultural Anthropology,* New York: Columbia University Press, 1973.

DALTON, GEORGE (ed.), *Tribal and Peasant Economies: Reading in Economic Anthropology,* New York: Natural History Press, 1967.

DAVIES, JAMES C., 'Toward a Theory of Revolution,' *American Sociological Review,* vol. 27, February 1962, pp. 5-19.

DAVIS, KINGSLEY, 'Population Policy: Will Current Programs Succeed?' *Science,* no. 158, November 10, 1957, pp. 730-9.

DERRETT, J. DUNCAN M., *Religion, Law and the State in India,* New York: Free Press, 1968.

DESAI, A. R. (ed.), *Essays on Modernization of Underdeveloped Societies,* 2 vols, New York: Humanities Press, 1972, vols I and II.

DESAI, A. R., *Recent Trends in Indian Nationalism,* Bombay: Popular Book Depot, 1960.

DEUTSCH, KARL W., *Nationalism and Social Communication: An Inquiry into the Formation of Nationality,* Cambridge, Mass.: MIT Press, 1966.

DEUTSCH, KARL W., *The Nerves of Government: Models of Communication and Control,* New York: Free Press, 1963.

'Development Myths,' in *Bulletin,* Institute of Development Studies, University of Sussex, vol. 1, no. 4, May 1969.

DE WAAL MALEFIJT, ANNEMARIE, *Religion and Culture: An Introduction to Anthropology of Religion,* New York: Macmillan, 1968.

DJILAS, MILOVAN, *The New Class: An Analysis of the Communist System,* New York: Frederick A. Praeger, 1957.

DOBB, MAURICE, *Economic Growth and Underdeveloped Countries,* New York: International Publishers, 1963.

DUBE, S. C., 'Bureaucracy and Nation Building in Transitional Societies,' *International Social Science Journal,* vol. 16, 1964, pp. 229-36.

DUBE, S. C., *India's Changing Village: Human Factors of Community Development,* London: Routledge & Kegan Paul, 1958.

DURKHEIM, EMILE, *The Division of Labor in Society,* Chicago: Free Press, 1933.

DURKHEIM, EMILE, *The Elementary Forms of the Religious Life,* New York: Collier Books, 1961.

EAMES, EDWIN and JUDITH GOODE, 'Urban Anthropology: A Critical Survey,' in Baidya Nath Varma (ed.), *The New Social Science,* Westport, Conn.: Greenwood Press, 1976.

EAMES, EDWIN and JUDITH GRANICH GOODE, *Urban Poverty in a Cross-Cultural Context,* New York: Free Press, 1973.

EASTON, DAVID, *The Political System,* New York: Alfred A. Knopf, 1953.

EASTON, DAVID, *Varieties of Political Theory,* Englewood Cliffs: Prentice-Hall, 1966.

EISENSTADT, S. N. (ed.) *The Protestant Ethic and Modernization: A Comparative View,* New York: Basic Books, 1968.

EISENSTADT, S.N.(ed.), *Comparative Perspective on Social Change*, New York: Little, Brown, 1968.

EISENSTADT, S.N., *Modernization, Diversity, and Growth*, Bloomington: Indiana University, Department of Government, 1953.

EISENSTADT, S.N. *Modernization: Protest and Change*, Englewood Cliffs: Prentice-Hall, 1966.

EISENSTADT, S.N., *The Political Systems of Empires*, New York: Free Press, 1963.

EMERSON, RUPERT, *From Empire to Nation: The Rise to Self-Assertion of Asian and African Peoples*, Boston: Beacon Press, 1962 [1960].

ETZIONI, AMITAI, *The Active Society: A Theory of Societal and Political Process*, New York: Free Press, 1971 [1968].

ETZIONI, AMITAI and EVA ETZIONI (eds), *Social Change: Sources, Patterns and Consequences*, New York: Basic Books, 1969.

EULAU, HEINZ, *The Behavioral Persuasion in Politics*, New York: Random House, 1963.

FAIRCHILD, HENRY PRATT, *Versus: Reflections of a Sociologist*, New York: Philosophical Library, 1950.

FESTINGER, LEON, *A Theory of Cognitive Dissonance*, Stanford University Press, 1957.

FINKLE, JASON L. and RICHARD W. GABLE (eds), *Political Development and Social Change*, New York: John Wiley, 1966.

FIRTH, RAYMOND, *Elements of Social Organization*, Boston: Beacon Press, 1963.

FIRTH, RAYMOND, *Malay Fishermen: Their Peasant Economy*, London: Routledge & Kegan Paul, 1946.

FIRTH, RAYMOND, *Primitive Polynesian Economy*, London: Routledge & Kegan Paul, 1939.

FIRTH, RAYMOND and BASIL S. YAMEY (eds), *Capital, Saving and Credit in Peasant Societies*, Chicago: Aldine, 1964.

FISHER, MARGARET W. (ed.) and JOAN V. BONDURANT (assoc. ed.), *Indian Approaches to a Socialist Society*, Indian Press Digests-Monograph Series, Berkeley: Institute of International Studies, University of California, no. 2, July 1956.

FORTES, MEYER and E. E. EVANS-PRITCHARD, *African Political Systems*, London: Oxford University Press, 1940.

FRANK, PIERRE, et al. (eds), *Key Problems of the Transition from Capitalism to Socialism*, New York: Pathfinder Press, 1969.

FRIED, MORTON H. (ed.), *Explorations in Anthropology: Readings in Culture, Man, and Nature*, New York: Thomas Y. Crowell, 1973.

FRIED, MORTON H., *The Evolution of Political Society: An Essay in Political Anthropology*, New York: Random House, 1967.

FRIEDLAND, WILLIAM H. and CARL G. ROSBERG, JR. (eds), *African Socialism*, Stanford University Press, 1964.

FRYE, R. N. (ed.), *Islam and the West*, The Hague: Mouton, 1959.

FURNIVALL, J. S., *Colonial Policy and Practice: A Comparative Study of Burma and Netherlands India*, Cambridge University Press, 1948.

FURNIVALL, J. S., *Netherlands India: A Study of Plural Economy*, Cambridge University Press, 1939.

GALBRAITH, JOHN KENNETH, *Economic Development in Perspective*, Cambridge, Mass.: Harvard University Press, 1962.

GANS, HERBERT, *More Equality*, New York: Pantheon Books, 1974.

GEERTZ, CLIFFORD (ed.), *Old Societies and New States*, New York: Free Press, 1963.

GEERTZ, CLIFFORD, *Peddlers and Princes: Social Development and Economic Change in Two Indonesian Towns*, University of Chicago Press, 1963.

GEIGER, THEODORE and LEO SOLOMON (eds), *Motivations and Methods in Development and Foreign Aid*, Washington, D.C.: Society for International Development, 1964.

204

GINSBURG, NORTON, *Atlas of Economic Development*, University of Chicago Press, 1961.

GOODE, WILLIAM J., *World Revolution and Family Patterns*, New York: Free Press, 1970 [1963].

GRAS, N. S. B., 'Anthropology and Economics,' in W. F. OGBURN and A. A. GOLDEN-WEISER (eds), *The Social Sciences and their Interrelations*, Boston: Houghton Mifflin, 1927.

GRUNEBAUM, GUSTAVE E. VON (ed.), *Unity and Variety in Muslim Civilization*, University of Chicago Press, 1955.

GUSFIELD, JOSEPH R., 'Tradition and Modernity: Misplaced Polarities in the Study of Social Change,' *American Journal of Sociology*. vol. 72, no. 4, January 1967, pp. 351-62.

HAGEN, EVERETT E., *On the Theory of Social Change: How Economic Growth Begins*, Homewood, Ill.: Dorsey Press, 1962

HAIM, SYLVIA G. (ed.), *Arab Nationalism: An Anthology*, Berkeley: University of California Press, 1962.

HALPERN, MANFRED, *The Politics of Social Change in the Middle East and North Africa*, Princeton University Press, 1963.

HARRINGTON, MICHAEL, *The Other America: Poverty in the United States*, New York: Macmillan Company, 1962.

HARROD, R.F., *Towards a Dynamic Economics*, London: Macmillan, 1948.

HATT, PAUL K. and ALBERT J. REISS, JR (eds), *Cities and Society*, Chicago: Free Press, 1951.

HEILBRONER, ROBERT L., *The Great Ascent: The Struggle for Economic Development in Our Time*, New York: Harper & Row, 1963.

HIGGINS, BENJAMIN, *Economic Development: Problems, Principles, and Politics*, New York: W.W. Norton, 1959.

HIRSCHMAN, ALBERT O., *A Bias for Hope: Essays on Development and Latin America*, New Haven: Yale University Press, 1971.

HIRSCHMAN, ALBERT O., *Development Projects Observed*, Washington, D.C.: Brookings Institution, 1967.

HIRSCHMAN, ALBERT O., *The Strategy of Economic Growth*, New York: 1958.

HOFFMAN, STANLEY (ed.), *Conditions of World Order*, New York: Simon & Schuster, 1966.

HOLT, ROBERT T. and JOHN E. TURNER (eds), *The Methodology of Comparative Research*, New York: Free Press, 1972.

HONIGMANN, JOHN J. (ed.), *Handbook of Social and Cultural Anthropology*, Chicago: Rand McNally, 1973.

HORNEY, KAREN, *The Neurotic Personality of Our Time*, New York: W.W. Norton, 1937.

HOROWITZ, IRVING LOUIS, *Three Worlds of Development: The Theory and Practice of International Stratification*, New York: Oxford University Press, 1966.

HOSELITZ, BERT F. (ed.), 'Agrarian Societies in Transition,' *The Annals of the American Academy of Political and Social Science*, Philadelphia, May 1956.

HOSELITZ, BERT F., *Sociological Aspects of Economic Growth*, Chicago: Free Press, 1960.

HOSELITZ, BERT F., 'The City, the Factory, and Economic Growth,' *American Economic Review*, vol. 45, May 1955, pp. 166-84.

HOSELITZ, BERT F. (ed.), *The Progress of Underdeveloped Areas*, University of Chicago Press, 1952.

HOSELITZ, BERT F., *et al.* (eds), *Theories of Economic Growth*, Chicago: Free Press, 1960.

HOSELITZ, BERT F. and WILBERT E. MOORE (eds), *Industrialization and Society*, The Hague: UNESCO-Mouton, 1963.

HUBERMAN, LEO and PAUL M. SWEEZY (eds), *Introduction to Socialism*, New York: Modern Reader Paperbacks. 1968.

HUNTER, GUY, *Modernizing Peasant Societies: A Comparative Study in Asia and Africa*, New York: Oxford University Press, 1969.

HUNTER, GUY, *The New Societies of Tropical Africa*, New York: Frederick A. Praeger, 1962.

HYMAN, HERBERT, *Political Socialization*, Chicago: Free Press, 1959.

INKELES, ALEX, 'The Modernization of Man,' in Myron Weiner (ed.), *Modernization*, New York: Basic Books, 1966.

INKELES, ALEX, 'The OM Scale: A Comparative Socio-Psychological Measure of Individual Modernity,' *Sociometry*, vol. 29, no. 4, December 1966, pp. 353-77.

JACOB, PHILIP E. (ed.), *Values and the Active Community*, New York: Free Press, 1971.

JANOWITZ, MORRIS (ed.), *The New Military: Changing Patterns of Organization*, New York: John Wiley, 1967 [1964].

JOHNSON, JOHN J. (ed.), *The Role of the Military in Underdeveloped Countries*, Princeton University Press, 1962.

KAUTSKY, JOHN H. (ed.), *Political Change in Underdeveloped Countries: Nationalism and Communism*, New York: John Wiley, 1962.

KENISTON, KENNETH, *Youth and Dissent*, New York: Harcourt, Brace & Jovanovich, 1971.

KINGSLEY, J. DONALD, *Representative Bureaucracy*, Yellow Springs, Ohio: Antioch Press, 1944.

KOHN, HANS, *The Idea of Nationalism: A Study in Its Origins and Background*, New York: Macmillan, 1961 [1944].

KORNHAUSER, WILLIAM, *The Politics of Mass Society*, Chicago: Free Press, 1959.

KOTLER, MILTON, *Neighborhood Government: The Local Foundations of Political Life*, New York: Bobbs-Merrill, 1969.

KRADER, LAWRENCE, *Formation of the State*, Englewood Cliffs: Prentice-Hall, 1968.

KRISHNA, DAYA, 'Some Reflections on the Concept of Political Development as Represented in the Writings of Some American Political Scientists of the Sixties,' East-West Center, University of Hawaii (mimeographed).

KROEBER, A.L. (ed.), *Anthropology Today*, University of Chicago Press, 1953.

KROEBER, A. L. and CLYDE KLUCKHOHN, *Culture: A Critical Review of Concepts and Definitions*, New York: Vintage Books, 1963.

KUHN, THOMAS S., *The Structure of Scientific Revolutions*, 2nd edition, University of Chicago Press, 1970.

KUPER, LEO and MARION G. SMITH (eds), *Pluralism in Africa*, Berkeley: University of California Press, 1969.

KUZNETS, SIMON, *Six Lectures on Economic Growth*, Chicago: Free Press, 1959.

KUZNETS, SIMON, 'Notes on the Take-off,' Paper presented at the International Economic Association's Conference at Konstanz in September, 1960, on 'The Economics of Take-off into Sustained Growth,' and reprinted in Paul A. Samuelson (ed.), *Readings in Economics*, New York: McGraw-Hill Book Company, 1973, 7th edition, pp. 262-5.

LAMBERT, JACQUES, *Latin America: Social Structure and Political Institutions*, Berkeley: University of California Press, 1967.

LAPALOMBARA, JOSEPH (ed.), *Bureaucracy and Political Development*, Princeton University Press, 1963.

LAPALOMBARA, JOSEPH and MYRON WEINER (eds), *Political Parties and Political Development*, Princeton University Press, 1966.

LASSWELL, HAROLD D., *Politics: Who Gets What, When, How*, New York: McGraw-Hill, 1936.

LAZARSFELD, PAUL F. and FRANK N. STANTON (eds), *Communications Research 1948-49*, New York: Harper, 1949.

LEACOCK, ELEANOR BURKE (ed.), *The Culture of Poverty: A Critique*, New York: Simon & Schuster, 1971.

LECLAIR, EDWARD E., 'Economic Theory and Economic Anthropology,' *American Anthropologist*, vol. 64, 1962.

LEE, ALFRED MCCLUNG (ed.), *New Outline of the Principles of Sociology*, New York: Barnes & Noble, 1946.

LEEDS, ANTHONY, 'Locality Power in Relation to Supralocal Power Institutions,' in Aiden Southall (ed.), *Urban Anthropology: Cross-Cultural Studies of Urbanization*, New York: Oxford University Press, 1973.

LEIBENSTEIN, HARVEY, *Economic Backwardness and Economic Growth*, New York: John Wiley, 1957.

LENIN, V.I., *Collected Works*, Moscow, 1963-9.

LENIN, V.I. *Collected Works*, New York: International Publishers, 1936.

LERNER, DANIEL, *The Passing of Traditional Society: Modernizing the Middle East*, New York: Free Press, 1958.

LEVY, MARION J., JR, *Modernization and the Structure of Societies: A Setting for International Relations*, Princeton University Press, 1966.

LEWIS, A.B., 'Local Self-Government: A Key to National Economic Advancement and Political Stability,' *Philippine Journal of Public Administration*, vol. II, no. 1, 1958, pp. 54-7.

LEWIS, OSCAR, *Five Families: Mexican Studies in the Culture of Poverty*, New York: Basic Books, 1959.

LEWIS, OSCAR, *La Vida: A Puerto Rican Family in the Culture of Poverty, San Juan and New York*, New York: Random House, 1966.

LEWIS, OSCAR, *Life in a Mexican Village, Tepoztlan Restudied*, Urbana: University of Illinois Press, 1951.

LEWIS, OSCAR, Review of Charles A. Valentine, *Culture and Poverty: Critique and Counterproposals*, University of Chicago Press, 1968, in *Current Anthropology*, vol. 10, nos 2-3, 1969, p. 192.

LEWIS, OSCAR, *The Children of Sanchez*, New York: Random House, 1961.

LEWIS, OSCAR, 'The Culture of Poverty,' *Scientific American*, vol. 215, 1966, pp. 19-25.

LEWIS, W. ARTHUR, *The Principles of Economic Planning*, Washington, D.C.: Public Affairs Press, 1951.

LEWIS, W. ARTHUR, *The Theory of Economic Growth*, London: Allen & Unwin, 1955.

LIEBOW, ELLIOT, *Tally's Corner: A Study of Negro Street Corner Men*, Boston: Little, Brown, 1967.

LIFTON, ROBERT J., *Boundaries: Psychological Man in Revolution*, New York: Random House, 1969.

LINTON, ERICA, *Gramdan—Revolution by Persuasion*, London: Friends Peace and International Relations Committee, n.d.

LIPSET, SEYMOUR MARTIN, *Political Man: The Social Bases of Politics*, Garden City, New York: Doubleday, 1960.

LIPSET, SEYMOUR MARTIN, *Revolution and Counterrevolution: Change and Persistence in Social Structures*, Garden City, New York: Doubleday, 1970, revised edition [1963, 1968].

LIPSET, SEYMOUR MARTIN, *The First New Nation: The United States in Historical and Comparative Perspective*, Garden City, New York: Doubleday, 1967 [1963].

LIPSET, SEYMOUR MARTIN and REINHARD BENDIX, *Social Mobility in Industrial Society*, Berkeley: University of California Press, 1960 [1959].

LITTLE, KENNETH, *West African Urbanization: A Study of Voluntary Associations in Social Change*, Cambridge University Press, 1965.

LOOMIS, C.P. and Z.K. LOOMIS (eds), *Socio-Economic Change and the Religious Factor in India*. New York: Van Nostrand Reinhold, 1969.

LYND, ROBERT S., *Knowledge for What?* Princeton University Press, 1948.

MACIVER, ROBERT M., *The Web of Government*, New York: Macmillan, 1947.

MCCLELLAND, DAVID C., 'Community Development and the Nature of Human

Motivation: Some implications of Recent Research,' paper presented at the Conference on Community Development and National Change, MIT, CIS, December 1957 (mimeographed).

MCCLELLAND, DAVID C., 'Motivational Trends in Society,' a module, Morristown, New Jersey: General Learning Press, 1971.

MCCLELLAND, DAVID C., *The Achieving Society*, Princeton, New Jersey: D. Van Nostrand, 1961.

MCCLELLAND, DAVID C. and DAVID G. WINTER, *Motivating Economic Achievement*, New York: Free Press, 1969.

MCCORD, WILLIAM, *The Springtime of Freedom: The Evolution of Developing Societies*, New York: Oxford University Press, 1965.

MAINE, SIR HENRY SUMNER, *Ancient Law*, New York: Henry Holt & Co., 1885.

MALRAUX, ANDRÉ, *Anti-Memoirs*, translated by Terence Kilmartin, New York: Holt, Rinehart & Winston, 1968.

MANDEL, ERNEST (ed.), *Fifty Years of World Revolution: An International Symposium*, New York: Pathfinder Press, 1968.

MANGIN, W., *Peasants in Cities*, New York: Houghton Mifflin, 1970.

MARRIOTT, MCKIM, 'Cultural Policy in the New States,' in Clifford Geertz (ed.), *Old Societies and New States*, New York: Free Press, 1963.

MARX, KARL and FRIEDRICH ENGELS, *Correspondence 1864-1895*, New York: International Publishers, 1936.

MARX, ENGELS, LENIN, *The Essential Left: Four Classic Texts on the Principles of Socialism*, London: George Allen & Unwin, 1961.

MBOYA, TOM, *Freedom and After*, Boston: Little, Brown, 1963.

MERTON, ROBERT K., *Social Theory and Social Structure*, Glencoe, Ill.: Free Press, 1957, rev. edition.

MÉTRAUX, GUY S. and FRANÇOISE CROUZET, *The New Asia*, New York: Mentor, 1965.

MILLER, S. M. and P. ROBY, *The Future of Inequality*, New York: Basic Books, 1970.

MILLS, C. WRIGHT, *Listen, Yankee: The Revolution in Cuba*, New York: Ballantine Books, 1960.

MINER, HORACE, 'The Folk-Urban Continuum,' *American Sociological Review*, vol. 17, October 1952, pp. 525-37.

MISRA, VIKAS, *Hinduism and Economic Growth*, London: Oxford University Press, 1962.

MOORE, BARRINGTON JR, *Social Origins of Dictatorship and Democracy: Lord and Peasant in the Making of the Modern World*, Boston: Beacon Press, 1966.

MOORE, WILBERT E. and ARNOLD S. FELDMAN (eds.), *Labor Commitment and Social Change in Developing Areas*, New York: Social Science Research Council, 1960.

MORGAN, HENRY L., *Ancient Society*, edited by Eleanor B. Leacock, Cleveland, Ohio: World Publishing, 1963 [1874].

MYINT, H., *Economic Theory and the Underdeveloped Countries*, New York: Oxford University Press, 1971.

MYRDAL, GUNNAR, *An American Dilemma*, New York: Harper, 1944.

MYRDAL, GUNNAR, *Asian Drama: An Inquiry into the Poverty of Nations*, 3 vols, New York: Pantheon, 1968.

MYRDAL, GUNNAR, *Economic Theory and Underdeveloped Regions*, London: Duckworth, 1957.

MYRDAL, GUNNAR, *Rich Lands and Poor*, New York: Harper, 1957.

NADAR, LAURA and BARBARA YNGVESSON, 'On Studying the Ethnography of Law and Its Consequences,' in JOHN J. HONIGMANN (ed.), *Handbook of Social and Cultural Anthropology*, Chicago: Rand McNally, 1973.

NAROLL, RAOUL, 'A Preliminary Index of Social Development,' *American Anthropologist*, vol. 58, 1956.

NAROLL, RAOUL and RONALD COHEN (eds), *A Handbook of Method in Cultural Anthropology*, New York: Columbia University Press, 1973.

'Nature and Extent of Social Change in India,' *Sociological Bulletin*, Decennial Celebration Symposium, October 1961, vol. XI, Nos. 1 and 2, March-September 1962.

NEARING, HELEN SCOTT, *Living the Good Life*, New York: Schoeken, 1971.

NEUMANN, S. (ed.), *Modern Political Parties*, University of Chicago Press, 1956.

NISBET, ROBERT, *Social Change and History: Aspects of the Western Theory of Development*, New York: Oxford University Press, 1969.

NISBET, ROBERT, *The Social Philosophers: Community and Conflict in Western Thought*, New York: Thomas Y. Crowell, 1973.

NOVACK, GEORGE, *Democracy and Revolution*, New York: Pathfinder Press, 1971.

NOVACK, GEORGE, *Understanding History: Marxist Essays*, New York: Pathfinder Press, 1972.

NURKSE, RAGNAR, *Problems of Capital Formation in Underdeveloped Countries*, New York: Oxford University Press, 1953.

OGBURN, W. F and A. A. GOLDENWEISER (eds), *The Social Sciences and Their Interrelations*, Boston, Mass.: Houghton Mifflin, 1927.

ORGANSKI, A. F. K., *The Stages of Political Development*, New York: Alfred A. Knopf, 1965.

ORTEGA Y GASSET, JOSÉ, *The Revolt of the Masses*, New York: W.W. Norton, 1932.

PARK, ROBERT E., *Race and Culture*, Chicago: Free Press, 1950.

PARSONS, TALCOTT, 'Pattern Variables Revisited,' *American Sociological Review*, vol. 25, no. 4, August 1960, pp. 470, 476.

PARSONS, TALCOTT, *Societies: Evolutionary and Comparative Perspectives*, Englewood Cliffs: Prentice-Hall, 1966.

PARSONS, TALCOTT, *Structure and Process in Modern Societies*, Chicago: The Free Press of Glencoe, 1960.

PARSONS, TALCOTT, *The Social System*, Chicago: Free Press, 1951.

PARSONS, TALCOTT, *The Structure of Social Action*, 2 vols, New York: Free Press, 1968 [1937].

PARSONS, TALCOTT, *The System of Modern Societies*, Englewood Cliffs: Prentice-Hall, 1971.

PARSONS, TALCOTT and EDWARD A. SHILS (eds), *Toward a General Theory of Action*, Cambridge, Mass.: Harvard University Press, 1951.

PEACOCK, JAMES L. and THOMAS KIRSCH, *The Human Direction: An Evolutionary Approach to Social and Cultural Anthropology*, New York: Appleton-Century-Crofts, 1970.

PETERSON, WILLIAM, *Population*, New York: Macmillan Company, 1969.

PIERS, GERHART and MILTON SINGER (eds), *Shame and Guilt: A Psychological and Cultural Study*, Springfield, Illinois: Charles C. Thomas, 1953.

POLANYI, KARL, *et al.* (eds), *Trade and Market in the Early Empires*, Chicago: Free Press, 1957.

PRASAD, NARMADESHWAR, *Change Strategy in a Developing Society: India*, Meerut, India: Meenakshi Prakashan, 1970.

PYE, LUCIEN W. (ed.), *Communications and Political Development*, Princeton University Press, 1963.

PYE, LUCIEN W., *Politics, Personality, and Nation Building: Burma's Search for Identity*, New Haven: Yale University Press, 1962.

PYE, LUCIEN W. and SIDNEY VERBA (eds), *Political Culture and Political Development*, Princeton University Press, 1965.

REDFIELD, ROBERT, *Peasant Society and Culture*, University of Chicago Press, 1956.

REDFIELD, ROBERT, 'The Folk Society,' *American Journal of Sociology*, vol. LII, 1947.

REDFIELD, ROBERT, *The Little Community* and *Peasant Society and Culture*, University of Chicago Press, 1960.

REDFIELD, ROBERT and MILTON SINGER, 'The Cultural Role of Cities,' *Economic Development and Cultural Change*, vol. III, 1954.

209

RIESMAN, DAVID. *et al.*, *The Lonely Crowd*, New York: Doubleday, 1955.

ROSENBERG, BERNARD and DAVID MANNING WHITE (eds), *Mass Culture and the Popular Arts in America*, Chicago: Free Press, 1957.

ROSTOW, WALT W., *The Economics of Take-Off into Sustained Growth*, Proceedings of a conference held by the International Economic Association, New York: St Martin's Press, 1963.

ROSTOW, WALT W., *The Stages of Economic Growth: A Non-Communist Manifesto*, Cambridge University Press, 1960.

RUDOLPH, LLOYD I. and SUSANNE HOEBER RUDOLPH, *The Modernity of Transition*, University of Chicago Press, 1967.

RUMMEL, R., *Dimensions of Nations*, forthcoming.

RUSSETT, B., H. R. ALKER, JR, K. DEUTSCH and H. LASSWELL, *World Handbook of Political and Social Indicators*, New Haven: Yale University Press, 1964.

RUSTOW, DUNKART A., *A World of Nations: Problems of Political Modernization*, Washington, D.C.: Brookings Institution, 1967.

SAHLINS, MARSHALL, 'Economic Anthropology and Anthropological Economics,' *Social Science Information*, vol. 8, no. 5, 1973, pp. 13-33.

SAKSENA, R. N., 'Modernization and Development Trends in India,' *Sociological Bulletin*, Journal of the Indian Sociological Society, vol. 21, no. 2, September 1972, pp. 91-102.

SAMUELSON, PAUL A., *Economics*, New York: McGraw-Hill, 1973, 9th edition.

SCHAPERA, I., *Government and Politics in Tribal Societies*, New York: Schocken Books, 1967 [1956].

SCHUMPETER, JOSEPH A., *The Theory of Economic Development*, Cambridge, Mass.: Harvard University Press, 1934.

SEAL, ANIL, *The Emergence of Indian Nationalism: Competition and Collaboration in the Later Nineteenth Century*, Cambridge University Press, 1968.

SEERS, DUDLEY, 'The Meaning of Development,' Communication Series no. 44, Sussex: Institute of Development Studies at the University of Sussex (mimeographed), n.d.

SEERS, DUDLEY, 'The Meaning of Development,' *International Development Review*, Presidential Address by Dudley Seers at the Society for International Development, The World Congress in New Delhi, November 1969.

SELIGMAN, EDWIN R.A. and ALVIN JOHNSON (eds), *Encyclopedia of the Social Sciences*, New York: Macmillan Company, 1937.

SENNETT, RICHARD (ed.), *Classic Essays on the Culture of Cities*, New York: Appleton-Century-Crofts, 1969.

SHAH, A.B. and C.R.M.RAO (eds), *Tradition and Modernity in India*, Bombay: Monaktalas, 1965.

SHARMA, G. S. (ed.), *Essays in Indian Jurisprudence*, Lucknow and Delhi: Eastern Book Company, 1964.

SHILS, EDWARD A., *Political Development in the New States*, New York: Humanities Press, n.d.

SHILS, EDWARD A., *The Intellectual Between Tradition and Modernity: The Indian Situation*, The Hague: Mouton, 1961.

SHILS, EDWARD A., 'The Intellectuals in the Political Development of the New States,' *World Politics*, vol. XII, no. 3, April 1960, pp. 329-68.

SHILS, EDWARD A., 'The Military in the Political Development of the New States,' in JOHN J. JOHNSON (ed.), *The Role of the Military in Underdeveloped Countries*, Princeton University Press, 1962.

SHOSTAK, ARTHUR B., *et al.*, *Privilege in America: An End to Inequality?*, Englewood Cliffs: Prentice-Hall, 1973.

SIFFIN, WILLIAM J. (ed.). *Toward the Comparative Study of Public Administration*, Bloomington: Indiana University Press, 1959.

SILLS, DAVID L. (ed.), *International Encyclopedia of the Social Sciences*, New York: Crowell Collier and Macmillan, 1967.

SILVERBERG, JAMES, *Social Mobility in the Caste System in India*, The Hague: Mouton, 1968.

SILVERT, K. H. (ed.), *Discussion at Bellagio*, New York: American Universities Field Staff, 1964.

SILVERT, K. H. (ed.), *Expectant Peoples: Nationalism and Development*, New York: Random House, Vintage Books, 1963.

SILVERT, KALMAN H., *The Conflict Society: Reaction and Revolution in Latin America*, New York: American Universities Field Staff, 1966, rev. edition.

SIMMEL, GEORG, *The Sociology of Georg Simmel*, translated and edited by Kurt H. Wolff, New York: Free Press, 1950.

SINGER, HANS, 'The Concept of Balanced Growth and Economic Development: Theory and Facts,' University of Texas Conference on Economic Development, April 1958.

SINGER, HANS W., 'Social Development: Key Growth Sector Philosophy, Plans, and First Results of the UN Research Institute,' *International Development Review*, vol. VII, no. 1, March 1965, pp. 3-8.

SINGER, HANS, 'The Distribution of Gains Between Investing and Borrowing Countries,' *American Review Papers and Proceedings*, May 1950.

SINGER, MILTON, 'Changing Craft Traditions in India,' in WILBERT E. MOORE and ARNOLD S. FELDMAN (eds), *Labor Commitment and Social Change in Developing Areas*, New York: Social Science Research Council, 1960.

SINGER, MILTON, 'Cultural Values in India's Economic Development,' *The Annals of the American Academy of Political and Social Science*, vol. 305, May 1956.

SINGER, MILTON, 'Shame Cultures and Guilt Cultures,' in Gerhart Piers and Milton Singer (eds), *Shame and Guilt: A Psychological and Cultural Study*, Springfield, Illinois: Charles C. Thomas, 1953.

SINGER, MILTON and BERNARD S. COHN (eds), *Structure and Change in Indian Society*, Chicago: Aldine, 1968.

SJOBERG, GIDEON, ' "Folk" and "Feudal" Societies,' *The American Journal of Sociology*, vol. 58, November 1952, pp. 231-9.

SMELSER, NEIL J. and SEYMOUR MARTIN LIPSET (eds), *Social Structure and Mobility in Economic Development*, Chicago: Aldine, 1966.

SMITH, DONALD EUGENE, *India as a Secular State*, Princeton University Press, 1963.

SMITH, T. E., *Elections in Developing Countries*, New York: St Martin's Press, 1960.

SOUTHALL, AIDAN (ed.), *Urban Anthropology: Cross-Cultural Studies of Urbanization*, New York: Oxford University Press, 1973.

SPENCER, HERBERT, *The Principles of Sociology*, New York: D. Appleton, 1898.

SPENCER, R. (ed.), *Migration and Anthropology*, Seattle: University of Washington Press, 1970.

SPRADLEY, J., *You Owe Yourself a Drunk*, Boston: Little, Brown, 1970.

SRINIVAS, M.N., *Social Change in Modern India*, Berkeley: University of California Press, 1966.

STALIN, *Foundations of Leninism*, New York: International Publishers, 1939.

STEWARD, JULIAN H., *Theory of Culture Change: The Methodology of Multilinear Evolution*, Urbana: University of Illinois Press, 1955 [1951].

STONEQUIST, E. V., *The Marginal Man: A Study in Personality and Culture Conflict*, New York: Russell, 1937.

SUTTON, F. X., 'Social Theory and Comparative Politics,' in David E. Apter and H. Eckstein (eds), *Comparative Politics*, New York: Free Press, 1963.

TAX, SOL, *Penny Capitalism*, University of Chicago Press, 1963 [1953].

THOMSON, D., *England in the Nineteenth Century*, London: Pelican Books, 1950.

THOMSON, D., *Europe Since Napoleon*, New York: Alfred A. Knopf, 1962.

DE TOCQUEVILLE, ALEXIS, *Democracy in America*, 2 vols, New York: Alfred A. Knopf, 1945.

TÖNNIES, FERDINAND, *Community and Society (Gemeinschaft und Gesellschaft)*, translated by Charles P. Loomis, East Lansing: Michigan State University Press, 1957.

Transactions of the Seventh World Congress of Sociology, held at Varna, September 14-19, 1970, Sofia: The Bulgarian Academy of Sciences Publishing House, 1973, vol. V.

TURNER, ROY (ed.), *India's Urban Future*, Berkeley: University of California Press, 1962.

UPHOFF, NORMAN T. and WARREN F. JOHNSON (eds), *The Political Economy of Development*, Berkeley: University of California Press, 1972.

USEEM, JOHN and RUTH HILL USEEM, *The Western-Educated Man in India: A Study of His Social Roles and Influence*, New York: Dryden Press, 1955.

VAN DEN BERGHE, PIERRE L., 'Pluralism,' in JOHN J. HONIGMANN (ed.), *Handbook of Social and Cultural Anthropology*, Chicago: Rand McNally, 1973, pp. 959-77.

VARMA, BAIDYA NATH (ed.), *Contemporary India*, New York: Asia Publishing House, 1965.

VARMA, BAIDYA NATH (ed.), *A New Survey of the Social Sciences*, New York: Asia Publishing House, 1962.

VASSILEV, R., M. DRAGANOV and S. MIKHAILOV, *Sociology in Bulgaria*, Sofia: Bulgarian Academy of Sciences, Institute of Sociology, 1970.

VIDYARTHI, L. P. (ed.), *Aspects of Religion in Indian Society*, Meerut, India: Kedar Nath Ram Nath, 1961.

VON BERTALANFFY, LUDWIG, 'The Theory of Open Systems in Physics and Biology,' *Science*, vol. CXI, 1950.

VON DER MEHDEN, FRED R., *Politics of the Developing Nations*, Englewood Cliffs: Prentice-Hall, 1964.

WALLERSTEIN, IMMANUEL (ed.), *Social Change: The Colonial Situation*, New York: John Wiley, 1966.

WARD, BARBARA, *The Rich Nations and the Poor Nations*, New York: W. W. Norton, 1962.

WARD, BARBARA, *et al.* (eds), *The Widening Gap*, New York: Columbia University Press, 1971.

WARD, ROBERT E. (ed.), *Studying Politics Abroad*, Boston: Little, Brown, 1964.

WARNER, W. LLOYD and PAUL S. LUNT, *The Social Life of a Modern Community*, New York: Yale University Press, 1941.

WARNER, W. LLOYD and PAUL S. LUNT, *The Status System of a Modern Community*, New Haven: Yale University Press, 1942.

WEBB, BEATRICE, *Our Partnership*, London; Longmans, Green, 1948 [1894].

WEBER, MAX, *From Max Weber: Essays in Sociology*, translated by H. H. Gerth and C. Wright Mills, New York: Oxford University Press, 1946.

WEBER, MAX, *Max Weber on Law in Economy and Society*, edited by Max Rheinstein and translated by Edward Shils and Max Rheinstein, New York: Simon & Schuster, 1967 [1954].

WEBER, MAX, *The Methodology of the Social Sciences*, Chicago: Free Press, 1949.

WEBER, MAX, *The Protestant Ethic and the Spirit of Capitalism*, New York: Charles Scribner's Sons, 1958.

WEBER, MAX, *The Religion of China: Confucianism and Taoism*, translated by H. H. Gerth, New York: Free Press, 1964 [1951].

WEBER, MAX, *The Religion of India: The Sociology of Hinduism and Buddhism*, translated by H. H. Gerth and Don Martindale, Chicago: Free Press, 1958.

WEBER, MAX, *The Theory of Social and Economic Organization*, New York: Free Press, 1947.

WEINER, MYRON (ed.), *Modernization*, New York: Basic Books, 1966.

WEINER, MYRON, 'Political Integration and Political Development,' in *The Annals of the American Academy of Political and Social Science,* vol. 358, March 1965, pp. 52-64.

WHITE, LEONARD D. (ed.), *The State of the Social Sciences,* Chicago: University of Chicago Press, 1956.

WHITE, LESLIE, 'Energy and the Evolution of Culture,' *American Anthropologist,* vol. 45, 1943, pp. 335-56.

WHITE, LESLIE, *The Evolution of Culture,* New York: McGraw-Hill, 1959.

WISEMAN, H.V. *Political Systems: Some Sociological Approaches,* New York: Frederick A. Praeger, 1966.

WOLF, ERIC R., *Peasant Wars of the Twentieth Century,* New York: Harper & Row, 1969.

WOLF, ERIC R., *Peasants,* Englewood Cliffs: Prentice-Hall, 1966.

WOOD, ROBERT S., 'Integration Theories,' *European Community,* no. 174, March 1974, pp. 17-19.

WRIGGINS, W. HOWARD, 'Impediments to Unity in New Nations: The Case of Ceylon,' *American Political Science Review,* vol. 55, June 1961, pp. 313-20.

ZAMORA, MARIO D. *et al.* (eds), *Theories in Culture,* Quezon City, Philippines: Kayumanggi Publishers, 1971.

ZETTERBERG, HANS L., *On Theory and Verification in Sociology,* Totowa, New Jersey: Bedminster Press, 1963, rev. edition.

Subject index

Aspiration, 22; level of, 4
Association, 2; voluntary, 2
Authoritarianism, 19; economic, 13; political, 13
Autonomy, 15, 42, 49, 64, 81, 132, 161; community, 18, 57, 81; cultural, 122, 124, 132, 138; individual, 1, 18, 43, 49, 132; national, 152

Bourgeois, 34, 91, 96, 97, 98, 101, 119, 120, 127, 144, 149, 156
Bourgeoisie, 11, 119, 120, 144, 149, 151
Bureaucracy, 3, 4, 18, 19, 21, 24, 33, 38, 42, 46, 59, 62, 65, 66, 71, 80, 85, 86, 88, 90, 94-6, 99, 100, 102-3, 106, 112, 115-17, 118, 123, 129, 130, 134, 143, 157, 161, 163, 168, 172
Bureaucrat, 3
Bureaucratization, 49

Capital, 2, 22, 52, 53, 55, 99, 104, 105, 107, 131, 146, 149, 154, 171; formation, 2, 54, 106, 107, 166; investment, 55
Capitalism, 16, 20, 26, 27, 34, 35, 41, 42, 53, 54, 72, 85, 88, 90, 91, 96-101, 120, 122, 130-1, 135, 136, 139, 140, 141, 142-3, 144, 145, 146, 148, 149, 150-2, 170-1, 173; anti-, 21; bourgeois, 34; post-, 22
Casteism, 3
Centralization, 18, 36, 38-9, 53, 78, 86, 93, 95-6, 99, 117, 127-8
Class, 2, 22, 27, 42, 59, 72, 74, 76, 81, 96-101, 107, 109, 119, 120, 125, 128-9, 131, 133, 141, 144, 147, 150-1,

154, 156-7, 158, 159, 168; abolition, 162; antagonism, 144; business, 171, 172; capitalist, 171, 172; cleavage, 144; consciousness, 72, 144-5; formation, 163; hierarchy, 168; intellectual, 46; laboring, 170; merchant, 166; middle, 3, 22; power, 155; professional, 157; relationship, 41; ruling, 22; society, 21; structure, 2, 3, 22, 23; urban, 3; variables, 74; war, 145
Colonial, 70, 85, 90, 112, 121; anti-, 21, 120
Colonization, 36
Communism, 22, 34, 35, 75, 96-101, 133, 141, 145, 157, 162, 164
Community, 22, 45, 67, 70, 75-6, 80-2, 85, 109, 116, 128-9, 132, 133, 135, 144, 156, 157; autonomy, 18, 19, 39, 49, 57, 64, 76, 78, 80, 132; development, 15, 18, 39, 81, 128, 169-70; extension, 169-70; leadership, 40; little, 70; peasant, 70; political, 23; strength, 1; studies, 67; village, 15
Conservative, 8, 91, 107, 166, 167, 168
Cultural: monist, 14; relativist, 14

Decentralization, 18, 25, 49, 66, 78, 95-6, 108-11, 117, 127-8, 162, 164
Democracy, 3, 15, 18, 19, 21, 22, 36, 41, 42, 44, 58, 64, 65-6, 81, 85-6, 89, 92, 93, 94, 96, 101, 103, 107, 108, 113, 115, 118, 120, 121, 123, 128-30, 132, 137, 140, 144, 151, 152, 168
Dialectical, 7, 35, 62, 125; analysis, 29,

214

Author index

Routledge Social Science Series

Routledge & Kegan Paul   London, Henley and Boston

39 Store Street, London WC1E 7DD
Broadway House, Newtown Road,
Henley-on-Thames, Oxon RG9 1EN
9 Park Street, Boston, Mass. 02108

Contents

Authors wishing to submit manuscripts for any series in
this catalogue should send them to the Social Science Editor,
Routledge & Kegan Paul Ltd, 39 Store Street,
London WC1E 7DD

●*Books so marked are available in paperback*
All books are in Metric Demy 8vo format (216 × 138mm approx.)

International Library of Sociology

General Editor   John Rex

GENERAL SOCIOLOGY

Barnsley, J. H. The Social Reality of Ethics. *464 pp.*
Brown, Robert. Explanation in Social Science. *208 pp.*
●   Rules and Laws in Sociology. *192 pp.*
Bruford, W. H. Chekhov and His Russia. *A Sociological Study. 244 pp.*
Burton, F. and **Carlen, P.** Official Discourse. *On Discourse Analysis, Government Publications, Ideology. About 140 pp.*
Cain, Maureen E. Society and the Policeman's Role. *326 pp.*
●**Fletcher, Colin.** Beneath the Surface. *An Account of Three Styles of Sociological Research. 221 pp.*
Gibson, Quentin. The Logic of Social Enquiry. *240 pp.*
Glucksmann, M. Structuralist Analysis in Contemporary Social Thought. *212 pp.*
Gurvitch, Georges. Sociology of Law. *Foreword by Roscoe Pound. 264 pp.*
Hinkle, R. Founding Theory of American Sociology 1883-1915. *About 350 pp.*
Homans, George C. Sentiments and Activities. *336 pp.*
Johnson, Harry M. Sociology: *a Systematic Introduction. Foreword by Robert K. Merton. 710 pp.*
●**Keat, Russell** and **Urry, John.** Social Theory as Science. *278 pp.*
Mannheim, Karl. Essays on Sociology and Social Psychology. *Edited by Paul Keckskemeti. With Editorial Note by Adolph Lowe. 344 pp.*
Martindale, Don. The Nature and Types of Sociological Theory. *292 pp.*
●**Maus, Heinz.** A Short History of Sociology. *234 pp.*
Myrdal, Gunnar. Value in Social Theory: *A Collection of Essays on Methodology. Edited by Paul Streeten. 332 pp.*
Ogburn, William F. and **Nimkoff, Meyer F.** A Handbook of Sociology. *Preface by Karl Mannheim. 656 pp. 46 figures. 35 tables.*
Parsons, Talcott, and **Smelser, Neil J.** Economy and Society: *A Study in the Integration of Economic and Social Theory. 362 pp.*
Podgórecki, Adam. Practical Social Sciences. *About 200 pp.*
Raffel, S. Matters of Fact. *A Sociological Inquiry. 152 pp.*
●**Rex, John.** (Ed.) Approaches to Sociology. *Contributions by Peter Abell, Sociology and the Demystification of the Modern World. 282 pp.*
·●**Rex, John** (Ed.) Approaches to Sociology. *Contributions by Peter Abell, Frank Bechhofer, Basil Bernstein, Ronald Fletcher, David Frisby, Miriam Glucksmann, Peter Lassman, Herminio Martins, John Rex, Roland Robertson, John Westergaard and Jock Young. 302 pp.*
Rigby, A. Alternative Realities. *352 pp.*
Roche, M. Phenomenology, Language and the Social Sciences. *374 pp.*
Sahay, A. Sociological Analysis. *220 pp.*

Strasser, Hermann. The Normative Structure of Sociology. *Conservative and Emancipatory Themes in Social Thought. About 340 pp.*
Strong, P. Ceremonial Order of the Clinic. *About 250 pp.*
Urry, John. Reference Groups and the Theory of Revolution. *244 pp.*
Weinberg, E. Development of Sociology in the Soviet Union. *173 pp.*

FOREIGN CLASSICS OF SOCIOLOGY

● **Gerth, H. H.** and **Mills, C. Wright.** From Max Weber: *Essays in Sociology. 502 pp.*
● **Tönnies, Ferdinand.** Community and Association. *(Gemeinschaft and Gesellschaft.) Translated and Supplemented by Charles P. Loomis. Foreword by Pitirim A. Sorokin. 334 pp.*

SOCIAL STRUCTURE

Andreski, Stanislav. Military Organization and Society. *Foreword by Professor A. R. Radcliffe-Brown. 226 pp. 1 folder.*
Carlton, Eric. Ideology and Social Order. *Foreword by Professor Philip Abrahams. About 320 pp.*
Coontz, Sydney H. Population Theories and the Economic Interpretation. *202 pp.*
Coser, Lewis. The Functions of Social Conflict. *204 pp.*
Dickie-Clark, H. F. Marginal Situation: *A Sociological Study of a Coloured Group. 240 pp. 11 tables.*
Giner, S. and **Archer, M. S.** (Eds.). Contemporary Europe. *Social Structures and Cultural Patterns. 336 pp.*
● **Glaser, Barney** and **Strauss, Anselm L.** Status Passage. *A Formal Theory. 212 pp.*
Glass, D. V. (Ed.) Social Mobility in Britain. *Contributions by J. Berent, T. Bottomore, R. C. Chambers, J. Floud, D. V. Glass, J. R. Hall, H. T. Himmelweit, R. K. Kelsall, F. M. Martin, C. A. Moser, R. Mukherjee, and W. Ziegel. 420 pp.*
Kelsall, R. K. Higher Civil Servants in Britain: *From 1870 to the Present Day. 268 pp. 31 tables.*
● **Lawton, Denis.** Social Class, Language and Education. *192 pp.*
McLeish, John. The Theory of Social Change: *Four Views Considered. 128 pp.*
● **Marsh, David C.** The Changing Social Structure of England and Wales, 1871-1961. *Revised edition. 288 pp.*
Menzies, Ken. Talcott Parsons and the Social Image of Man. *About 208 pp.*
● **Mouzelis, Nicos.** Organization and Bureaucracy. *An Analysis of Modern Theories. 240 pp.*
Ossowski, Stanislaw. Class Structure in the Social Consciousness. *210 pp.*
● **Podgórecki, Adam.** Law and Society. *302 pp.*
Renner, Karl. Institutions of Private Law and Their Social Functions. *Edited, with an Introduction and Notes, by O. Kahn-Freud. Translated by Agnes Schwarzschild. 316 pp.*

Rex, J. and **Tomlinson, S.** Colonial Immigrants in a British City. *A Class Analysis. 368 pp.*
Smooha, S. Israel: Pluralism and Conflict. *472 pp.*
Wesolowski, W. Class, Strata and Power. *Trans. and with Introduction by G. Kolankiewicz. 160 pp.*
Zureik, E. Palestinians in Israel. *A Study in Internal Colonialism. 264 pp.*

SOCIOLOGY AND POLITICS

Acton, T. A. Gypsy Politics and Social Change. *316 pp.*
Burton, F. Politics of Legitimacy. *Struggles in a Belfast Community. 250 pp.*
Etzioni-Halevy, E. Political Manipulation and Administrative Power. *A Comparative Study. About 200 pp.*
● **Hechter, Michael.** Internal Colonialism. *The Celtic Fringe in British National Development, 1536–1966. 380 pp.*
Kornhauser, William. The Politics of Mass Society. *272 pp. 20 tables.*
Korpi, W. The Working Class in Welfare Capitalism. *Work, Unions and Politics in Sweden. 472 pp.*
Kroes, R. Soldiers and Students. *A Study of Right- and Left-wing Students. 174 pp.*
Martin, Roderick. Sociology of Power. *About 272 pp.*
Myrdal, Gunnar. The Political Element in the Development of Economic Theory. *Translated from the German by Paul Streeten. 282 pp.*
Wong, S.-L. Sociology and Socialism in Contemporary China. *160 pp.*
Wootton, Graham. Workers, Unions and the State. *188 pp.*

CRIMINOLOGY

Ancel, Marc. Social Defence: *A Modern Approach to Criminal Problems. Foreword by Leon Radzinowicz. 240 pp.*
Athens, L. Violent Criminal Acts and Actors. *About 150 pp.*
Cain, Maureen E. Society and the Policeman's Role. *326 pp.*
Cloward, Richard A. and **Ohlin, Lloyd E.** Delinquency and Opportunity: *A Theory of Delinquent Gangs. 248 pp.*
Downes, David M. The Delinquent Solution. *A Study in Subcultural Theory. 296 pp.*
Friedlander, Kate. The Psycho-Analytical Approach to Juvenile Delinquency: *Theory, Case Studies, Treatment. 320 pp.*
Gleuck, Sheldon and **Eleanor.** Family Environment and Delinquency. *With the statistical assistance of Rose W. Kneznek. 340 pp.*
Lopez-Rey, Manuel. Crime. *An Analytical Appraisal. 288 pp.*
Mannheim, Hermann. Comparative Criminology: *a Text Book. Two volumes. 442 pp. and 380 pp.*
Morris, Terence. The Criminal Area: *A Study in Social Ecology. Foreword by Hermann Mannheim. 232 pp. 25 tables. 4 maps.*
Podgorecki, A. and **Łos, M.** *Multidimensional Sociology. About 380 pp.*
Rock, Paul. Making People Pay. *338 pp.*

● **Taylor, Ian, Walton, Paul,** and **Young, Jock.** The New Criminology. *For a Social Theory of Deviance. 325 pp.*

● **Taylor, Ian, Walton, Paul** and **Young, Jock.** (Eds) Critical Criminology. *268 pp.*

SOCIAL PSYCHOLOGY

Bagley, Christopher. The Social Psychology of the Epileptic Child. *320 pp.*

Brittan, Arthur. Meanings and Situations. *224 pp.*

Carroll, J. Break-Out from the Crystal Palace. *200 pp.*

● **Fleming, C. M.** Adolescence: Its Social Psychology. *With an Introduction to recent findings from the fields of Anthropology, Physiology, Medicine, Psychometrics and Sociometry. 288 pp.*

● The Social Psychology of Education: *An Introduction and Guide to Its Study. 136 pp.*

Linton, Ralph. The Cultural Background of Personality. *132 pp.*

● **Mayo, Elton.** The Social Problems of an Industrial Civilization. *With an Appendix on the Political Problem. 180 pp.*

Ottaway, A. K. C. Learning Through Group Experience. *176 pp.*

Plummer, Ken. Sexual Stigma. *An Interactionist Account. 254 pp.*

● **Rose, Arnold M.** (Ed.) Human Behaviour and Social Processes: *an Interactionist Approach. Contributions by Arnold M. Rose, Ralph H. Turner, Anselm Strauss, Everett C. Hughes, E. Franklin Frazier, Howard S. Becker et al. 696 pp.*

Smelser, Neil J. Theory of Collective Behaviour. *448 pp.*

Stephenson, Geoffrey M. The Development of Conscience. *128 pp.*

Young, Kimball. Handbook of Social Psychology. *658 pp. 16 figures. 10 tables.*

SOCIOLOGY OF THE FAMILY

Bell, Colin R. Middle Class Families: *Social and Geographical Mobility. 224 pp.*

Burton, Lindy. Vulnerable Children. *272 pp.*

Gavron, Hannah. The Captive Wife: *Conflicts of Household Mothers. 190 pp.*

George, Victor and **Wilding, Paul.** Motherless Families. *248 pp.*

Klein, Josephine. Samples from English Cultures.
  1. Three Preliminary Studies and Aspects of Adult Life in England. *447 pp.*
  2. Child-Rearing Practices and Index. *247 pp.*

Klein, Viola. The Feminine Character. *History of an Ideology. 244 pp.*

McWhinnie, Alexina M. Adopted Children. *How They Grow Up. 304 pp.*

● **Morgan, D. H. J.** Social Theory and the Family. *About 320 pp.*

● **Myrdal, Alva** and **Klein, Viola.** Women's Two Roles: *Home and Work. 238 pp. 27 tables.*

Parsons, Talcott and **Bales, Robert F.** Family: Socialization and Inter-action Process. *In collaboration with James Olds, Morris Zelditch and Philip E. Slater. 456 pp. 50 figures and tables.*

SOCIAL SERVICES

Bastide, Roger. The Sociology of Mental Disorder. *Translated from the French by Jean McNeil. 260 pp.*

Carlebach, Julius. Caring For Children in Trouble. *266 pp.*

George, Victor. Foster Care. *Theory and Practice. 234 pp.*
    Social Security: *Beveridge and After. 258 pp.*

George, V. and **Wilding, P.** Motherless Families. *248 pp.*

● **Goetschius, George W.** Working with Community Groups. *256 pp.*

Goetschius, George W. and **Tash, Joan.** Working with Unattached Youth. *416 pp.*

Heywood, Jean S. Children in Care. *The Development of the Service for the Deprived Child. Third revised edition. 284 pp.*

King, Roy D., Ranes, Norma V. and **Tizard, Jack.** Patterns of Residen-tial Care. *356 pp.*

Leigh, John. Young People and Leisure. *256 pp.*

● **Mays, John.** (Ed.) Penelope Hall's Social Services of England and Wales. *About 324 pp.*

Morris, Mary. Voluntary Work and the Welfare State. *300 pp.*

Nokes, P. L. The Professional Task in Welfare Practice. *152 pp.*

Timms, Noel. Psychiatric Social Work in Great Britain (1939-1962). *280 pp.*

●   Social Casework: *Principles and Practice. 256 pp.*

SOCIOLOGY OF EDUCATION

Banks, Olive. Parity and Prestige in English Secondary Education: a Study in Educational Sociology. *272 pp.*

● **Blyth, W. A. L.** English Primary Education. *A Sociological Description.* 2. Background. *168 pp.*

Collier, K. G. The Social Purposes of Education: *Personal and Social Values in Education. 268 pp.*

Evans, K. M. Sociometry and Education. *158 pp.*

● **Ford, Julienne.** Social Class and the Comprehensive School. *192 pp.*

Foster, P. J. Education and Social Change in Ghana. *336 pp. 3 maps.*

Fraser, W. R. Education and Society in Modern France. *150 pp.*

Grace, Gerald R. Role Conflict and the Teacher. *150 pp.*

Hans, Nicholas. New Trends in Education in the Eighteenth Century. *278 pp. 19 tables.*

●   Comparative Education: *A Study of Educational Factors and Tra-ditions. 360 pp.*

● **Hargreaves, David.** Interpersonal Relations and Education. *432 pp.*

●   Social Relations in a Secondary School. *240 pp.*

    School Organization and Pupil Involvement. *A Study of Secondary Schools.*

● **Mannheim, Karl** and **Stewart, W.A.C.** An Introduction to the Sociology of Education. *206 pp.*

● **Musgrove, F.** Youth and the Social Order. *176 pp.*

● **Ottaway, A. K. C.** Education and Society: An Introduction to the Sociology of Education. *With an Introduction by W. O. Lester Smith. 212 pp.*

Peers, Robert. Adult Education: *A Comparative Study. Revised edition. 398 pp.*

Stratta, Erica. The Education of Borstal Boys. *A Study of their Educational Experiences prior to, and during, Borstal Training. 256 pp.*

● **Taylor, P. H., Reid, W. A.** and **Holley, B. J.** The English Sixth Form. *A Case Study in Curriculum Research. 198 pp.*

SOCIOLOGY OF CULTURE

Eppel, E. M. and **M.** Adolescents and Morality: *A Study of some Moral Values and Dilemmas of Working Adolescents in the Context of a changing Climate of Opinion. Foreword by W. J. H. Sprott. 268 pp. 39 tables.*

● **Fromm, Erich.** The Fear of Freedom. *286 pp.*

● The Sane Society. *400 pp.*

Johnson, L. The Cultural Critics. *From Matthew Arnold to Raymond Williams. 233 pp.*

Mannheim, Karl. Essays on the Sociology of Culture. *Edited by Ernst Mannheim in co-operation with Paul Kecskemeti. Editorial Note by Adolph Lowe. 280 pp.*

Zijderfeld, A. C. On Clichés. *The Supersedure of Meaning by Function in Modernity. About 132 pp.*

SOCIOLOGY OF RELIGION

Argyle, Michael and **Beit-Hallahmi, Benjamin.** The Social Psychology of Religion. *About 256 pp.*

Glasner, Peter E. The Sociology of Secularisation. *A Critique of a Concept. About 180 pp.*

Hall, J. R. The Ways Out. *Utopian Communal Groups in an Age of Babylon. 280 pp.*

Ranson, S., Hinings, B. and **Bryman, A.** Clergy, Ministers and Priests. *216 pp.*

Stark, Werner. The Sociology of Religion. *A Study of Christendom.*
Volume II. *Sectarian Religion. 368 pp.*
Volume III. *The Universal Church. 464 pp.*
Volume IV. *Types of Religious Man. 352 pp.*
Volume V. *Types of Religious Culture. 464 pp.*

Turner, B. S. Weber and Islam. *216 pp.*

Watt, W. Montgomery. Islam and the Integration of Society. *320 pp.*

SOCIOLOGY OF ART AND LITERATURE

Jarvie, Ian C. Towards a Sociology of the Cinema. *A Comparative Essay on the Structure and Functioning of a Major Entertainment Industry. 405 pp.*

Rust, Frances S. Dance in Society. *An Analysis of the Relationships between the Social Dance and Society in England from the Middle Ages to the Present Day. 256 pp. 8 pp. of plates.*

Schücking, L. L. The Sociology of Literary Taste. *112 pp.*

Wolff, Janet. Hermeneutic Philosophy and the Sociology of Art. *150 pp.*

SOCIOLOGY OF KNOWLEDGE

Diesing, P. Patterns of Discovery in the Social Sciences. *262 pp.*

● **Douglas, J. D.** (Ed.) Understanding Everyday Life. *370 pp.*

Glasner, B. Essential Interactionism. *About 220 pp.*

● **Hamilton, P.** Knowledge and Social Structure. *174 pp.*

Jarvie, I. C. Concepts and Society. *232 pp.*

Mannheim, Karl. Essays on the Sociology of Knowledge. *Edited by Paul Kecskemeti. Editorial Note by Adolph Lowe. 353 pp.*

Remmling, Gunter W. The Sociology of Karl Mannheim. *With a Bibliographical Guide to the Sociology of Knowledge, Ideological Analysis, and Social Planning. 255 pp.*

Remmling, Gunter W. (Ed.) Towards the Sociology of Knowledge. *Origin and Development of a Sociological Thought Style. 463 pp.*

URBAN SOCIOLOGY

Aldridge, M. The British New Towns. *A Programme Without a Policy. About 250 pp.*

Ashworth, William. The Genesis of Modern British Town Planning: *A Study in Economic and Social History of the Nineteenth and Twentieth Centuries. 288 pp.*

Brittan, A. The Privatised World. *196 pp.*

Cullingworth, J. B. Housing Needs and Planning Policy: *A Restatement of the Problems of Housing Need and 'Overspill' in England and Wales. 232 pp. 44 tables. 8 maps.*

Dickinson, Robert E. City and Region: *A Geographical Interpretation. 608 pp. 125 figures.*

The West European City: *A Geographical Interpretation. 600 pp. 129 maps. 29 plates.*

Humphreys, Alexander J. New Dubliners: *Urbanization and the Irish Family. Foreword by George C. Homans. 304 pp.*

Jackson, Brian. Working Class Community: *Some General Notions raised by a Series of Studies in Northern England. 192 pp.*

● **Mann, P. H.** An Approach to Urban Sociology. *240 pp.*

Mellor, J. R. Urban Sociology in an Urbanized Society. *326 pp.*

Morris, R. N. and **Mogey, J.** The Sociology of Housing. *Studies at Berinsfield. 232 pp. 4 pp. plates.*

Rosser, C. and **Harris, C.** The Family and Social Change. *A Study of Family and Kinship in a South Wales Town. 352 pp. 8 maps.*

● **Stacey, Margaret, Batsone, Eric, Bell, Colin** and **Thurcott, Anne.** Power, Persistence and Change. *A Second Study of Banbury. 196 pp.*

RURAL SOCIOLOGY

Mayer, Adrian C. Peasants in the Pacific. *A Study of Fiji Indian Rural Society. 248 pp. 20 plates.*

Williams, W. M. The Sociology of an English Village: *Gosforth. 272 pp. 12 figures. 13 tables.*

SOCIOLOGY OF INDUSTRY AND DISTRIBUTION

Dunkerley, David. The Foreman. *Aspects of Task and Structure. 192 pp.*

Eldridge, J. E. T. Industrial Disputes. *Essays in the Sociology of Industrial Relations. 288 pp.*

Hollowell, Peter G. The Lorry Driver. *272 pp.*

● **Oxaal, I., Barnett, T.** and **Booth, D.** (Eds) Beyond the Sociology of Development. *Economy and Society in Latin America and Africa. 295 pp.*

Smelser, Neil J. Social Change in the Industrial Revolution: *An Application of Theory to the Lancashire Cotton Industry, 1770–1840. 468 pp. 12 figures. 14 tables.*

Watson, T. J. The Personnel Managers. *A Study in the Sociology of Work and Employment. 262 pp.*

ANTHROPOLOGY

Brandel-Syrier, Mia. Reeftown Elite. *A Study of Social Mobility in a Modern African Community on the Reef. 376 pp.*

Dickie-Clark, H. F. The Marginal Situation. *A Sociological Study of a Coloured Group. 236 pp.*

Dube, S. C. Indian Village. *Foreword by Morris Edward Opler. 276 pp. 4 plates.*

India's Changing Villages: *Human Factors in Community Development. 260 pp. 8 plates. 1 map.*

Firth, Raymond. Malay Fishermen. *Their Peasant Economy. 420 pp. 17 pp. plates.*

Gulliver, P. H. Social Control in an African Society: a Study of the Arusha, Agricultural Masai of Northern Tanganyika. *320 pp. 8 plates. 10 figures.*

Family Herds. *288 pp.*

Jarvie, Ian C. The Revolution in Anthropology. *268 pp.*

Little, Kenneth L. Mende of Sierra Leone. *308 pp. and folder.*

Negroes in Britain. *With a New Introduction and Contemporary Study by Leonard Bloom. 320 pp.*

Madan, G. R. Western Sociologists on Indian Society. *Marx, Spencer, Weber, Durkheim, Pareto. 384 pp.*

Mayer, A. C. Peasants in the Pacific. *A Study of Fiji Indian Rural Society. 248 pp.*

Meer, Fatima. Race and Suicide in South Africa. *325 pp.*

Smith, Raymond T. The Negro Family in British Guiana: *Family Structure and Social Status in the Villages. With a Foreword by Meyer Fortes. 314 pp. 8 plates. 1 figure. 4 maps.*

SOCIOLOGY AND PHILOSOPHY

Barnsley, John H. The Social Reality of Ethics. *A Comparative Analysis of Moral Codes. 448 pp.*

Diesing, Paul. Patterns of Discovery in the Social Sciences. *362 pp.*

● **Douglas, Jack D.** (Ed.) Understanding Everyday Life. *Toward the Reconstruction of Sociological Knowledge. Contributions by Alan F. Blum, Aaron W. Cicourel, Norman K. Denzin, Jack D. Douglas, John Heeren, Peter McHugh, Peter K. Manning, Melvin Power, Matthew Speier, Roy Turner, D. Lawrence Wieder, Thomas P. Wilson and Don H. Zimmerman. 370 pp.*

Gorman, Robert A. The Dual Vision. *Alfred Schutz and the Myth of Phenomenological Social Science. About 300 pp.*

Jarvie, Ian C. Concepts and Society. *216 pp.*

Kilminster, R. Praxis and Method. *A Sociological Dialogue with Lukács, Gramsci and the early Frankfurt School. About 304 pp.*

● **Pelz, Werner.** The Scope of Understanding in Sociology. *Towards a More Radical Reorientation in the Social Humanistic Sciences. 283 pp.*

Roche, Maurice. Phenomenology, Language and the Social Sciences. *371 pp.*

Sahay, Arun. Sociological Analysis. *212 pp.*

Slater, P. Origin and Significance of the Frankfurt School. *A Marxist Perspective. About 192 pp.*

Spurling, L. Phenomenology and the Social World. *The Philosophy of Merleau-Ponty and its Relation to the Social Sciences. 222 pp.*

Wilson, H. T. The American Ideology. *Science, Technology and Organization as Modes of Rationality. 368 pp.*

International Library of Anthropology

General Editor Adam Kuper

Ahmed, A. S. Millenium and Charisma Among Pathans. *A Critical Essay in Social Anthropology. 192 pp.*
Pukhtun Economy and Society. *About 360 pp.*

Brown, Paula. The Chimbu. *A Study of Change in the New Guinea Highlands. 151 pp.*

Foner, N. Jamaica Farewell. *200 pp.*

Gudeman, Stephen. Relationships, Residence and the Individual. *A Rural Panamanian Community. 288 pp. 11 plates, 5 figures, 2 maps, 10 tables.*

The Demise of a Rural Economy. *From Subsistence to Capitalism in a Latin American Village. 160 pp.*

Hamnett, Ian. Chieftainship and Legitimacy. *An Anthropological Study of Executive Law in Lesotho. 163 pp.*

Hanson, F. Allan. Meaning in Culture. *127 pp.*

Humphreys, S. C. Anthropology and the Greeks. *288 pp.*

Karp, I. Fields of Change Among the Iteso of Kenya. *140 pp.*

Lloyd, P. C. Power and Independence. *Urban Africans' Perception of Social Inequality. 264 pp.*

Parry, J. P. Caste and Kinship in Kangra. *352 pp. Illustrated.*

Pettigrew, Joyce. Robber Noblemen. *A Study of the Political System of the Sikh Jats. 284 pp.*

Street, Brian V. The Savage in Literature. *Representations of 'Primitive' Society in English Fiction, 1858–1920. 207 pp.*

Van Den Berghe, Pierre L. Power and Privilege at an African University. *278 pp.*

International Library of Social Policy

General Editor   Kathleen Jones

Bayley, M. Mental Handicap and Community Care. *426 pp.*

Bottoms, A. E. and **McClean, J. D.** Defendants in the Criminal Process. *284 pp.*

Butler, J. R. Family Doctors and Public Policy. *208 pp.*

Davies, Martin. Prisoners of Society. *Attitudes and Aftercare. 204 pp.*

Gittus, Elizabeth. Flats, Families and the Under-Fives. *285 pp.*

Holman, Robert. Trading in Children. *A Study of Private Fostering. 355 pp.*

Jeffs, A. Young People and the Youth Service. *About 180 pp.*

Jones, Howard, and **Cornes, Paul.** Open Prisons. *288 pp.*

Jones, Kathleen. History of the Mental Health Service. *428 pp.*

Jones, Kathleen, with **Brown, John, Cunningham, W. J., Roberts, Julian** and **Williams, Peter.** Opening the Door. *A Study of New Policies for the Mentally Handicapped. 278 pp.*

Karn, Valerie. Retiring to the Seaside. *About 280 pp. 2 maps. Numerous tables.*

King, R. D. and **Elliot, K. W.** Albany: Birth of a Prison—End of an Era. *394 pp.*

Thomas, J. E. The English Prison Officer since 1850: *A Study in Conflict.* *258 pp.*

Walton, R. G. Women in Social Work. *303 pp.*

● **Woodward, J.** To Do the Sick No Harm. *A Study of the British Voluntary Hospital System to 1875. 234 pp.*

International Library of Welfare and Philosophy

General Editors Noel Timms and David Watson

● **McDermott, F. E.** (Ed.) Self-Determination in Social Work. *A Collection of Essays on Self-determination and Related Concepts by Philosophers and Social Work Theorists. Contributors: F. B. Biestek, S. Bernstein, A. Keith-Lucas, D. Sayer, H. H. Perelman, C. Whittington, R. F. Stalley, F. E. McDermott, I. Berlin, H. J. McCloskey, H. L. A. Hart, J. Wilson, A. I. Melden, S. I. Benn. 254 pp.*

● **Plant, Raymond.** Community and Ideology. *104 pp.*

Ragg, Nicholas M. People Not Cases. *A Philosophical Approach to Social Work. About 250 pp.*

● **Timms, Noel** and **Watson, David.** (Eds) Talking About Welfare. *Readings in Philosophy and Social Policy. Contributors: T. H. Marshall, R. B. Brandt, G. H. von Wright, K. Nielsen, M. Cranston, R. M. Titmuss, R. S. Downie, E. Telfer, D. Donnison, J. Benson, P. Leonard, A. Keith-Lucas, D. Walsh, I. T. Ramsey. 320 pp.*

● (Eds). Philosophy in Social Work. *250 pp.*

● **Weale, A.** Equality and Social Policy. *164 pp.*

Primary Socialization, Language and Education

General Editor Basil Bernstein

Adlam, Diana S., *with the assistance of Geoffrey Turner and Lesley Lineker.* Code in Context. *About 272 pp.*

Bernstein, Basil. Class, Codes and Control. *3 volumes.*

● 1. *Theoretical Studies Towards a Sociology of Language. 254 pp.*

2. *Applied Studies Towards a Sociology of Language. 377 pp.*

● 3. *Towards a Theory of Educational Transmission. 167 pp.*

Brandis, W. and **Bernstein, B.** Selection and Control. *176 pp.*

Brandis, Walter and **Henderson, Dorothy.** Social Class, Language and Communication. *288 pp.*

Cook-Gumperz, Jenny. Social Control and Socialization. *A Study of Class Differences in the Language of Maternal Control. 290 pp.*

● **Gahagan, D. M** and **G. A.** Talk Reform. *Exploration in Language for Infant School Children. 160 pp.*

Hawkins, P. R. Social Class, the Nominal Group and Verbal Strategies. *About 220 pp.*

Robinson, W. P. and **Rackstraw, Susan D. A.** A Question of Answers. *2 volumes. 192 pp. and 180 pp.*

Turner, Geoffrey J. and **Mohan, Bernard A.** A Linguistic Description and Computer Programme for Children's Speech. *208 pp.*

Reports of the Institute of Community Studies

Baker, J. The Neighbourhood Advice Centre. A Community Project in Camden. *320 pp.*

● **Cartwright, Ann.** Patients and their Doctors. *A Study of General Practice. 304 pp.*

Dench, Geoff. Maltese in London. *A Case-study in the Erosion of Ethnic Consciousness. 302 pp.*

Jackson, Brian and **Marsden, Dennis.** Education and the Working Class: *Some General Themes raised by a Study of 88 Working-class Children in a Northern Industrial City. 268 pp. 2 folders.*

Marris, Peter. The Experience of Higher Education. *232 pp. 27 tables.*
● Loss and Change. *192 pp.*

Marris, Peter and **Rein, Martin.** Dilemmas of Social Reform. *Poverty and Community Action in the United States. 256 pp.*

Marris, Peter and **Somerset, Anthony.** African Businessmen. *A Study of Entrepreneurship and Development in Keyna. 256 pp.*

Mills, Richard. Young Outsiders: *a Study in Alternative Communities. 216 pp.*

Runciman, W. G. Relative Deprivation and Social Justice. *A Study of Attitudes to Social Inequality in Twentieth-Century England. 352 pp.*

Willmott, Peter. Adolescent Boys in East London. *230 pp.*

Willmott, Peter and **Young, Michael.** Family and Class in a London Suburb. *202 pp. 47 tables.*

Young, Michael and **McGeeney, Patrick.** Learning Begins at Home. *A Study of a Junior School and its Parents. 128 pp.*

Young, Michael and **Willmott, Peter.** Family and Kinship in East London. *Foreword by Richard M. Titmuss. 252 pp. 39 tables.*
The Symmetrical Family. *410 pp.*

Reports of the Institute for Social Studies in Medical Care

Cartwright, Ann, Hockey, Lisbeth and **Anderson, John J.** Life Before Death. *310 pp.*

Dunnell, Karen and **Cartwright, Ann.** Medicine Takers, Prescribers and Hoarders. *190 pp.*

Farrell, C. My Mother Said. . . . *A Study of the Way Young People Learned About Sex and Birth Control. 200 pp.*

Medicine, Illness and Society

General Editor W. M. Williams

Hall, David J. Social Relations & Innovation. *Changing the State of Play in Hospitals. 232 pp.*

Hall, David J., and **Stacey, M.** (Eds) Beyond Separation. *234 pp.*

Robinson, David. The Process of Becoming Ill. *142 pp.*

Stacey, Margaret *et al.* Hospitals, Children and Their Families. *The Report of a Pilot Study. 202 pp.*

Stimson G. V. and **Webb, B.** Going to See the Doctor. *The Consultation Process in General Practice. 155 pp.*

Monographs in Social Theory

General Editor Arthur Brittan

● **Barnes, B.** Scientific Knowledge and Sociological Theory. *192 pp.*

Bauman, Zygmunt. Culture as Praxis. *204 pp.*

● **Dixon, Keith.** Sociological Theory. *Pretence and Possibility. 142 pp.*

Meltzer, B. N., Petras, J. W. and **Reynolds, L. T.** Symbolic Interactionism. *Genesis, Varieties and Criticisms. 144 pp.*

● **Smith, Anthony D.** The Concept of Social Change. *A Critique of the Functionalist Theory of Social Change. 208 pp.*

Routledge Social Science Journals

The British Journal of Sociology. *Editor – Angus Stewart; Associate Editor – Leslie Sklair. Vol. 1, No. 1 – March 1950 and Quarterly. Roy. 8vo. All back issues available. An international journal publishing original papers in the field of sociology and related areas.*

Community Work. *Edited by David Jones and Marjorie Mayo. 1973. Published annually.*

Economy and Society. *Vol. 1, No. 1. February 1972 and Quarterly. Metric Roy. 8vo. A journal for all social scientists covering sociology, philosophy, anthropology, economics and history. All back numbers available.*

Ethnic and Racial Studies. *Editor – John Stone. Vol. 1 – 1978. Published quarterly.*

Religion. Journal of Religion and Religions. *Chairman of Editorial Board, Ninian Smart. Vol. 1, No. 1, Spring 1971. A journal with an interdisciplinary approach to the study of the phenomena of religion. All back numbers available.*

Sociology of Health and Illness. *A Journal of Medical Sociology. Editor – Alan Davies; Associate Editor – Ray Jobling. Vol. 1, Spring 1979. Published 3 times per annum.*

Year Book of Social Policy in Britain, The. *Edited by Kathleen Jones. 1971. Published annually.*

Social and Psychological Aspects of Medical Practice

Editor Trevor Silverstone

Lader, Malcolm. Psychophysiology of Mental Illness. *280 pp.*

● **Silverstone, Trevor** and **Turner, Paul.** Drug Treatment in Psychiatry. *Revised edition. 256 pp.*

Whiteley, J. S. and **Gordon, J.** Group Approaches in Psychiatry. *256 pp.*

Printed in Great Britain by
Lowe & Brydone Printers Limited, Thetford, Norfolk